PHOTOSHOP
for NONLINEAR
EDITORS

Richard Harrington

EXPERT SERIES

San Francisco, CA • New York, NY • Lawrence, KS

Published by CMP Books
an imprint of CMP Media LLC
Main office: 600 Harrison Street, San Francisco, CA 94107 USA
Tel: 415-947-6615; fax: 415-947-6015
Editorial office: 1601 West 23rd Street, Suite 200, Lawrence, KS 66046 USA
www.cmpbooks.com
email: books@cmp.com

Designations used by companies to distinguish their products are often claimed as trademarks. In all instances where CMP is aware of a trademark claim, the product name appears in initial capital letters, in all capital letters, or in accordance with the vendor's capitalization preference. Readers should contact the appropriate companies for more complete information on trademarks and trademark registrations. All trademarks and registered trademarks in this book are the property of their respective holders.

The publisher does not offer any warranties and does not guarantee the accuracy, adequacy, or completeness of any information herein and is not responsible for any errors or omissions. The publisher assumes no liability for damages resulting from the use of the information in this book or for any infringement of the intellectual property rights of third parties that would result from the use of this information.

Acquisitions editor:	Dorothy Cox
Technical editor:	Glen Stephens
Managing editor:	Michelle O'Neal
Copyeditors:	Madeleine Reardon Dimond, Frank Kresen, and Catherine Janzen
Layout design:	Michelle O'Neal and Justin Fulmer
Cover design:	Richard Harrington and Damien Castaneda

Distributed to the book trade in the U.S. by:
Publishers Group West
1700 Fourth Street
Berkeley, CA 94710
1-800-788-3123

Distributed in Canada by:
Jaguar Book Group
100 Armstrong Avenue
Georgetown, Ontario M6K 3E7 Canada
905-877-4483

For individual orders and for information on special discounts for quantity orders, please contact:
CMP Books Distribution Center, 6600 Silacci Way, Gilroy, CA 95020
Tel: 1-800-500-6875 or 408-848-3854; fax: 408-848-5784
email: cmp@rushorder.com; Web: www.cmpbooks.com

Library of Congress Cataloging-in-Publication Data
Harrington, Richard Michael, 1972–
  Photoshop for nonlinear editors / by Richard Harrington.
        p. cm.
    ISBN 1-57820-209-4 (softcover : alk. paper)
      1. Motion pictures–Editing–Data processing. 2. Digital video–Editing–Data processing. 3. Adobe Photoshop. I. Title.
TR899.H39 2003
006.6'869–dc21   2003003896

Printed in the United States of America
03 04 05 06 07   5 4 3 2 1

ISBN: 1-57820-209-4

CMP**Books**

Dedication

To my parents. Thanks for teaching me about hard work and giving me your love and support throughout the years. The sacrifices you have made for my education and well-being are deeply appreciated. Who would have guessed that all those video games and early computers would lead to this?

To my wife, Meghan. Thanks for your incredible patience and support throughout this project, for your understanding that the long hours and demands of the video industry do not diminish my love and desire to spend more time with you. You are the single most important part of my life.

To my extended family. Your guidance and support have helped with the many twists in life's road. Thanks for helping me get on my feet and stay there.

Table of Contents

Foreword

Given the wide adoption of Adobe Photoshop® in professional print and Web publishing workflows, as well as the incredible growth of digital photography in the past few years, it can be easy to forget that the very first version of Photoshop was developed in part by an engineer doing motion picture work at Industrial Light and Magic. Perhaps it shouldn't be surprising that Photoshop has long been an indispensable tool for digital video work.

Adobe Photoshop is the world's most widely used professional tool for image manipulation—regardless of whether those images will be printed in a brochure, linked together in a Web page, or streamed as frames in a video. In fact, it's even finding increasing use in fields as diverse as medical imaging and forensic analysis. How is it possible for a single application to be used in so many different ways? The answer lies at the core of the application, once you strip away Web export options, CMYK printing controls, and other specialized workflow features. What you'll find is a set of powerful tools and commands that allow you to take a collection of image pixels and turn them into just about anything you can imagine.

Photoshop is fabled for its formidable learning curve. I believe that reputation owes more to the extreme flexibility of the application than it does to the challenge of mastering any particular function. There is rarely one right way to do anything in Photoshop. There are sometimes dozens. What Photoshop gives you is a set of powerful imaging building blocks. You're the one who decides how to put those blocks together to build the result you want. You're the one in control.

Of course, having so much control—and so many choices—can be intimidating to the uninitiated. What you need is a guide to help you to narrow the choices to the ones that matter. What are the most valuable functions for the type of work you're doing? What are the key techniques for combining these functions? What's the fastest way to take what's in your head and realize it on your computer monitor?

Before writing this foreword, I conducted a quick online search and discovered more than 500 available books about Photoshop. What's almost as remarkable as the sheer number of books is the variety. There are books written for Web designers, prepress professionals, photographers, and fine artists. There are a variety of books focused on type effects, special effects tricks, color correction, retouching, and portraiture. What I didn't find, however, was a book focused on using Photoshop for digital video.

In fact, motion picture and video professionals rely on Adobe Photoshop every day to retouch frames, design titles, and create sophisticated graphics for animation. They've learned where to find the features they need in Photoshop, how to combine these features to solve the problems they encounter every day, and how to streamline and automate their workflow for maximum efficiency. Over the years, a wealth of tips and techniques have been developed—things you won't find documented in the manual we include in the box.

But now, finally, they are documented in Richard Harrington's new book. If you're just beginning to use Photoshop for video work, then this book will help you get up to speed by focusing on just the things you need to know. If you're already an experienced user, you're still bound to pick up a variety of techniques that can make a difference in your daily work. It's taken a dozen years, but video professionals finally have a Photoshop book to call their own.

–Kevin Connor
Director of Product Management
Adobe Systems Incorporated

Introduction: The Gift of Giving

Throughout my professional life, I have been very fortunate to know a great number of talented people. These cutting-edge pioneers worked in small corners of a diverse industry and never received recognition or fame. Fortunately, many of them were generous in their giving of knowledge, never fearing that teaching a young upstart would jeopardize their career or prestige.

When I entered the workforce, the practice of apprenticeship was essentially dead. Due to budget cuts and the emerging digital tools, video and television were being made by fewer people on tighter deadlines. Many people pulled inward, set up small shops, and became fiercely competitive.

Many great tools emerged that let the industry reinvent itself. The advent and subsequent widespread adoption of computer-based editing carried us into a world where even a small corporate video could have visual effects and a rich graphic identity. Soon the tools of the print and emerging web industry were crossing paths with those used for video.

Unfortunately, there were few, if any, books in those early days beyond the owner's manuals. Formalized training centers started to appear, but most companies did not (and many still don't) invest in their employees. Many creative individuals had to struggle with these new tools and spend many late and isolated hours working diligently to climb to the top of this rapidly shifting industry.

But things have started to change. Our industry has become a recognized art form. Students now formally study things like nonlinear editing and motion graphics. When I work with our future peers, the concept of physically editing videotape with two decks or making art cards to shoot with a camera seems arcane and foolish to them. These new co-workers are going to challenge the status quo. All they know is digital; all they have ever seen is visually rich and entertaining television. These students don't define themselves with narrow job titles such as editor, animator, or producer; they want to do it all.

All of these changes have dramatically reshaped the industry. Terms such as *preditor* are emerging (as in producer/editor) for situations where one person is guiding a creative project from start to end, being responsible for completing most of the hands-on work. Even the "traditional" editor is now being expected to create motion graphics, color correct, and understand sound. Because the same computer that can run the nonlinear editing software also runs graphic and sound applications, the editor is expected to grow (sometimes overnight).

So what's this have to do with you? If you bought this book (and thanks if you did!), you are probably working as an editor or motion graphic artist. I am sure that you want to make more visually interesting videos to meet your artistic (and client) demands. You have taken it upon yourself to learn what is often considered the world's best graphic application, Adobe Photoshop. You also need results immediately and don't have time for long-winded explanations or searching through several sources.

If you found this book in a store, it was probably surrounded by dozens of other Photoshop books. So why did I write this? And for that matter, why did CMP Books put it out? Despite all those other books, no one has put out a book exclusively for the video industry. While you'll find thicker books on Photoshop, it has been my goal to create a book that discusses only the issues facing a video professional. I believe I have succeeded, and I thank the wonderful contributors and editors who have helped shape this book.

It has been my goal to give back to an industry that has been nurturing to me. I sincerely hope that this book makes your job easier and your videos better. Be sure to explore the disc, try every tutorial, and make it through every page (even if you read them nonlinearly). No matter what your experience level, I am sure you will come out better for investing your time.

Because this is the first edition of the book, it is likely that technology will rapidly change, as will the way we work in Photoshop. Please be vocal in your feedback to help this effort grow. I wish you luck, and I look forward to seeing many of you at conferences, in a classroom, or online.

Have fun pushing your pixels around.

Richard Harrington
RHED Pixel
February 2003

Acknowledgments

I have a new respect for authors and publishers. I have worked in several deadline-driven industries: newspapers, broadcast news, waiting tables...writing books is harder. When I was asked to write this title, I chronically underestimated what I was getting myself into (like a newbie producer). Because this is my first book, I must thank *all* the people who have made things possible for me to write these words. I would do this all again, but only with this great team. Thanks to the following folks for keeping me on track and helping with the load:

My wife Meghan who was with me in the beginning. You are an inspiration.

CMP Books Paul Temme for the opportunity to write. Dorothy Cox for helping me get there. Michelle O'Neal and her team for making it look great (and making me sound literate). Brandy Ernzen for spreading the word.

FMC Ben Kozuch for letting me reach out to other pros. Jeff Greenberg for providing insight and support.

Technical Editor Thanks to Glen Stephens for tracking both the big and little details, as well as helping me see my blind spots.

Adobe Daniel Brown, Julieanne Kost, Kevin Connor, John Nack, and Gwyn Weisberg for being so helpful.

Contributors Thanks to my friends and peers who made the time to contribute great tutorials and share advice. There are so many people who believed in this project. I could not have done this by myself.

Trish Meyer Thanks for paving the way for this book to be written. I appreciate you refining my outline and raising the bar for professional video books.

Creative Cow My online home. Thanks for your support and resources. To the forum members, thanks for the challenges and keeping me sharp.

The Art Institute of Washington Thanks to Ron Hansen and Michael Davidson for encouraging me (and not questioning why my eyes have been bloodshot for six months). Your support has let me contribute to our industry. To my students past and present, you inspire and challenge me.

DVD-ROM Thanks in a big way to Tom White for authoring a great disc with many industry firsts. The videos would not have been possible without my favorite DP, James Ball, who graciously donated his time. Thanks for the great tunes to SR Audio and Mike Lawyer.

Software Developers and Stock Image Companies Thanks for filling our toolboxes.

Apple Patty Montesion and Abba Shapiro for helping me with Final Cut Pro.

Avid Greg Staten for being my Avid guy. The participants of Avid's Master Editor Workshop for showing me how many true professionals are out there.

NAPP for being a great organization and reaching out to video pros as well. Thanks for letting us reprint a great article.

Educators Mt. Carmel High School–for giving me confidence and courage, as well as introducing me to journalism. Drake University–for sharpening my skills and teaching me how to communicate visually. Keller Graduate School of Management–for teaching me the world of business and project management. Special thanks to great teachers like Billy Stone and John Lytle, who helped steer me.

KCCI John, Dave, Larry, Jack, and Eric for teaching me so much about being a pro.

You, the reader for being a concerned professional and improving our art form.

Caffeine Pepsi One, Diet Coke, Starbucks, and Caribou Coffee for keeping me going.

My wife Meghan who is with me in the end. Thanks for putting up with my deadlines and all-night writing. I am looking forward to our time together.

About the Author

Richard Harrington has had a long relationship with media. When he was seven, he was grounded for using magnets to rearrange the picture tube on the family's 13-inch color TV. (It works, but don't try it.) He has since gone on to many more interesting television experiments.

The author has surrounded himself with media for his entire professional career. Richard has held such diverse jobs as directing newscasts and producing children's television to managing a video production department and editing award-winning national commercials.

He has an extensive background with many cutting-edge video tools. He holds Adobe Certified Expert certificates in Photoshop and After Effects and has completed Avid's Master Editor Workshop and Avid Certified Instructor Program. Additionally, he was one of the first instructors certified by Apple as an instructor for Final Cut Pro. The Project Management Institute certifies Richard Harrington as a Project Management Professional. He holds a Master's Degree in Project Management as well.

The author frequently shares his expertise as a guest speaker at industry conferences and as a trainer for Future Media Concepts. Currently, Richard is a faculty member at the Art Institute of Washington. He also runs a successful consultancy named RHED Pixel which provides technical and design services to a wide range of clients. RHED Pixel creates motion graphics, produces video and multimedia projects, and delivers web-based content including QuickTimeVR.

He believes that we live in a world that is getting increasingly cluttered with confusing messages. His personal philosophy is "Communicate... Motivate...Create." He is a firm believer that media can have powerful results. He hopes that this book helps you to create better-looking, more effective videos.

Getting Started

How to Use This Book

> "Human salvation lies in the hands of the creatively maladjusted."
> —Martin Luther King, Jr., 1963

This book is different. I have approached it like an edit session. I have gathered the best source materials. I have "logged the tapes," so to speak, by pulling only the essential information that a video editor, motion graphic artist, or DVD designer would need. I've organized things into bins for you (except here they're called chapters). I've also loaded the system with tons of new effects and powerful tools to help you out. Think of me as the perfect edit assistant. I've prepared everything for you–now go to town.

This book and accompanying disc can be enjoyed in a nonlinear fashion. Work in whatever order you want (or need). I've included a detailed index and glossary to help you through any gaps caused by skipping around. If you're a little rusty, there are expert articles and tips on the DVD to help you through.

I want Photoshop to be fast and easy for you. I also want you to understand it, not just memorize things. While the chapters will often contain step-by-step instructions for certain skills, there is always a clear explanation of both how and *why* to do things. I want you to get immediate results every time you read a chapter.

I face the same problems you do. I have designed this book so it can live next to your NLE or compositing suite. I know that space is valuable, so I have tried to give you the best book out there on making graphics for video. All of the techniques in this book are *real-world solutions*. You have problems...I've got answers.

Iconography

The content in each chapter is grouped in a logical (and occasionally linear) form. A chapter can be read from start to finish, or by jumping through and stopping when a section catches your eye. Frequently, however, there are important tips or likely problems.

Key to the Icons

	Web Link. Go online to find out more.
	On the DVD. Resources on the DVD-ROM that are important to the current subject.
	Noteworthy. "Gotchas" (pitfalls) to avoid, new terminology, or Photoshop-related skills.
	Technical Tip. Shortcuts, tricks, and practical advice to solve problems.
	New in Photoshop. New, version 7 Photoshop features.

In addition to sidebars, which will give deeper insight into specific techniques or ideas, you will also encounter five kinds of icons–described in the adjoining Key. (Icon design courtesy of Alex Buffalo.)

Disc Access

Since this book is exclusively for the video audience, I am assuming you have access to a drive that can read DVDs. If you don't, buy one. There are so many free resources on the disc that the money spent will be worth it.

 The book and DVD-ROM are meant to be enjoyed together. Nearly every chapter has its own project files so you can try the techniques discussed in the chapter. Look throughout the chapter for the **On the DVD** icon to point out much of the bonus content.

You can explore the disc on your own or use the interactive Pixel Browser. The browser helps sort through the 4+ gigabytes of demos, source files, fonts, freebies, tutorials, and source files. You'll find helpful descriptions and a familiar browser environment to view content. For your browsing enjoyment, I've even added a jukebox filled with songs from up-and-coming bands, thanks to my friends at SR Audio and Cinemedia Productions (http://www.sraudio.com).

Installation

I assume that you are working on Photoshop 6 or newer. If not, a tryout copy of Photoshop 7 is included on the disc, courtesy of Adobe. The Mac version is an installer; double-click to run it. The Windows version is a self-extracting archive; copy it to your local hard drive and double-click. Then open the resulting folder and launch the *Setup.exe* file.

You will need QuickTime installed to open the video files and view the video tutorials. Download it from Apple's web site at http://www.apple.com/quicktime. You need to use version 5 or newer because several clips have the Sorenson version 3 codec applied.

You will need Adobe Acrobat to open the tutorials and several bonus articles. If you don't already have it installed, be sure to visit http://www.adobe.com to download the latest version of Acrobat Reader.

In a few instances, I have used Microsoft Office (http://www.microsoft.com). This is for cases where integration with the Office environment is needed. There are also a few documents that are provided in an editable form for you to use.

There are numerous free plug-ins and resources on the disc. In most cases, you will find a READ ME or User's Guide in the product folder. Consult your owner's manual for installing fonts and other resources; they vary by system. I've included links to most vendor sites; this is the *best* place to turn for troubleshooting advice.

If you are having trouble with your DVD-ROM, contact books@cmp.com for a replacement. This title is a DVD-ROM disc, intended for playback in computer drives capable of reading DVDs. It is *not* for playback in a set-top box. The publisher chose the DVD format instead of shipping this book with eight CDs or leaving things out.

Mac Versus PC

Adobe Photoshop runs the same on Windows as it does a Macintosh. The faster your machine, and the more memory you have, the better it runs (regardless of platform). People will always ask, "Why Mac or Windows? What do you recommend?" Here are the facts, as far as this book is concerned.

MAC	PC
Command	Control
Option	Alt
Control+click	Right mouse click

- The screen captures in this book are mostly from Mac OSX, because of the excellent screen-capture software available.
- My house has five Macs and two PCs.
- When I edit, I run Avid on both platforms and Final Cut Pro on one platform.
- When I freelance, I run whatever they have on whatever they give me.

Macs have a longer history with professional editing, so the Mac keyboard commands come first. Windows shortcuts are listed, too. In today's world, you need to work cross-platform. Don't stress.

The Future

As things change—as they always do—I will update. Those of you who would like to sign up for e-mail news updates can send a blank e-mail to photoshopdv@news.cmpbooks.com. Further, if you would like to contribute to the effort by reporting any errors you spot or things I've overlooked, please contact me at http://www.rhedpixel.com.

For Instructors

If you are an instructor, I sincerely hope that you will adapt this book to your specific curriculum. I have designed it to be a great resource for advanced courses in screen graphics or video production. This book is based on techniques that I have taught over the years. I am a college instructor, as well as a frequent speaker at industry conferences and training events.

There are several sample files that you can use for demonstration purposes during lessons or lectures. If students own the book, I recommend copying a chapter's files to their local computer. This way, they can save and work with the material.

You will also find an excellent series of articles from http://www.adobeevangelists.com included on the disc. These serve as excellent supplemental material or to fill in points that a new user might not know. This book is written assuming that the reader has completed a "beginner book." If this is not the case, please consult several of the supplemental materials. Be sure to check out the Adobe Evangelist site for more advanced articles on Photoshop and all other Adobe products.

An instructor's guide is available to qualified instructors on the CMP Books Web site, http://www.cmpbooks.com/educators. It contains outlines to each chapter, suggested exercises, sample exam questions, and project ideas that students can complete to refine their skills. Additionally, a list of resources for each chapter is also available to help you map the book and disc content to your lesson plans.

As a fellow instructor, you'll understand how much work goes into preparing lessons and sample exercises that are helpful and meaningful. The entire content of this book and DVD-ROM are copyrighted. Owners of the book are granted specific rights as granted in the End User's License or in supplemental licenses provided in each folder. While there are several excellent resources, many of them fully functional or "free," they are for those who purchased the book. In some cases, I have content on the disc that is also available online. I have placed it on the disc for convenience. (Downloading a 12 MB file to 25 lab machines over a network can be slow.) If students do not (yet) own the book, they *can* access some of the content this way.

If a school distributes copies of the source files, software, plug-ins, movies, or PDFs to anyone who has not purchased the book, that constitutes copyright infringement. Also, reproducing pages electronically or physically is a *bad thing*. Thanks for respecting my work and that of the project's contributors.

Your voluntary compliance with copyright enables this book to be updated and me to keep teaching others. Thanks again!

Qualified teaching professionals can acquire evaluation copies of this book by submitting the request form provided on the CMP Books Web site (http://www.cmpbooks.com/educators).

DVD-ROM Roadmap

The enclosed DVD-ROM contains hundreds of useful resources for you to explore. While the disc is likely too large to copy to your hard drive all at once, you will have a smoother experience if you copy over the files you need for each chapter or tutorial. Be sure to try out the interactive Pixel Browser to experience the disc's content in a more user-friendly and entertaining way.

Here is a general summary of what you will find on the DVD-ROM. This title is intended for playback on a computer equipped with a DVD drive, not a TV set-top box.

Tutorials	You'll find 20 bonus tutorials in PDF form for you to practice what you've learned. See the "Guide to the DVD-ROM Tutorials" (page 6). Most projects come with sample files to complete the exercise. Some tutorials are designed to integrate Photoshop with specific applications such as Adobe After Effects or an NLE system. Additionally, some projects use third-party software included on this disc. Some tutorials act as case studies and will give you a window to see another way of working. The best way to learn is to do. Do them all.
Videos	You'll find more than one-and-a half hours of video demonstrating some of the most important techniques. These are compressed QuickTime movies which can be viewed directly from the disc. If you have a slower disc drive, or want to keep a particular clip handy for quicker access, copy the movies to your hard drive.

1. **Welcome:** A short introduction

2. **Using workspaces:** Set up custom workspaces to speed up your productions.

3. **User preferences:** Take control of Photoshop with your preferences.

4. **Working with type:** An overview of the Type tool (including leading and kerning).

5. **Layer masking:** How to create a layer mask and achieve great compositing.

6. **Using Blending Modes:** Unlock Photoshop's most powerful feature.

7. **Using the History Brush:** Use this underused tool to paint backwards in time.

8. **Fading filters:** Get more use out of your filters.

9. **Using After Effect filters on a .psd file:** Access great After Effects plug-ins for your Photoshop files.

10. **Working with PMS colors:** Match your client's colors by using these specialized colors.

11. **Creating duotones:** Learn how to create RGB duotones that import cleanly into your NLE.

12. **Flattening layer styles:** Layer styles are great, but they do not travel well. Learn how to properly flatten them so they import cleanly.

13. **Creating alpha channels:** Learn how to create a "perfect" alpha channel in a few seconds.

14. **Creating seamless backgrounds:** Create useful backgrounds for use in your video projects.

15. **Calculations:** This powerful command can be used to generate mattes or selections that are very complex.

16. **Conclusion:** Good luck and keep in touch!

Chapter files	Here you'll find the source files for chapter exercises. Look for bonus articles and software as well. Be sure to get inside each chapter file so you can get the most out of this book.
Plug-Ins	Take Photoshop to a whole new level. You'll find demos and free software from top manufacturers. Discover some little-known and specialized gems, as well as see why some of the well-known plug-ins are so useful.
Supporting applications	Build your toolbox with these great utilities. You'll find demos of top add-ons and software packages. Be sure to also check out the shareware and freeware that make working in the digital world far easier.
Bonus	Let it be free! You'll find a bounty here: Free Styles, Actions, Articles, Fonts, Edges, more than 1,800 textures or gradients, stock photos, and backgrounds. This folder will keep you busy and ready for some of your toughest production deadlines.
Adobe® Photoshop® 7.0 Tryout	This version of Adobe Photoshop is intended to give you a preview of the features of Adobe Photoshop 7.0 and Adobe ImageReady™ 7.0. This tryout includes all of the core features found in the full retail version and a few of the sample files. It will run for 30 days from date of installation.

Guide to the DVD-ROM Tutorials

| TUTORIAL 1 | **Creating Layer Styles with Photos** |
| | *by Richard Harrington* |

Layer Styles are one of the most exciting things to happen to Photoshop. Flat images can take on a rich depth and visual excitement. This tutorial explores using multiple layers and photographic sources to create a logo.

- MODERATE
- STEP-BY-STEP

| TUTORIAL 2 | **High-Impact Photos with Blend Modes** |
| | *by Apollo 26* |

In this four-part tutorial, you will learn how to create a dramatic look for your photos. Through creative use of blend modes, texture layers, and compositing, a unique look can be accomplished. These "high impact" designs are from the creative collective called Apollo 26.

- MODERATE
- STEP-BY-STEP

| TUTORIAL 3 | **Video Bevel** |
| | *by Jeff Greenberg, Future Media Concepts* |

A video bevel is that neat bug in the corner of the screen (although it doesn't have to go there) that video passes through. It is often the logo or initials of a network or your client. This technique will work in all NLE systems. This lesson is taught by Jeff Greenberg, a certified instructor for both Avid and Apple, who is the Senior Instructor at Future Media Concepts.

- CHALLENGING
- STEP-BY-STEP

| TUTORIAL 4 | **DVD Studio Pro Fast and Easy Buttons** |
| | *by Rachel Max* |

This tutorial is designed for people looking for a quick solution to button interactivity in Apple's DVD Studio Pro. To complete this tutorial, you will need recent versions of Photoshop and DVD Studio Pro. Using PICT layers to highlight buttons is a fast and effective method, but you can't beat the design options when using Photoshop menus.

- MODERATE
- STEP-BY-STEP

TUTORIAL 5 What's New in Photoshop 7.0?

by Julieanne Kost, www.adobeevangelists.com

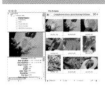

Adobe Photoshop 7.0 software keeps you ahead of the competition with an innovative toolset that delivers new and efficient ways to explore your creativity. The new release offers a number of new tools and features to help you produce even more exceptional imagery. This tutorial walks you through the new features of Adobe Photoshop 7.0. This tutorial comes from the excellent web site http://www.adobeevangelists.com. You'll find a partial collection of their articles and tutorials on the DVD-ROM, but be sure to visit their site for excellent resources for Adobe products.

- EASY–MODERATE
- STEP-BY-STEP + GUIDED TOUR

TUTORIAL 6 Making a Matte Painting

by Frank Rogers, Interface Media Group

Years ago, it took a really big sheet of glass and really good painting talent to do a believable matte painting. Now, with Photoshop, pieces of the set can be repeated, elements flipped or recolored. Additionally, perspectives can be changed, and models or actual location photos can be inserted and blended. All without a hint of oil paint.

- CHALLENGING
- STEP-BY-STEP + GUIDED TOUR

TUTORIAL 7 Fire!

by Jim Tierney, Digital Anarchy

This tutorial discusses how to use the Clouds filter and a simple gradient to create fire within After Effects. The Clouds filter, which uses the Perlin noise algorithm to produce the cloud effect, is an excellent way of creating all sorts of natural effects within AE when animated. The tutorial uses the Clouds image to distort a gradient to create realistic flames by using the Displacement Map filter within AE. It's a powerful technique that can be applied to other images to simulate rippling water going across an image or a flag waving in the wind.

- MODERATE
- STEP-BY-STEP

TUTORIAL 8 Enhancing Still Images for Video

by Jayse Hansen

As an editor, you may often receive still images to include in your video that aren't very inspiring, exciting, or fitting to the piece you're editing. Simply adding these to your video would make the end result look messy, inconsistent, and amateurish. Therefore, to make the video piece have a uniform quality, you'll want to adjust the photos so they all have a similar look to them.

- EASY
- STEP-BY-STEP

TUTORIAL 9   A Loop is a Loop is a Loop, Part 1
by Richard Harrington

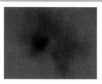

If you produce videos, television, motion graphics, or DVDs, you are probably quite familiar with looping backgrounds. These essential elements get used all the time under title graphics, inserted into lower-thirds, or as menus. There are plenty of outlets available for purchasing looping backgrounds (chances are you already own some). But that gets expensive and does not give your video a unique look. This first part explores making a single looping texture. Parts Two and Three will explore totally different techniques. All three tutorials require After Effects to complete.

- MODERATE
- STEP-BY-STEP

TUTORIAL 10   Case Study: Photoshop as an Animation Tool
by Markus Hofmann

Although Photoshop's uses as an artistic tool are readily apparent, its use as a supplement to animation tools like Adobe After Effects can be invaluable. It can be used to create and enhance digital matte paintings, prepare layers for compositing, cel cleanup, and even as a timesaver for various effects that would otherwise take time to render out in another program. This case study walks you through one artist's use of Photoshop to create promo trailers.

- CHALLENGING
- CASE STUDY

TUTORIAL 11   Making QuickTime Skins
by John Howell, Last Exit

You worked hard to make your video look the best it could, so don't stop at the final fade to black. QuickTime skins provide an easy way to add to the final presentation of your video. You can deliver your film's trailer in the middle of your poster. Your client's 30-second soft-drink spot can be delivered in a custom, branded player. Everything from a simple frame for your movie to play back in to a complicated interactive video player are possible with this technology built into QuickTime. This tutorial will show you how to complete a basic skin and can be easily customized for future projects.

- CHALLENGING
- STEP-BY-STEP

TUTORIAL 12   Creating Custom Backgrounds
by Glen Stephens

This tutorial explores using grayscale design elements to create a custom background. Through the use of blending modes, opacity, and gradients, a custom background can be quickly created. This lesson teaches you an important technique very quickly and can be used daily in your postproduction environment.

- EASY
- STEP-BY-STEP

TUTORIAL 13   Using Photoshop with Final Cut Pro

by Tom Wolsky, author, Final Cut Pro 3 Editing Workshop

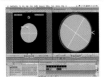

Want to use Photoshop with Apple's Final Cut Pro? Learn what works (and what doesn't) in this hands-on lesson. You'll discover how to get consistent, predictable results every time.

- MODERATE
- STEP-BY-STEP

TUTORIAL 14   A Loop is a Loop is a Loop, Part 2

by Richard Harrington

This continues a series on making seamless backgrounds. Here you'll learn how to take gradient layers made in Photoshop and create moving backgrounds in After Effects. This technique will show you how to create a usable background in minutes.

- EASY
- STEP-BY-STEP

TUTORIAL 15   Creating a Video Box Cover in Photoshop

by Jayse Hansen

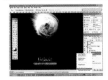

You've finished the project, and it looks great! Now all you need is a custom package. Don't know Quark or InDesign? No problem! Adobe's done such an excellent job with text and layout enhancements in the recent versions of Photoshop that it's robust enough to do a complete video cover.

- CHALLENGING
- STEP-BY-STEP + GUIDED TOUR

TUTORIAL 16   Integrating Adobe Products

by Raymond Soto

By combining Adobe Photoshop, After Effects, and Premiere, this designer developed an award-winning self-promotion piece. By using "found footage with guerilla videography," an aggressive, yet pleasing look is achieved. All of the work was done using desktop software, a DV camera, and a consumer scanner.

- MODERATE–CHALLENGING
- CASE STUDY

TUTORIAL 17   A Loop is a Loop is a Loop, Part 3

by Richard Harrington

Learn how to take complex Photoshop files and create three-dimensional backgrounds. This tutorial spends a lot of time in Photoshop, but then requires minimal work in After Effects to put the layers into motion.

- CHALLENGING
- STEP-BY-STEP

TUTORIAL 18   How to Age Your Photos
by Robert Lawson

Want to make your photos look *much* older? This quick technique can significantly age any modern photo. No third-party plug-ins are needed; everything is done with Photoshop's built-in tools.

- EASY
- STEP-BY-STEP

TUTORIAL 19   Making Textures
by Robert Lawson

Need a little photorealism? Photoshop excels at allowing you to incorporate photographic sources into your projects. But what happens if you need some texture but lack the photos? Don't worry about it. This tutorial shows you how to create three common textures: scratched metal, glass, and chrome.

- MODERATE
- STEP-BY-STEP

TUTORIAL 20   Inside Digital Vision
by Richard Harrington

Learn how three designers create high-end graphics in Adobe Photoshop. Find out how to integrate different graphic tools for great results. There are shortcuts and tricks from top pros. We hear from three designers from the popular Infinity series of layered stock images.

- MODERATE–CHALLENGING
- CASE STUDY

Make It Happen

This book and the accompanying DVD are intended to be a teaching guide, a reference book, and a source of inspiration. It is my hope to make your job easier and your projects more professional looking. To move you towards this goal, I will occasionally take related tangents. Photoshop is a companion to many other applications; so don't be surprised to occasionally dip into specific nonlinear editing systems (NLEs) or even After Effects.

Reality Check

Photoshop is one of the most elegantly designed, yet feature-deep pieces of software available. Before you get defensive and proudly stamp your feet in support of Apple, Avid, Media 100, etc., hear me out. No other application has so many tools and processing power with the ability to export to multiple formats. If you design for print, web, interactive, animation, or video, you likely use Photoshop.

Because it is the tool-for-everybody, Photoshop sometimes gets a little crowded. There are many features (distractions) that have nothing to do with video. I am not suggesting that you write Adobe asking for a refund on unused features. Instead, accept that all you need (and more) is waiting for you.

Be prepared to change your viewpoint. Editors often want to understand every bell and whistle in a particular application. This book won't go there. What it will do is show you tools that are likely to be used by video artists. It will also dip into some third-party plug-ins and related technologies that may help you. Will I cover everything? No, and if you want that, I suggest you pick up the *Photoshop Bible* by Deke McClelland.

I will waste no time talking about achieving great four-color printing or how to get faster download times. This is a video book, and you work (or want to work) in the video industry—a fast-paced, deadline-

Did you know that Photoshop has an alternate startup screen? Liquid Sky was the code name for Photoshop 7 in development. All versions of Photoshop have these "secret" screens. Hold down the Cmd (Ctrl) key and choose About Photoshop from the Help menu.

Honestly evaluate your skill level. It is OK to be a beginner in some applications and an expert at others. Photoshop requires a "strong bench" of skills.

driven, technical industry. I respect that, because I am right there with you, and it is my goal to help you get faster and feel more confident in using the world's best image-editing application.

Suggested Hardware

Pick up a combo TV/VCR unit for checking your graphics. These low-cost consumer models are helpful to give you a real-world view of your graphics.

Photoshop is a great tool right out of the box. Here are a few things that will help you get more work done, however. The order in which you add these items on will vary, depending on your work environment and budget. I will not assume you have any of these, other than access to an RGB video monitor in either NTSC or PAL (depending upon your country).

A second computer monitor. Once you've gotten used to having your palettes open, you'll never be able to go back to opening and closing windows and tabs all day long.

As much RAM as you can hold. RAM has been getting cheaper and cheaper. Fill your computer up all the way.

A video card with S-Video out. These are not very expensive anymore and will let you plug your system into a standard television or NTSC monitor. These cards are useful for checking interlace and flicker issues, but are not necessarily good for checking color because they do not use an accurate video setup. You might consider moving up to a higher-end video card with component or digital outputs for more accurate color monitoring.

An NTSC monitor.

For Mac users, a two-button mouse. Because Ctrl+clicking gets a little old after a while. Many options are available these days, since USB became a common standard between Mac and Windows.

An NTSC monitor. So that you can check your work before going into the edit suite.

A scanner that matches your imaging needs. I own four scanners. None of them had a price tag of more than $400, and they all work great for video. In fact, the $99 portable one scanned several photos in this book. Scanners have come a long way in recent years.

Keep your Pantone color book in its sleeve and in the drawer. Exposure to light speeds up fading (and reduces accuracy).

A Pantone color book. So that you have some sort of reference guide for matching the PMS logo colors that your clients give you.

A tablet and pressure-sensitive pen. This can be for both fun and serious work. A little bit of digital doodling can be a relaxing activity. Moreover, a pen is often an easier input device than a mouse or trackpad for realistic brushstrokes and tracing activities.

A card reader for transferring digital photos. There are multiple format readers available. Get one that is self-powered and supports what you use—compact flash, smart media, memory stick, etc.

A good set of keyboard and mouse wrist guards. Sore wrists get in the way of what you are trying to accomplish.

An optical storage device. I am a big fan of the new generation of DVD burners. It is possible to back up 4.5GB of project data onto a single $3 disc. A CD or DVD burner will also allow you to burn your projects to disc for testing in a Video CD/DVD player on consumer televisions.

Setting Up Photoshop

Success takes preparation. I cannot promise you overnight success, although I can tell you that this book can make you faster and more confident with each chapter you complete. To get the most out of this book, it will help if you and I are operating in a similar environment. I will make suggestions on how to configure Photoshop to operate more like the nonlinear edit system you are used to. So please take the extra time to reset Photoshop. But if you are strongly opposed to any of these cosmetic changes, skip them. These are merely suggestions to prepare you for success.

Help! I Can't See My Cursors! This is the #1 tech support call to Adobe. If you have the Caps Lock key on, Brush Size painting cursors are disabled.

Photoshop has its roots as a video and film application. The print—and more recently, web—industries have claimed it as their own. Now it's our turn. Digital video has emerged as the fastest growing technology area; more and more books and applications are popping up on the shelves, promising solutions for all skill levels. It is my goal to help you reclaim Photoshop and learn to harness its diverse imaging abilities to enhance your video projects. The program has all the tools you need (and many you don't). Let's get started by setting up Photoshop to work with our video applications. To begin, call up your Preferences panel with Cmd+K (Ctrl+K).

Smart Quotes will automatically insert true, curly quotation marks when you press the ' (feet) or the " (inches) key.

General

Under the **General** pane, choose:
- Adobe Color Picker
- Bicubic Interpolation
- Set the Redo key as Cmd+Y (Ctrl+Y)
- Allow at least 20 history states (levels of Undo). You will vary this number based on RAM and personal experience as you grow less (or more) dependent on undos.
- Show Tool Tips checked
- Keyboard Zoom Resizes Windows checked
- Save Palette Locations checked
- Use Shift Key for Tool Switch unchecked
- Use Smart Quotes checked. Click **NEXT**.

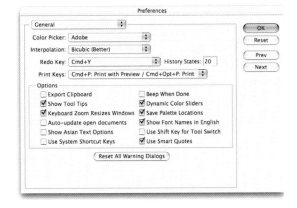

File Handling

Under **File Handling**, you need to make some changes to ensure cross-platform functionality. Even if your shop only uses Macs or PCs, you *will* work with others who are different. Trust me. Be cross-platform compliant when saving your Photoshop files.

- Always choose the **Save an Icon** and **Thumbnail** option. This will allow you to quickly locate files through visual cues. If you do a lot of web work, you may want to disable this feature to decrease file size (thus speeding download times).
- Always append file extension with lowercase tags.
- Always maximize compatibility for Photoshop (.psd) files. Click **NEXT**.

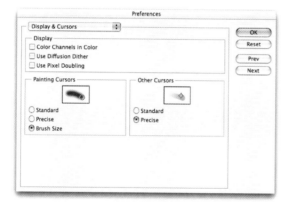

Display & Cursors

- Under Display & Cursors, leave the first three boxes unchecked. These options affect how your channels and images are viewed and diminish the on-screen viewing quality. You will never need these options for video work.
- Set Painting Cursors to Brush Size. (**Caps Lock** key disables this preview feature.)
- Set Other Cursors to **Precise**. This way, you can actually see your sample point for your Eyedropper and Stamp tools. Click **NEXT**.

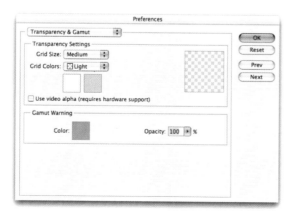

Transparency & Gamut

Under Transparency & Gamut, you can generally leave these options alone. Personal preferences do vary however.

- You can change the grid color if you despise light gray. You can also disable the grid altogether. Remember, the grid will not print or show up in your video graphics.
- *Do not* check **Use Video Alpha** unless you have an advanced video card and intend to use Photoshop as a live keyer. Chances are there are only eight people reading this book who are doing this. Click **NEXT**.

Units & Rulers

Under Units & Rulers, modify Photoshop's measuring system to match video. If you work in a web or print environment, you can quickly jump back and change your measurement units by double-clicking on the ruler.

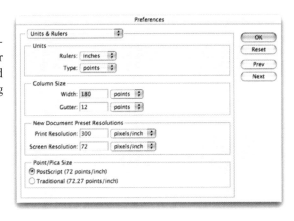

- Set Rulers to pixels
- Set Type to points
- Ensure that screen resolution is set to 72 pixels/inch
- Ensure that the Point/Pica Size is set to PostScript (72 points/inch) so that type acts like other video applications. Click **NEXT**.

Guides, Grid, & Slices

Set up gridlines every 25 pixels and 5 subdivisions. Pick a color such as a dark gray by clicking on the color swatch. You can now turn the grid off and on from the View menu or from the keyboard using Cmd+" (Ctrl+").

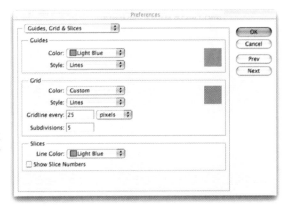

Disable Show Slice Numbers unless you are doing a lot of web work—in which case you should be using ImageReady anyway. Slices are used with rollover graphics to trigger button effects on web pages. Click **NEXT**.

Plug-Ins & Scratch Disks

Under Plug-Ins & Scratch Disks, you can specify additional hard drives to use as scratch disks. Photoshop uses hard-drive space when it runs out of physical RAM. This virtual memory is efficient, but real RAM is a better solution.

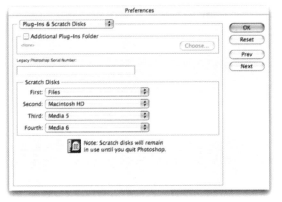

Memory will generally not be a big deal because you'll work primarily with low-resolution sources in this book. However, if you have extra (local) drives, make Photoshop aware of them. Set your emptiest drive as the First Scratch Disk. The changes take place the next time you launch Photoshop. Click **NEXT**.

When you choose New Document, you'll notice that the Window menu is **not** grayed out. You can steal the window size of an open document to create a new document. Make a new document, and then access the Window menu for a list of open documents (and sizes).

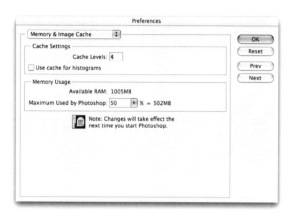

Memory & Image Cache

Under Memory & Image Cache, specify how much RAM you want to allow to Photoshop. With dynamic memory management under OSX and Windows, this is not a big deal. I recommend allowing 40–60% of your RAM, for a total of at least 200MB.

If you are running under OS9, you will need to quit Photoshop and set the memory allowances at the finder level. Locate the application's icon, highlight it, and choose File>Get Info>Memory and specify the maximum and minimum size. Click **OK**.

Color Settings

Now it is time to modify how Photoshop handles color. Press Shift+Cmd+K (Shift+Ctrl+K) to bring up the Color Settings dialog. The default configuration is optimized for web and print graphics, which can result in color shifts when opening video frames. Choose Color Management Off for consistent results with video graphics.

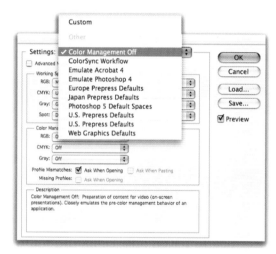

Remember, the only way to see accurate video colors is to hook your machine up to an NTSC monitor. If this is not an option, you will need to test your graphics. For more on checking your colors, see Chapter 12, "The Road to the NLE."

Video's Unique Requirements

Already maxed out your RAM slots? A dedicated drive or partition makes the perfect scratch disk. This will greatly improve Photoshop's efficiency in opening large images.

Video is a unique creature; it does not enjoy the careful management that other formats do. Web designers have the benefit of designing on computers, for computers. Print designers have precise control during the printing stage, with dedicated professionals calibrating their output devices. The general population installs $199 color televisions but won't even read the instruction manuals. To make things worse, there's a standards war going on between multiple formats, digital versus analog, standard versus widescreen. Let's just say, your job isn't easy. I want to establish a few key terms immediately, however, to help us move forward. Many of these may seem familiar, so I will keep the introduction short.

Canvas size. This is the area in which you will work. In Photoshop, specify your work area in pixels. It is a good idea to check with the manufacturer of your nonlinear edit system for requirements. These can be found in your owner's manual or on the NLE manufacturer's web site. You can also check the appendices for recommendations from top manufacturers.

Aspect ratio. Television is generally a 4×3 aspect ratio, while widescreen is a 16×9 aspect ratio. You will find more information, as well as information on templates, in Chapter 2, "Pixels: Time for Tech."

Image mode. Photoshop supports eight image modes, including bitmap, grayscale, RGB, and CMYK color spaces. For video, work in RGB mode for consistent results with nonlinear edit systems.

Standard video is shown at a 4×3 aspect ratio. In the print world, this is referred to as *landscape orientation.*

Bit depth. Also called color depth or pixel depth. A measurement of how much color information is available to be displayed for each pixel in an image. Photoshop users generally work in 8-bits per channel mode because it provides a full set of tools. These 8 bits combine to a total of 24 bits for an RGB image or 32 bits for an RGB image with an alpha channel.

Some high-end scanners can capture information at 16 bits per channel. These files are twice the size of their 8-bit counterparts, but contain more detail. Adobe After Effects can work with 16-bit images on a limited basis. Currently, 16-bit images do not support layers, nor do they support many of the editing tools or filters. You will likely always work in 8-bits-per-channel mode.

Luminance ranges. The range of colors supported by video. There are two major color spaces in use for nonlinear edit systems, RGB mapping and 601 Mapping. You should check your system to see which is in use. For more details, see Chapter 2, "Pixels: Time for Tech."

Anti-aliasing is critical for smooth edges. However, for really small type, leave it off to improve legibility.

Alpha channels. An alpha channel contains information about all of the transparent areas in your composition. All objects should be on transparent layers when creating an alpha channel. Do not place any of your objects on the background layer. For more details, see Chapter 3, "What About Transparency?" and Chapter 4, "Why Layers?".

If you need to archive an image, a 16-bit scan is the best format. You may have to down-convert to 8 bits for compositing or if your NLE does not support the mode, but at least you have the extra data for future applications.

Anti-aliasing. Anti-aliasing causes a gentle blending of the colors along the edge of an image. It is often used to reduce flicker. This technique is effective for straight lines and text, to create a smoother composite of foreground and background elements. It is most common for low-resolution output (such as video or web). There are four different types of anti-aliasing, which can be accessed from the Options bar or the Character palette. (See the following figure.)

Nonsquare pixels. Your own personal demon. These cause more problems for more people than anything else about Photoshop. In a nutshell, computers and Photoshop work with square pixels (1.0 aspect); most digital video works with nonsquare pixels (0.9 aspect). I attempt to squash this problem thoroughly in Chapter 2, "Pixels: Time for Tech."

A Few Basics

Working with layers

Virtually every modern edit system is adding at least partial support for Photoshop layers. These efforts are worth praise, but they still do not eliminate the need for saving specialized formats or creating alpha channels. There are times you want layers, and times you don't.

You will import a layered file into Adobe After Effects or your edit system if you want to animate the layers. This is particularly helpful for segment bumpers and show titles. It is also common to import a layered file that contains multiple elements that you intend to use in your edit. By importing just one file, it is easier to manage media on your hard drive.

Anti-aliasing helps elements containing curved lines (such as text) appear smoother on screen.

So why flatten layers? Do you really want a lower third eating up five tracks of your timeline? What about unsupported features like blending modes, grouping, and layer styles? Never flatten your design files, but rather choose Save As and specify a new file type. When saving a .psd file as a PICT or TARGA file, it is flattened to a single layer, with the option to include an alpha channel.

I will go very deeply into layer management, masking, blending, and alignment. You should come to appreciate how powerful and flexible a layered file can be. You will work hard for your layers, so do not ever flatten your file and trash all of your efforts. Simply choose Save A Copy and a flattened format.

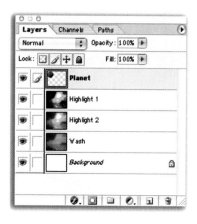

Backing up your work

Your work is what keeps you from enjoying the rest of your life. Do you ever want to have to redo something you've already done? Growing up in Chicago, we were always taught "Vote Early. Vote often." I've adapted this to the Chicago method of file backups: "Save Early! Save Often."

Saving your work is critical because, unlike your nonlinear edit system, Photoshop does not have an autosave feature. There is no "attic" to help cover you. Saving is your responsibility. Make the act of saving a reflex reaction. Every time you are sitting idle, tap Cmd+S (Ctrl+S). I often find myself tapping this five times in a row if I am in the middle of a creative thought.

Continue these good habits after the project. Gather up all design and production files, as well as fonts and source materials. Burn them to CD or DVD twice. Maintain two separate project archives so that you always have a copy of the work.

If you click directly on the layer name, you can edit it with the palette. One less pop-up window to deal with.

Toolbox

Many tools share space in the toolbox and a keyboard shortcut. Call up the Preferences with Cmd+K (Ctrl+K) and make sure the following option is disabled: Use Shift Key for Tool Switch. You can now tap a shortcut key (such as M for marquee) and cycle through the tools contained in that tool's drawer. This will speed up your ability to switch tools. While you are in your general preferences panel, you may also want to enable the Show Tool Tips feature to assist in learning keyboard shortcuts.

Your hands-on tools are all contained in the toolbox. Similar tools are often nested together. You can access these hidden tools by clicking and holding on a particular tool. Whenever you see a triangle in Photoshop, clicking will open additional options. The first keyboard shortcuts you should master are those for the toolbox. In general, the first letter of the tool is the keyboard shortcut. If you can't remember the shortcut, click on the tool while holding down the Option (Alt) key to cycle through the available tools.

Mnemonic: Devil's Xylophone. Pressing D will load the default colors of black and white; the X key will toggle between colors.

Not every tool is useful to the video editor. It is important to remember that Photoshop is the #1 image editor for other industries as well. Many of the tools in Photoshop are designed for print and web professionals. A color-coded chart is provided to point out the "video-friendly" tools. Green tools are ones you will need right way, yellow tools will be used occasionally, and video professionals may use red tools infrequently or not at all.

Double-clicking on the magnifying glass will zoom your image to 100%.

Next you'll find the foreground and background colors. Many other tools use these colors. The most obvious usage is for the painting tools. Lesser known is that these colors drive the results for many filters.

When working with the Artistic, Brush Stroke, or Sketch filters, you will see great variety when switching colors. These colors are often used in painting masks.

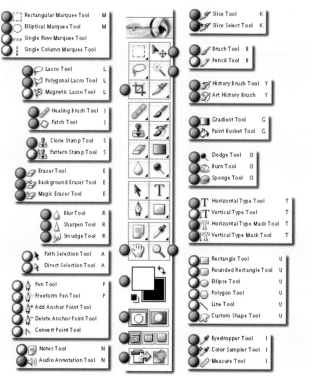

The toolbox contains a few other useful features for a video editor. Clicking on the Photoshop icon at the top of the box will take you to Adobe Online. This is the quickest way to check for software updates and extensive resources. You can tell Photoshop to check for resources manually or configure it to check monthly, weekly, or daily.

The remaining three rows will be used in very special circumstances. The Quick Mask mode is useful for creating advanced selections or masks. We'll dig deeper into masks and alpha channels in Chapter 3, "What About Transparency?". Next are the screen mode switches, which change how the workspace is presented.

Palette popping

We're not talking about a night of dim sum. One of the biggest wastes of times frequently committed is "palette popping." Many advanced users open and close tools all day long–dragging windows all over the place, closing and opening the same windows over and over. Stop! There are many solutions to this problem.

Temporary banishment. Pressing the Tab key hides all of your tools. Press it again and they come back. Not good enough for you? Using Shift+Tab, you can hide everything except the Options bar and toolbox. This useful command is best combined with full-screen mode for a video workspace. Tap the F key twice to blank out all other images and darken the edges of your screen. Use Cmd++ or – (Ctrl++ or –) to zoom in and out of your image. Press F and Tab again to go back to standard screen mode with menus and tools.

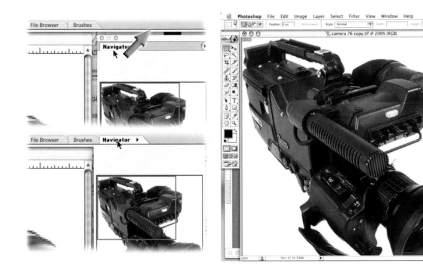

Palettes can now be docked in the Options Bar for quick access.

Sitting on a dock. Wish you could keep tools nearby in a virtual drawer? Photoshop 6 brought the welcome addition of the Options bar and its palette well. You can drag tool tabs to the well, where they are docked as dropdown menus. Put useful but rarely used tools like the Brushes palette and File Browser here.

A workspace of your own. One of Photoshop's coolest new features is workspaces. Like to work with different tools for different situations? Maybe you use the Channels and Brushes palette a lot when masking, but really wish Layer Styles and the Color Picker were there for text work. You can have any combo you want in one click with workspaces. Open the windows you want, and arrange them into the desired position. To save the current workspace layout, choose Winow>Workspace>Save Workspace. Enter a unique name for the workspace, and click OK.

To activate a workspace, simply Choose Window>Work-space, and choose a workspace from the submenu. There are no built-in keys for workspaces, but you can create actions and map them to an available F Key if you've foresworn menus. You update a workspace by resaving it with a new name. To delete a workspace, choose Window>Work-space>Delete Workspace. There is, unfortunately, no way to share workspaces with other users or machines, because they are tied to your preference files.

Instead of minimizing palettes, just hide them. Press the Tab key to toggle your palettes on and off.

Workspaces (custom window arrangements) are familiar concepts in several video-editing applications. They can now be found in Photoshop (v7 or newer).

Font overload. Upon startup, Photoshop must examine all of the fonts that will be available for the type tools. Large quantities of fonts installed on your system means long load times. This can cause Photoshop to take longer to start up. If you find the startup time for Photoshop to be too long, remove any unused fonts from your system (see your OS manual). Or use a font management program such as Suitcase or Font Foundry. Shareware fonts are often a source of instability as well, due to conflicting font IDs that may confuse your OS.

Changing the Plug-Ins folder at launch time. By holding Cmd+Shift keys (Ctrl+Shift) immediately after launch, the Additional Plug-Ins Folder dialog will appear. You can specify an additional folder from which Photoshop will load plug-ins. Many editors will carry a zip disc with extra plug-ins (although this won't work with serialized plug-ins).

Resetting preferences at launch time. If you would like to reset all of your Photoshop preferences, simultaneously hold down the Cmd+Option+Shift keys (Ctrl+Alt+Shift) when you launch Photoshop.

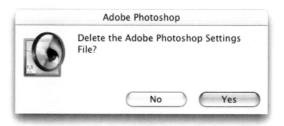

 Be sure to check out the many great materials on the disc. You'll find goodies in every chapter's folder, plus free and trial software. Fully explore the disc for extra articles, tutorials, and training movies. You'll be amazed at how much good stuff is packed in there.

Profile: Frank Rogers

Frank Rogers has a diverse background in film and video. He's designed props, make-up, prosthetics, table top, and special effects for movies such as *True Lies*, *Homicide*, *Contact*, and *Mars Attacks*. Frank started working for Interface Media in all the same capacities, but he's adding more digital tools to his palette.

"Coming from a traditional effects background and moving more and more to computer/real effects has made sense to me," said Rogers. "I do motion control, miniatures, set building, and all the traditional art department effects work. That's led to working on cel animation in a miniature world for PBS or working out how to shoot an Eskimo in the arctic (in a studio) believably or how to run down an Arab street and through a hole in a wall to see the Ark of the Covenant."

"Rather than a friction between traditional effects and production with the digital world, I see what's perceived as the ease of effects in the digital world driving clients to ask for more effects," said Rogers. "In the case of movies, more are nondigital than digital. Of course, the real beauty of digital is the ability to finesse those floor effects miniatures and CG into a believable whole. Most people aren't aware of how many of the CG backgrounds are actually miniatures beautifully finessed in the correction stage."

One area where several purists disagree is motion control photography. Rogers says that there's room for digital tools there as well.

"Even though you would think real-world motion control be to antithetical to Photoshop, clients really enjoy showing up with a double spread of the Sistine Chapel and hoping that I'll be able to take the staple out of God's navel," said Rogers. "Photoshop and a decent DeskJet sit next to the Moco. When lower thirds are needed and the Chyrons are already booked out, Photoshop is there."

Rogers is among a growing group that is harnessing Photoshop's powerful text engine to produce effects. The flexibility of the Character and Paragraph palettes, along with layer styles, makes it a powerful CG machine.

"I like title creation because I have so many choices and inputs to nudge my approach to type," said Rogers. "I also do storyboards in Photoshop to widen my choices."

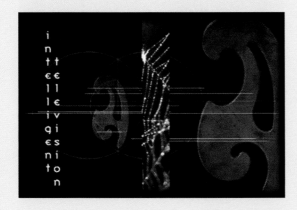

This open attitude has allowed Rogers to adapt and grow with changing technology. When you sit down with him, you quickly discover that he is as tech savvy as a recent college grad, current with what the industry is doing. Combine that with his extensive background, and you have a key individual, one who is indispensable to the production team.

"I see a lot of people get very comfortable in one set of skills, and I've seen highly paid experts in fields like Airbrush Retouching suddenly be unemployable," said Rogers. "Even if you are God's gift to _____, pray that _____ stays around."

This realization has led to a lifelong approach to learning. Rogers is working to be solid in type, color correction, photo retouching, and effects; all of these are skills important to the video and film industry. The most important skill, however, is still speed.

"I really admire people with speed and shortcut ability. I find that each job I do in a specific area is a chance to repeat and learn a new set of shortcuts."

Two of Frank Rogers' favorites:

- the ability to change type styles on a line of type that's already been set
- the ability to scroll blending modes using the Shift++ or – keys

Rogers encourages other pros to put the time into learning Photoshop.

"Learning to use Photoshop well is like knowing how to play piano in music or type in the real world," said Rogers. "It's a core program you wind up back in whether you are a compositor, motion graphic expert, or 3D code warrior."

Pixels: Time for Tech

The pixel is the building block upon which our industry is based. When creating computer graphics, they are either raster or vector images. Photoshop supports both types of images, and it is common to mix the two in a single project. Newer versions of Photoshop contain vector type, giving it the ability to be resized and edited within Photoshop. While all graphics for video end up as raster images, a clear understanding of the two categories will help you build, modify, and import artwork.

Pixel by Any Other Name

The term *pixel* is a fusion of the words *picture element,* and it is aptly named. The pixel is the smallest amount of space that exists in our creative universe. Pixels contain color, and these colors combine to form images. Bitmaps are used for continuous tone or photorealistic images. If you continue to zoom in on an image, you can eventually see the pixel grid that forms an image. To zoom, use the **Zoom** tool, or the Cmd++ or – to navigate (Ctrl++ or – on Windows). To fill the screen, press Cmd+0 (Ctrl+0), or to view at 100% magnification, press Cmd+Option+0 (Ctrl+Alt+0).

 Picture elements, more commonly known as pixels, are the building blocks of the video industry. In Photoshop, you will edit pixels when working with your source photos and video frames.

Raster images. When working with raster images, you edit pixels rather than shapes or objects directly. Proper selection techniques are important to get accurate results (see *Selecting and Extracting Images* on page 50 of Chapter 3). Raster images are resolution dependent in that they contain a specific number of pixels. Therefore, images will lose detail and appear jagged if they are scaled above 100% in the nonlinear edit system. If you need to scale an object such as a logo or title within the edit session, bring it in at maximum screen size, and scale down rather than up. For achieving a documentary pan-and-zoom effect, a wide variety of plug-ins is available for most edit systems. The best solution, however, is to create the effect in Adobe After Effects (see *Professional Motion Control "Photography" with After Effects and Photoshop* on page 42).

Always ask for the client logo as a vector file. It will give you greater flexibility when scaling. If you own Illustrator, splitting it up is easy. (See Chapter 5, "Some Words on Words, Logos, and Symbols.")

Vector Graphics. An understanding of vector graphics may seem out of place to many readers. Traditionally artists turn to Adobe Illustrator to work with vector graphics. While it is still necessary to use Illustrator for complex vector editing, Adobe Photoshop now provides its own set of powerful vector tools.

Vector graphics are often used for corporate logos and print pieces. Vector graphics are resolution independent because they are composed of lines and curves defined by mathematical objects called vectors. Vectors describe an image by its geometric characteristics or shapes. These vectors allow the graphic to be scaled to any size without losing detail or clarity. Adobe After Effects supports the use of vector graphics, and most motion graphic artists swear by vectors for achieving dramatic type effects involving scaling. Vector graphics are best used for shapes or logos, especially if scaling is involved. Because video monitors represent images by displaying them as pixels along a grid, all vector graphics are rasterized at some point for use in video. Vectors still offer great flexibility, which makes them desirable during the initial design phase. They also are resolution independent, an advantage if you ever need to take your work into a print environment.

Display Resolution

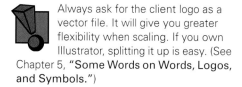

Newer monitors support a wide range of resolutions. Television monitors display only one resolution.

The quantity of pixels along the height and width of a raster image determines its screen (or display) size. Older computer monitors display 72 pixels per inch (ppi); newer monitors often display 96 ppi or higher. These display settings will often vary, ranging higher or lower, depending on your computer's video card. On the other hand, video monitors are not variable. Standard video places 648×486 square pixels for the NTSC format, and 768×576 for the PAL format. I'll go deeper into setting up pixel dimensions and pixel aspect ratio later in this chapter.

In order to get the maximum quality out of Photoshop, you must understand video's limitations. These limitations can be a hindrance, causing flicker on the screen if you improperly anti-alias fine details such as text or thin lines. They can also be a benefit, in that many affordable stock-photography collections exist with low-resolution files, as well as filters and image-processing techniques that are many times faster for video-sized images.

It is possible to view many more pixels on your computer at one time than will fit in a standard video frame. For example, a 15-inch monitor can be configured to display 800 pixels horizontally and 600 pixels vertically. An 800×600 image would appear to fill the screen. On a 21-inch monitor configured to the same display settings, the same image would appear to fill the screen, but each pixel would be significantly larger. Changing the monitor's settings, however, could allow more pixels to fit on the screen, leaving empty space around our 800×600 image. However, while most computer monitors support multiple resolutions, video monitors do not.

Display size does matter! Be sure to view your image at 100% to make accurate decisions. If your monitor is not wide enough, then view in even increments of 50% or 25%.

Check the display size in Photoshop. You'll usually want to view images at 100%, so that you can make accurate decisions about the display quality of effects. If this is not possible, view in even increments of 50% or 25%, because computers are very good at dividing by two.

Image Resolution

The requirements of print differ greatly from those for video. It is necessary to work with a much higher quantity of pixels to produce satisfactory results when outputting to the printed page.

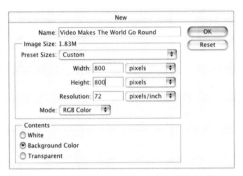

If you have an object loaded on the clipboard, the new document dialog will automatically size itself to match.

A common problem occurs when video professionals talk to their cousins in the print and web worlds. Although all camps speak the same language, some unique terms are used that often result in confusion and extra work by both. The most common problem is resolution. Video makers may use the term pixels per inch or ppi; other industries use dots per inch, or dpi. The two terms are interchangeable.

Print resolution. In print, using too low of a resolution results in *pixelization*–output with large, rough-looking pixels. Using too high a resolution image increases processing time and storage requirements and slows the output. Video and print pros have very different definitions of full size and high quality.

There is no "dots per inch" (dpi) with video graphics. All that matters are the total pixels on screen.

If you translate a 648×486 television screen into inches, it would be approximately 8.88×6.66 inches. At 72 ppi, the file size is approximately 900 kilobytes. If you asked a print professional for the same size image at high quality, you would likely get a file in the range of 4–60 megabytes. This is because print professionals often use resolutions of 150–600 ppi, depending upon output requirements.

Photoshop 7 lets you create new, preset file sizes. Modify the *New Doc Sizex.txt* file in the Photoshop 7>Presets folder.

Be sure to specify image resolution when working with outside artists and clients, or you will spend a lot of wasted time downsampling images. Print-ready images will quickly eat up your disk space and are difficult to transport electronically due to their large size. Filters and image adjustments take "forever" on large images, especially if you are used to video or web work. The only advantage to this extra information is that you can have more control over cropping and scaling of the final photo. Unless I plan on doing dramatic moves on an image in After Effects, I request outside artists to provide me images at 150 dpi; this involves the least work for all parties.

Web resolution. High-resolution images won't always be your problem, though. With the proliferation of image-rich Web sites, clients are often providing artwork directly from Web sites. While this is a convenient way to find things, it offers many problems. Web images are a low-resolution medium. While web and video images are both built at 72 ppi, it is rare to find full-screen web graphics due to download times. Larger images tend to be sliced up as well, making it difficult to reformat them for video. The worst problem, however, is compression.

Web graphics generally employ three file types: GIF, JPEG, and PNG. These compression schemes discard information, especially color detail, to achieve smaller file size. The Graphics Interchange Format (GIF) is most commonly used to display indexed-color graphics. Indexed color supports only 256 colors and should never be used for video source material.

Web formats are great... for the Internet! Don't use JPEG, GIF, or PNG in your video projects. If you have to use a web format, choose PNG-24. It is the most versatile of all the web formats.

The Joint Photographic Experts Group (JPEG) format is extremely common. It can be found in web pages and digital cameras. Most web images are highly compressed and do not hold up well when reformatted for video. Digital cameras that use at least a 2.1 megapixel system and are set to high or fine quality can produce acceptable results. Be careful when working with JPEGs; they may be set to CMYK or grayscale color modes. It is necessary to convert these to RGB before using them in the nonlinear edit system, or unpredictable color changes may occur.

The least likely format you may encounter is PNG. The Portable Network Graphics (PNG) format can be used for lossless compression and for display of images on the World Wide Web. There are two varieties of PNG, 8-bit (PNG-8) and 24-bit (PNG-24). These two formats support RGB, indexed color, and grayscale modes, as well as interlacing. Of all the web formats, the PNG-24 is most desirable (least awful) for video purposes. The file size of a PNG file is significantly larger than GIF or JPEG. This will give you more information to work with. PNG files are very uncommon because older web browsers do not support them and the large file size deters many web designers.

Salvaging Web Images for Use in Video

One of the worst things to happen to graphic artists was the proliferation of Web pages for corporate clients and associations. Firms are moving virtually all of their assets on to the Internet and have placed such emphasis on their Web sites that they have abandoned or lost track of traditional assets. It used to be far easier to get a high quality, "camera-ready" ad slick with logos on it. Annual reports or brochures could always be found and scanned as well.

These days you ask for a logo and you get a 200×200 pixel GIF from the client's Web site. These images suck and should be avoided at all costs. No matter what your client says, the logo exists as a higher quality file. If they have a business card, it exists. There are several approaches you can try before accepting Garbage In.

- Ask if there's an in-house web department or printer. Call these people and ask for a better logo. While you're at it, ask for a style guide.

- Search the Web site for a press area. Many times high-quality logos are available for download to the media.

- Download an annual report or brochure as a PDF. Often times these are saved at 150dpi or better (or even as vector files!). You can import a multi-page PDF into Photoshop (File>Automate>Multi-Page PDF to PSD). You can also import a single page by choosing File>Import>PDF Image.

- Ask for the business card and scan it at as high a ppi setting as you can. If you scanner has a de-screen filter, use it.

So how to salvage these images? I have seen editors and art departments spend days recreating logos. In larger facilities, this ordeal is often repeated due to poor communication and archives. So always ask everyone remotely experienced in using a computer if they have ever done work for the client before.

But if you must "salvage" a Web logo, remember this: Garbage In = Garbage Out. Vector programs as such as Adobe Illustrator—or the unfortunately nearly forgotten Adobe Steamline—can help here, but it is very hard to pull something from a 50×50 pixel source. The results you get will be mediocre at best.

The fastest solution I have developed involves "up-rezzing" via the image size command (Image>Image size). Computers are good at duplication, so blow the logo up 200% and choose Nearest Neighbor as the Interpolation method. The resulting image is soft, but may pass quality control. Some adventurous souls attempt to rebuild the text by font matching. If you know the name of the font used, this is a fair approach. If you are hunting, you will need a *huge* font collection and chances are you will get close, but not exactly right. You do not want to be to blamed when the "logo police" arrive.

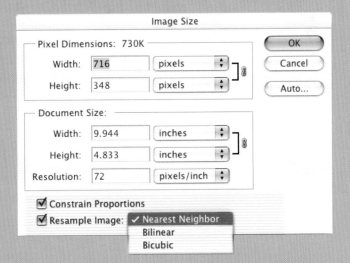

Avoid web graphics at all costs. Both you and the client will be *very* disappointed with the results when using a web-ready graphic. If clients insist that the web-ready format is all that's available, dig deeper. Ask them for a business card. If their logo is on that card, then it must exist in a print-ready format (somewhere). Ask who designs the cards or how they get additional cards at work. After a phone call or two, you will have the appropriate EPS or AI file.

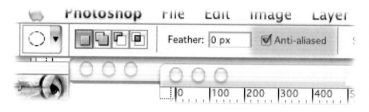

Anti-aliasing. Anti-aliasing will generate smoother results—especially when using selection or vector-based tools. Anti-aliasing works by softening the color transition between edge pixels. Since only the edge pixels are changed, you lose no detail in the image itself. Anti-aliasing is a useful option for creating text, making selections for filters, or copying and pasting. It will be a recurrent topic throughout this book. You can adjust the anti-aliasing for many tools directly in the **Options** bar. You must apply this option before a selection is made.

Feathering. Feathering can be applied once a selection is made. It works by blurring the edges, thus building a transition between a selection and the surrounding pixels. This blurring will result in loss of detail at the edge of a selection. The **Marquee** and **Lasso** Tools can be feathered from the **Options** bar. All selections can be feathered from the **Select** menu, and this is often the last step in creating a selection because it produces a more gradual edge. This edge produces smoother results when filtering, masking, or pasting the image.

Computer and Video Issues

NTSC: The National Television Standards Committee developed the North American broadcast standard in 1953. The group is jokingly referred to as, "Never Twice the Same Color."

PAL: Developed in the early 1960s, the Phase Alternate Line format is the standard for most of Europe.

Video traces its history to early pioneers such as John Logie Baird, who managed to record a recognizable human face on video in 1925. The first microcomputer appeared in 1960, developed by Digital Equipment. For a mere $120,000, it did include a keyboard and mouse. These two technologies existed very independently of each other for many years. All computer pixels are square in their native format. Professional video applications generally use pixels that are nonsquare.

The National Television Standards Committee, known as the NTSC, has set the standard that television fits to the 4×3 aspect ratio. This is often seen as an image that is 648×486 pixels. All analog televisions that use the NTSC standard display video at this size. Those countries that use the PAL format contain images that measure 768×576 square pixels. Designing for square systems is easy because no conversions are necessary.

Of course, if you offer a standard, it will be broken. In an effort to pack more pixels and increase resolution, the 601 video standard was developed. It is often called D1 (after the D1 format invented by Sony in the 1980s). In NTSC, the native size of a D1 frame is 720×486 nonsquare pixels. The PAL format uses 720×576 nonsquare pixels. This format has evolved into the Digital Video (DV) standard, which is employed in the consumer DV format, as well as DVCAM and DVCPRO tape and DVD authoring. The native size for DV frames is 720×480 nonsquare pixels for NTSC, six frames less than the D1 format. The PAL DV format is identical to the standard PAL format and remains unchanged at 720×576 nonsquare pixels.

These pixels are played back on analog televisions, which must display them as square pixels at the 4×3 aspect ratio.

Houston, we have a problem.

Discussing pixel aspect ratio is about as much fun as going to the Art Institute of Chicago and spending all your time discussing the doorknobs. Yes, they too are important, but hardly interesting. Please bear with me as I try to resolve this dilemma in a clear and orderly fashion.

Easy Solutions

- 720×540 is the most versatile square-pixel graphic size
- Use Image size to resize to 486 for D1
- Crop to 720×534; then resize vertically to 480 for DV
- If you are designing for a specific system, check the manufacturer's Web site.

Pixel aspect ratio

Remember, video is displayed on standard televisions at a 4×3 aspect ratio. Even video that has a different native size must be eventually converted. Natively, an NTSC D1/DV pixel is taller than it is wide, approximately 0.9 to 1. Many video edit systems, as well as Adobe After Effects, can work with square pixel images, ensuring that they display correctly throughout the editing stage.

To avoid this problem, however, many designers choose to manually stretch their images within Photoshop, which offers powerful interpolation tools that produce exceptional scaling. Before going any further, let me say two things:

- First, there are many conflicting opinions on what size to build graphics and what application to use when resizing them.
- Second, *read the manual* that shipped with your editing software because different companies have their own procedures for each editing system.

A standard square and NTSC D1 pixel.

With those two points cleared, I will present a method that will work for most users on most systems.

Need a "Frame Grab"? See Chapter 8 for some tips.

Step 1　Determine the native size of your video frame. This can be found in your NLE's manual, or you can export out a single frame. If you are working with a traditional (switcher-based) analog system, the frame is likely 648×486 for NTSC or 768×576 for PAL square pixels. Most hardware-dependent nonlinear systems, such as Avid Media Composers and Symphonys, Media 100s, or Accelerated Premiere-based systems, use the D1 format. The native D1 size is 720×486 nonsquare pixel image for NTSC or 720×576 nonsquare pixel image for PAL. Recently, many DV solutions have appeared. These use a 720×480 nonsquare pixel image for NTSC and 720×576 nonsquare pixel image for PAL.

Step 2　Design your graphics in Photoshop using square pixels. There are two major camps: those who recommend stretching horizontally and those who prefer vertically. In the spirit of Dr. Seuss' Sneetches, I'll call them the 'Zontals and the Verts.

Every edit system and manufacturer has unique requirements. Be sure to see Appendix D for specific suggestions for leading editing and motion graphics applications.

The 'Zontals argue that it is best to maintain the same number of scan lines throughout. This method helps maintain fine details, such as text, by not compressing them. Using this approach, the final image is stretched horizontally (Image>Image Size, Constrain Proportions unchecked) to fill the video screen. Eventually this image will be squeezed back when playing back on televisions.

The Verts counter that it is always better to shrink raster images than to blow them up. By employing a 720×540 image in Photoshop, the files can be scaled down (as opposed to up). Before saving the file out for video editing, the file must be resized (Image>Image Size>Constrain Proportions unchecked). The 720×540 file is squeezed vertically to 720×486. This vertical stretch will be counteracted by the horizontal stretch when the image is transferred to video.

(Left) Original image viewed in D1 editing system such as Avid Media Composer.

(Middle) Same image viewed in Photoshop with NTSC standard.

(Right) Same image viewed in Photoshop with PAL standard.

There are strengths to both arguments. Because DV is having such an impact, I recommend designing at 720×540, using a 4×3 aspect ratio. This means you are only scaling a single direction when sizing for D1 or DV. This size also works for PAL graphics as well. Graphics intended for DV merely need to be cropped, since DV lacks six lines of pixels (480 versus 486).

Format	4×3 Aspect Ratio (Square Pixels)	16×9 Aspect Ratio (Square Pixels)	Native Size Nonsquare Pixel
NTSC D1	648×486 or 720×540	864×486	720×486
PAL D1	768×576 or 720×540	1024×576	720×576
NTSC DV	640×480 or 720×534	853×480	720×480
PAL DV	768×576 or 720×540	1024×576	720×576

Interlaced displays

Interlacing video is another leftover technology meant to serve as a temporary fix. When television was invented, it was decided that 30 frames per second generated smooth motion. However, it took 60 images per second to reduce flicker. The problem is that the broadcast signal could not hold that much information without significant softening, and the slow speed of phosphors produced banding.

In order to maintain a relatively crisp picture, the solution of interlacing was decided upon by the first National Television Standards Committee in 1940. By showing half an image 60 times per second, both goals could be met. The electron beam would scan across the tube, painting every other line. It would then return to the top and paint the remaining lines. These alternating lines are known as upper (or odd field first) and lower (or even field first). This solution solved the problem between bandwidth, flicker, and smooth motion.

It's important to note that only analog televisions are interlaced. If your video is intended for traditional output, you need to keep this in mind. Standard analog televisions display interlaced video, but newer digital televisions may show progressive scan (or noninterlaced). If you are designing for web or CD output, you will work with noninterlaced video. Interlacing is not a big issue when you start in Photoshop, but becomes very important when importing video freeze frames or working in Adobe After Effects. The only issue to keep in mind is to avoid lines thinner than three pixels, or you will definitely introduce flicker to the image.

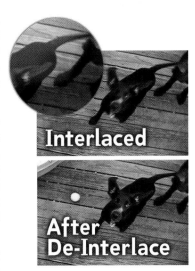

With NTSC video, the image updates 60 times per second. These fields reduce image flickering by refreshing every other line. To clean up an exported video frame, you will likely need the De-Interlace filter.

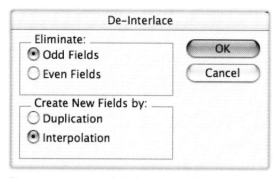

Choose to create new fields by interpolation; field elimination is a subjective choice.

If you import a freeze frame with visible fields, you can choose to run the De-Interlace filter (Video>De-Interlace). You will have the choice of keeping the odd or even field, as well as creating the replacement through duplication or interpolation. This step is especially important for broadcast designers who are working with freeze frames. If you video contains movement (and you didn't remove interlacing during export from the NLE), you will definitely see the need for this filter. Many lower-cost digital cameras will show a similar problem because they use a similar, image-capture device. It is a good idea to run this filter on video freeze frames every time if the work is to be done in Photoshop.

When animating your graphics inAfter Effects, interlacing provides smoother movement between frames. The render times are longer, but the quality is worth it. You need to do nothing different inside of Photoshop; just make sure to turn on **Field Rendering** in After Effects' render settings. In fact, make it part of your presets in After Effects by modifying your output settings.

RGB versus YCC color

Black-and-white televisions were the roadblock to true RGB color. In an effort to preserve backwards compatibility, the YCC color space was developed.

As if the nonsquare pixels, aspect ratios, and interlacing weren't enough, let me present our next problem. Photoshop works in the RGB color space. Each pixel you see on your monitor is comprised of light being emitted by a red, a green, and a blue phosphor placed closely together. Our eyes perceive that light as a single-colored dot, or pixel. These red, green, and blue components are referred to as channels. More on channels and channel operations in later chapters.

So what's the problem? Televisions use the same red, green, and blue phosphors right? Not exactly. While it's true that both computers and most NLEs use eight bits of information for each channel, television signals are not transmitted or stored in RGB. This is our final leftover problem. Initially, television was black and white. These images were actually a grayscale signal consisting of only one channel that contained the brightness information (known as *luminance*).

In an effort to keep consumers happy, color television was made backwards compatible. An RGB broadcast would not work on a black-and-white television, so broadcasters chose (and still use) the YCC color space. The Y is the luminance information, while the two Cs represented the color components (hue and saturation). These three signals would combine to form the composited pixels.

How does this affect you? Colors will look different on a television screen than they do on a computer monitor. The color shift is minor, but present. There is no setting in Photoshop to correct this. The best solution is to have an NTSC or PAL video monitor (or consumer television) connected to your system. Many video cards will let you output via S-Video. If a television monitor is not an option, periodically test your graphics by importing them into your NLE, then outputting to tape.

Many editors choose to look at HSB sliders (hue, saturation, and brightness). This color model is very compatible with RGB and allows you to examine color information in a more video-like manner.

RGB versus 601

When working in Photoshop, black is black and white is white. In other words, Photoshop uses absolute values. Black is assigned a value of 0 and white a value of 255. There is no allowance for anything beyond this range. This process is referred to as computer graphics or RGB mapping. Adobe Photoshop and After Effects both work with RGB mapping. These programs do not understand the concept of *superblack*, or *whiter than white*.

RGB mapping assumes that video black (NTSC 7.5 IRE, PAL 0 mV) is assigned a value of 0, and video white (NTSC 100 IRE, PAL 700 mV) a value of 255. If you import or export video from your edit system as RGB, signals above or below this range will be clipped.

The ITU-R BT.601 digital video standard (commonly referred to as *601 mapping*) does not handle black and white as absolutes. It is allowable to go above white and below black. One reason for this is superblack, which places a darker black in areas that are meant to be luma keyed. Many hardware-based switchers will use a luma key, instead of tying up two channels of a still store to use the fill and alpha matte. Another reason is to allow the storage of camera data for overexposed frames.

601 mapping specifies that video black (NTSC 7.5 IRE, PAL 0 mV) is assigned a value of 16, and video white (NTSC 100 IRE, PAL 700 mV) a value of 235. This allows for reasonable footroom and headroom in the signal.

Apple's Final Cut Pro system can warn you when your pixels are not broadcast safe. Go back to Photoshop and fix the original photo when this happens. Otherwise, you have additional rendering.

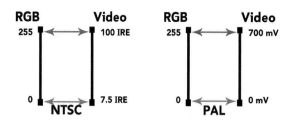

RGB mapping

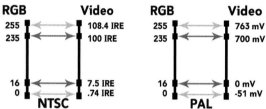

601 mapping

When importing or exporting your frames, it is important to use a consistent color mapping method. Avid, Media 100, Sonic Foundry, and many others support the 601 color space. Currently Adobe Premiere and Apple's Final Cut Pro do not. More support across all edit systems is very likely as software-based NLEs improve in quality. Specifying the color method is part of the import dialog box on these systems. To make things easier, I suggest that you add 601 to the file name of graphics prepared in this fashion.

When to use RGB levels. You want to use RGB for exporting frames from your NLE to be used in print, web, or CD-ROM. You also may choose RGB if you plan to modify the image greatly with filters, and then reimport the image. Using RGB levels on export will clip the image and video black and white, making it less likely to go beyond safe luminance ranges.

When to use 601 levels. If you plan to create graphics that use superblack for keying, export from your NLE as a 601 image, if it is an option. Also, if you are exporting a frame for touch up, such as to paint out a scratch or dropout, export as 601. This will allow you to keep the full color range of your video image, thus avoiding color shift when moving between applications. 601 is best used when you intend to export from video, do minor processing on the image, and import the frame back into the timeline.

 If it is a still image, color correct it in Photoshop. Otherwise you have more rendering. A 10-second still graphic would require you to render approximately 300 frames of color correction; Photoshop would require one frame.

 Superblack (aka, Zero Black). A pure luma value of 0 IRE, which falls below the legal limit of 7.5 IRE for NTSC broadcasting. It is often used for luma-keying, a process of transparency generation that would not tie up a second channel of a switcher (for the matte) in order to perform a key.

"Whiter Than White." Cameras have extra headroom in capturing luminance. These values beyond broadcast white may need to be adjusted in the edit environment to bring the video signal in compliance with broadcast standards.

Luminance and Saturation

The issue of color choice has two issues, broadcast safe and good taste. Many excellent books are available to assist you with color choice. The principles of a color wheel and selecting harmonious colors are worth your time to study. To get you started, I've included a demo of Color Theory, a Photoshop plug-in, on the disc. Color Theory helps you select color combinations that look good on video. Use this as a starting point to selecting good colors.

Unfortunately, video is a limited medium with a limited color palette. You need to learn what colors look good on video and, even more importantly, which colors look good on VHS tapes played back on $59 VCRs. It is a good idea to test your graphics often on a vectorscope and waveform monitor, especially for your first few years of working in Photoshop. For more on testing graphics, see Chapter 12, "The Road to the NLE."

Without proper contrast, details may be difficult for your audience to perceive. Combinations such as red and green do not offer sufficient contrast. To test your graphic, use a Saturation Adjustment Layer to desaturate your composition.

To make things simpler, here's a crash course in building your own "big box of crayons." Here are a few color rules to keep in mind:

- Certain colors do not look good on video. Reds have a tendency to bleed on screen; light yellows look like a dog used your TV as a fire hydrant.
- Oversaturated colors will cause problems. Consumer televisions ship with the saturation and red tones turned up too high. You can't tell the customers that they're wrong (even if their TVs are), so turn down the saturation on bright colors. Muted colors will become more vibrant once they make it out to televisions.
- Avoid extremely dark colors. On video, there is very little difference between indigo, charcoal, and slate. Dark tones tend to gravitate towards black in the viewer's eyes.

A gradient map is identical to After Effects' Colorama filter. Both provide a great way to map new colors to an image and give it identity.

- Maintain proper contrast. Some viewers will view your work on black-and-white sets; others may be color blind. Even those with perfect eyes will have a hard time seeing a difference in luminance between blue and purple or red and green. Print your graphics out in grayscale, tape them on the wall, and stand back 15 feet. Can you read it?

- Avoid "pure" white. It will bloom on screen, making it difficult to read. Use off-white, especially for text. Also stroke the text with a contrasting color. For more on making readable text, see Chapter 5, "Some Words on Words, Logos, and Symbols."
- Not all graphics need to be full chroma. Using one color—for example, a base blue—with multiple shades, with darker and lighter accents often looks very good. Duotone effects, where a grayscale image has a new color mapped to it, often look good as well.

When in doubt, use the NTSC Colors filter (**Filter>Video>NTSC Colors**) to check your work. But do not rely on the NTSC color filter to fix problems as it produces visible banding. See Chapter 8, "Color Correction: How to Get It Right" for more information.

Working with Photoshop's Presets

In an effort to make life easier, Photoshop 7 has introduced preset document sizes. These can be picked from a dropdown menu when you create a new document Cmd+N (Ctrl+N). You have the choice between NTSC and PAL sizes, Standard or Widescreen, and 601, DV/DVD, or HDTV. These presets are a welcome addition, but they have a few flaws.

 You can quickly find out the details of a document by Option+clicking (Alt+click) on the Document Info bar.

First, always check your **Image** menu. Photoshop presents you with five choices; RGB is the correct one. The second problem: no title- or action-safe guidelines. *Action safe* shows the portion of the frame that should show on all TVs. *Title safe* is the area in which titles should be created, to minimize any text crowding at the edges. If you want to manually add these, the safe action area is 10% of the original image, and the title-safe area is 20% of the original frame size.

There are many sources for title-safe documents. Most manufacturers will provide you a template with your edit system. Numerous online sites and user groups post them. Possibly the best, and most versatile solution I've ever seen, are those included with the Tools for Television Photoshop Toolbox (http://www.toolsfortelevision.com). This solution provides actions for creating safe title documents (and many other cool things as well). The entire sets add up to only 704 kilobytes, far smaller than even a single template graphic. They work extremely well and are very accurate. You can find a demo for Tools for Television (as well as a discount offer) on the disc. What I like best about this product is that it does the thinking for you and lets you focus on the creative aspects, rather than memorizing a big table of information.

✓ Custom

Default Photoshop Size

Letter
Legal
Tabloid

2 x 3
4 x 6
5 x 7
8 x 10

640 x 480
800 x 600
1024 x 768
468 x 60 web banner

720 x 540 Std. NTSC 601
720 x 534 Std. NTSC DV/DVD
864 x 486 Wide NTSC 601
864 x 480 Wide NTSC DV/DVD
768 x 576 Std. PAL
1024 x 576 Wide PAL
1280 x 720 HDTV 720P
1920 x 1080 HDTV 1080i

A4
A3

B5
B4
B3

This dropdown list cuts down on the guesswork. The video templates do not offer safe-title area previews, however.

Resizing an Existing Image

If you have an existing image, chances are that it's not sized correctly for video. To change the size of an image, you can use the **Image Size** or **Canvas Size** menu commands or use the **Crop** tool for the adjustment. These three choices can be used individually or in combination to achieve the desired results.

Image Size. Image size lets you permanently reassign the total pixel count, as well as resolution, for a particular image. It is critical to make sure the **Resample Image** box is checked; otherwise you will not be able to change the document size. It is best to use bicubic interpolation for resizing most images. An exception is when enlarging a very small image; you can enlarge it 200% and select nearest neighbor. This should be a last-case scenario when using web sources.

Leave the **Constrain Proportions** box checked, or you will introduce additional squeezing. You are concerned with the pixel dimensions, so look at the total pixel count in the top boxes. Many editors choose to specify the resolution as 72 pixels per inch, although this is not necessary.

Canvas Size. The canvas size is your work area. Canvas size adjustments are a way to crop or extend the canvas of the work area. When you first launch the **Canvas Size** command, you are likely to see measurements in inches. The key is to change the units of measurement to pixels. You can temporarily change the units of measurement to pixels (with the dropdown lists) or permanently change your units of measure in **Units and Rulers** in the **Preferences** submenu.

Once you are measuring in pixels, type in the desired size, and specify an anchor point. The anchor point tells Photoshop whether you want to keep the image centered or expand/crop from a particular edge. Photoshop will either contract or expand based upon the input values. It is possible to extend the border of an image, particularly on a source with portrait aspect ratio. In this case, the empty space surrounding the image would be filled by the background color.

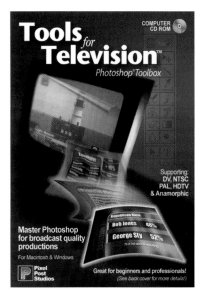

Tools for Television is a CD-ROM of actions, articles, and source files designed with video editors in mind. Look for a sample (including the awesome safe title area action) and a special upgrade offer on this book's disc.

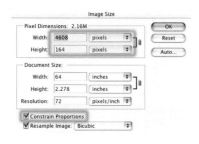

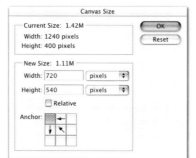

The new space created by changing canvas size is based upon the background color loaded. It is a good idea to have no design elements on your background layer.

Pay close attention to the pixel dimensions when sizing an image. The document size does not matter for video purposes.

These Crop tool presets can be found in this chapter's folder on the DVD.

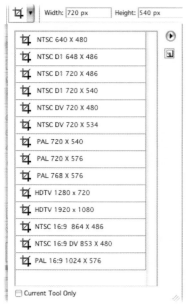

Tool presets are easy to make and offer many timesaving options to a video pro.

Crop Tool. The **Crop** tool is the fastest way to size an image for video. Cropping is a way to remove parts of an image permanently to create a focal point or resize the image. While **Crop** is available on a menu (Image>Crop), the **Crop** tool provides better control. You can select it by pressing the letter C on your keyboard.

The easy way to use the **Crop** tool is to type the desired size of your final image into the **Options** bar. When you drag to crop the image, your box will constrain to the proper aspect ratio. The shielded (darkened) areas will be cropped when you press Return/Enter or click on the **Commit** button in the **Options** bar. To toggle the shielded area off, press the forward slash (/). To hide the marching ants, press Cmd+H (Ctrl+H).

To make things even easier, harness the power of Photoshop 7's **Preset Manager**. You can create tool presets that already have the values for a tool loaded. In fact, on the disc you'll find a file called *Video Crop.tpl* in the *Goodies* folder for this chapter. Locate your *Tool Presets* folder (Adobe Photoshop 7>Presets >Tools) and copy the file in. The next time you launch Photoshop, the different aspect ratios required for video will be available from the Tool Presets tab or a dropdown menu in the **Options** bar.

You have an important choice to make when cropping. You can specify **Delete** or **Hide** in the **Options** bar for the **Crop** tool. Delete is the traditional method and will discard cropped material. Hide is more like changing the canvas size. The cropped pixels remain outside the viewable area for future editing. The Hide method may cause you problems when you import layered files for animation because you will have extra pixels that affect your anchor point.

Final Advice

I have sat in workshops where the entire time has been eaten up by conversations on frame size and pixel aspect ratio. We seem to accept our frame rates of 29.97 fps (or 25 fps) with little question. But the mixing of square and nonsquare pixels is often mind-boggling.

Pixel aspect ratio is the most boring and inflexible aspect of designing graphics for video. You can choose to fully understand it, use templates, or keep a list of presets and notes next to your computer. Whatever it takes, accept it, embrace it, use one of the aforementioned techniques consistently, and move on. On behalf of you, the reader, let's get to the fun stuff!

Professional Motion Control "Photography" with After Effects and Photoshop

Documentary-style motion control photography is becoming increasingly popular for use in all styles of video production. Why just show the pictures, static and full-screen? Most editors have traditionally had two options.

The first is setting up a camera and card stand, and then shooting the photos with a digital video camera. This method is prone to *keystoning* (due to the tilting to avoid light reflections) and does not allow for photo restoration or precise movement. The second method involved importing the photos into the edit system and enlarging (*zooming*) them. This method produced softening and had very limited results. Many plug-ins have recently been developed that work within edit systems that improve upon this technique, but there is still a better way.

After Effects provides convenient presets for choosing the right composition settings. After Effects will set everything except for the duration. That's up to you.

By combining Photoshop with Adobe After Effects, extremely high-quality motion control is possible. In fact, I have produced results that outperform those done on expensive motion control rigs. Everyone knows that Photoshop is the perfect tool for restoring damaged photos (see Chapter 9, "Repairing Damaged Photos"). When combined with Adobe After Effects, complex motion is possible.

I've included a project in this chapter's folder that contains a few motion control examples. You will find a movie on the disc as well that demonstrates this technique.

Step 1   Scan and prep all of your photos in Photoshop. If you want to do a zoom or a pan, you will need extra pixels. For example, an image that is 2160 pixels wide will allow you to perform a three-screen pan. Do not worry about cropping or sizing for the screen, but make sure that you have enough pixels for additional movement. The goal is to have extra pixels when you shrink the image. In other words, you scale the image down to zoom out and restore it to 100% to zoom in.

Step 2   Import your photos into After Effects. You can drag an entire folder in (provided there are no nested folders within it). Select the folder, hold down the **Option** (Alt) key and drag it into the project window. If you need to rename the folder, select it and press the Return (Enter) key.

Step 3   Create a new composition and size for your edit system. If you are unsure, check the owner's manual for your NLE or export a video clip from the NLE and import it to After Effects to check size. Set the duration to match your needs, plus add a little pad. After Effects will correctly interpret your Photoshop files as square pixels, unless you've sized them to a standard video size such as 720×480.

 Animate the anchor point, *not* Position. This produces a truer camera move.

Step 4   Drop in a photo. Highlight the layer, and press S to call up the Scale properties. Now hold down the Shift key and press A for anchor point and R for Rotation. The anchor point is where the "camera" is pointing, and is a *much* better option than using **Position**. Using an anchor point is like moving the camera; using Position is like locking the camera down and moving the picture instead. This is one of two key differences between building your motion control (MOCO) in After Effects instead of another system. If you want to drag in a visual interface, double-click on the layer to launch footage view. From the submenu, you can choose Anchor Point Path; this will show you the camera path. This path can be dragged to set the viewing position, and will give you a visual map of the motion that will be taken.

"Perfect" motion control is possible by combining Photoshop and After Effects. In fact, result can far exceed what is possible with an expensive MOCO rig.

Step 5   Add key frames for the initial position of the photo. Jump to the outpoint of the layer by pressing the letter O. Add your end key frames.

Step 6   If you will want to simulate a zoom, press S for Scale to access the scaling controls. Do not enlarge your image beyond 100% for best results. You can also add Rotation keyframes (**R**), if that is desired.

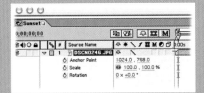

Step 7   (Optional) Use your animation assistants to add Ease on the rotation and anchor point key frames. If you own the production bundle, click on the word **Scale** to highlight both keyframes. From under the keyframe assistants, choose Exponential Scale. This powerful assistant will accurately simulate the speed of a camera zoom.

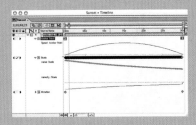

By using Exponential Scale (Production Bundle only) and Ease, realistic camera moves can be achieved.

Step 8   Double check that your quality switches are all set to **Best** and add your comp to the render queue. If you want, you can specify **Best** inside of the render queue, but I personally always switch it in the timeline to be certain. Render out to the specifications of your edit system by matching output size and codec (compressor-decompressor). For best results, choose to field render.

This is just a microscopic amount of the possibilities that exist for combining Photoshop and After Effects. Don't worry, After Effects is a *very* deep program, but getting into it is easy for Photoshop users because the interfaces are very similar.

To Be, or Not to Be (Square, That Is!)

By Glen Stephens, *Photoshop User Magazine*

Sometimes it is the little things that make your projects stand out above the others and tell your viewer that they are watching a professionally produced video. This article will explain a concept that will take you one step closer to mastering Photoshop for video.

Anyone who has worked in desktop video and incorporated Photoshop graphics into their projects has at one time or another asked themselves the question, "Why do my images and logos look stretched on my video monitor and not on my computer monitor?" This is a common problem that editors and graphic designers for video face, and it is a problem that has an easy solution. There is a way to fix this problem as you are working in Photoshop, and once you understand what is happening and how to fix it, your graphics will look better on screen than ever before.

My goal for you as the reader is not to just know how to fix the problem, but to understand what is causing the problem so that what I am telling you to do in Photoshop makes sense. That being said, let's start off by explaining exactly what is happening to your images when they are moved to a video output.

What is happening

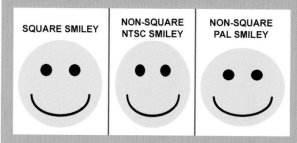

Most of you know that the aspect ratio for standard definition NTSC and PAL video is 4×3. That means that all NTSC and PAL television sets are four units wide by three units high. Most of you also know that the size of a DV video still from your camera or editing software is 720 pixels wide by 480 pixels. If you are working with D1 footage, your images are 720 pixels wide by 486, and 720 by 576 if you are working in PAL. If you do the math, neither 720×486, 720×480, nor 720×576 are in a 4×3 aspect ratio. They are off by approximately 10%. To make these image sizes fit into a 4×3 aspect ratio, the images are stretched vertically for NTSC and horizontally for PAL to fill the frame. This creates what is known as nonsquare pixels, and the effect of having images stretched on the screen. Circles now look like ovals, and squares are no longer perfectly square.

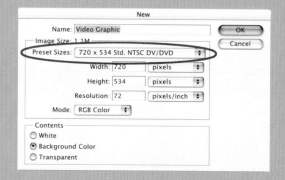

The result of this stretching is not extreme, but it is significant enough to notice. So what do you do? You have to emulate nonsquare pixels in Photoshop. Even though Photoshop does not have the ability to generate nonsquare pixels, there is a way in the design process to cancel the stretching that occurs.

What to do

The tendency for most designers is to design their images in Photoshop at the sizes listed previously, either 720×486, 720×480, or 720×576. The problem is that Photoshop only works with square pixels. When your editing system imports a square pixel image that it thinks is a nonsquare pixel image, stretching will occur. The first step in fixing this problem is to start initially in Photoshop with a canvas that is in a 4×3 aspect ratio and with square pixels. When you open a new document in Photoshop to begin designing, you want to use the file sizes in the following table as your starting point.

Video Format	Video Frame Size	Square or Nonsquare Pixels	Photoshop File Size	Aspect Ratio
NTSC (non D1 or DV)	640×480	square	640×480	4×3
NTSC D1 (CCIR 601)	720×486	nonsquare	720×540	4×3
NTSC DV	720×480	nonsquare	720×534	4×3
PAL	720×576	nonsquare	768×576	4×3

You can now create your designs and do all of your image preparation. Working in Photoshop at the file sizes listed allows you to see exactly what your images will look like when sent to video. This is because you are now working in Photoshop at a true 4×3 aspect ratio, which is how your final images end up on video. However, there is a final step that you must go through to make the move from Photoshop to your editing system. Because you are working in a square pixel environment, and moving your images to a nonsquare pixel environment in your editing system, you need to convert your Photoshop images to a nonsquare pixel format. Because Photoshop can-

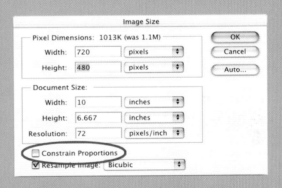

not create nonsquare pixels, you can emulate this by resizing your image and stretching it in the opposite direction than it will be stretched when it is sent to video. The two stretching processes cancel each other out, keeping your images looking correct on your video monitor. To do this, use the Image Size option under the Image menu and resize your image to the size of the video standard you are working with. For example, if you are working with DV footage, you start in Photoshop with an image that is 720×534, and then resize the final image to 720×480 with the Image Size command.

The result will be a squeezed version of your image. But that is fine, because your editing system will stretch the image in the opposite direction to return it to a 4×3 aspect ratio, canceling any stretching that takes place. Your image on your video monitor now looks exactly the same as it did on your computer monitor (except for the fact that you are seeing a completely different color gamut, but that's a completely different issue!)

If you are using Photoshop 7, they have added these file sizes as Preset Sizes in the New File dialog box.

Notice that the 640×480 format is designated as a square pixel format. This means that the size of the final video frame is not resized to fit the frame, and stretching of the image does not occur. Images in this format do not need any special attention. Simply start in Photoshop at the final video size and send those images straight to your editing software. This is a rare format anymore, and chances are you won't be using it. HDTV formats are also square pixel formats. A chart follows that shows what those formats are in the event that you are lucky enough to blaze the trail to High Definition television.

Video Format	Video Frame Size	Square or Nonsquare Pixels	Photoshop File Size	Aspect Ratio
HDTV 720p	1280×720	Square	1280×720	16×9
HDTV 1080i	1920×1080	Square	1920×1080	16×9

Make sure that you do *not* have the **Constrain Proportions** box checked; otherwise, you keep your image at a 4×3 aspect ratio.

Check with the manual that came with your editing system software to find out what video format you are using. Also, some video software editing packages such as Adobe Premiere, Apple's Final Cut Pro, Adobe After Effects, and a few others have the ability to take the original 4×3, square pixel images. Again, check in your non-linear software manual to find out how to properly handle these files. Most of the time it is simply a matter of telling the software that you are giving it an image that is either square pixel or non-square pixel.

Now that you understand the difference between square and nonsquare pixels and know how to work around the problems that they pose, you can consider yourself among the elite. I regularly see programming on major television networks that have stretched images that do not look correct. Applying this technique to your design process will guarantee that your corporate clients never come back to you to complain about their company logo not looking right.

Profile: Larry Hawk

Larry Hawk is one of those pros who is not well known, but should be. He has been making broadcast graphics since 1978. He is a pioneer and was one of the first video pros to switch to designing on-air graphics exclusively on a Macintosh using desktop software such as Adobe Photoshop and Illustrator. Hawk works for KCCI in Des Moines, Iowa, as Senior Broadcast Designer.

"I use Photoshop and Macs as the *only* graphic 2D paint program here at KCCI. That includes on-air news graphics for every newscast, promotion support graphics for the Avids, and sales graphics for use in the Avids and production studio," said Hawk. "I use Photoshop to design virtual sets for chroma-key walls and to visualize studio sets before they are built. I use Photoshop in almost all the stations' print graphics, like newspaper ads, billboards, banners, sales materials, and KCCI stationery and business cards."

Hawk's reliance on Photoshop over the years has led to him developing specific skills. Long before editable type or even layers, Hawk refined his Photoshop skills so that he could meet a tough broadcast schedule. Hawk's use of keyboard shortcuts and power tools has enabled him to turn out more than 50 graphics in a single day.

"The use of Photoshop for television graphics requires some special tricks and skills to get the final result and remember to watch your levels of black and white and NTSC colors," said Hawk. "Using the correct fonts and colors in video graphics is always a challenge, and I see a lot of bad fonts on television today—local and network broadcasts."

Hawk has mentored several interns and newbies (this author included). He truly is a power user—often leaving others wondering, "How did he do that?".

"I have had many college interns here at KCCI and new production employees who want to help or learn television graphics. First I ask how much Mac/PC experience they have, and, second, 'Do you know the basics of Photoshop?'" said Hawk. "It's the *most* important program to learn if you are going to do any multimedia graphics. That includes television, film, web, and presentations."

To speed your Photoshop work up, Hawk offers this expert-level tip:

"When removing light or dark spots from scanned photos, use the **Blur** tool at 100% set to the **Lighten** mode for light spots and set to **Darken** mode to darken the spot without using the **Cloning** tool. This works best with a soft-edge medium brush."

Hawk also extends some helpful advice to those working in broadcasting:

"Never stop learning or expanding your Photoshop skills, and if you are lucky enough to work at a broadcast television station, *never* stand still in the hallway, or someone from the newsroom will run you down on their way to the ENG room."

What About Transparency?

Perhaps Photoshop's greatest power lies in its ability to preserve complex transparency. Photoshop is very flexible when working with transparency, because it supports 256 levels. By employing masks, both in layers and embedded into the saved files, this transparency data can travel seamlessly into the nonlinear editing environment.

Some terminology worth locking in: A *foreground element* is any layer that contains objects to be composited over the background layer or plate. The *matte* determines the opacity of the foreground elements, as well as defining the edges of the foreground element. It is important to keep your background in mind when developing independent foreground elements (and their mattes/masks/alpha channels) inside of Photoshop. Know what you intend to key and where you intend to key it.

Photoshop is primarily an 8-bit image editor. That is to say, each channel contains eight bits of information. Eight bits is another way of saying two to the eighth power, or $2\times2\times2\times2\times2\times2\times2\times2$, which equals 256. These 256 different shades of gray combine to form a complex image. RGB images contain 24 bits of information, eight bits per channel. A grayscale image contains eight bits. It is a good idea to stick with RGB or grayscale images for video purposes. If you add an alpha channel, you have added another eight bits of information.

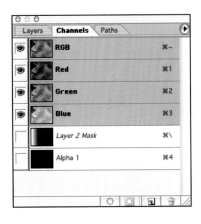

Each channel normally contains eight bits of information. It is best to view channels in grayscale to see contrast and detail.

The left screen shows a layered Photoshop file with transparency information stored in layers. The center screen has an added alpha channel, which also includes a drop shadow. This allows the image to be keyed or composited over other layers or video during the edit.

Photoshop does support 16-bit images on a limited basis. These 16-bit images would generally come from a high-end drum scanner or some stock image libraries. This extra data may be useful if you are doing a lot of color correction or are working in a higher resolution medium. For video purposes, you will not come across a need to work with 16-bit images very often. While they are higher quality, 16-bit images do not support layers, and they occupy twice as much disk space. In general, you will work with RGB images with eight bits per channel, for a total of 24 bits. If you add an alpha channel, you will have 32 bits.

Selecting and Extracting Images

In order to work with something in Photoshop, it must be selected. Photoshop must be told what you want done and where it should happen. This process involves making selections and is often done using the **Marquee**, **Magic Wand**, or **Lasso** Tools. A disadvantage of these tools is that once you deselect something, the selection data is not permanently saved with the document.

In order to facilitate a smoother workflow, many people isolate individual pieces of a composition to their own layer. It is possible to place only what you want on an isolated layer. The empty space, often represented by a checkerboard pattern inside of Photoshop, is called *transparency*. An advantage to isolating elements to their own layers is that you can quickly load them as a selection and make further changes.

There are many approaches to extracting images. Some are obvious, such as using an eraser or selecting and deleting. Word processor-like functions of copy, cut, and paste also exist. Photoshop has a built-in "dummy" tool called **Extract**, which is very tempting, but proves lacking. Intermediate techniques include layer masking. Of course, this transparency needs to travel out to the NLE, so you'll need to look at alpha channels and support for the .psd file format. Transparency is the foundation of compositing, and since there are many different situations, there are also many different tools.

Tool	Command
Magic Wand	W
Rectangular Marquee Tool	M
Elliptical Marquee Tool	M
Lasso Tool	L
Magnetic Lasso Tool	L
Polygonal Lasso Tool	L

The easy ways

There is an assortment of tools that you can learn quickly. With a little bit of practice, the **Lasso** and **Magic Wand** Tools can generate acceptable results. Once you have a selection, you can copy it to a new layer, inverse the selection, and delete the rest, or use the selection to generate a layer mask or alpha channel. Some new users are attracted to the **Eraser** Tools, but these tools are *very* inaccurate. They make a selection and delete in one step. The eraser tools produce destructive editing and should be avoided.

Accessing the **Options** bar on all of these tools is quick and easy. Select the tool you want to use; then press **Return/Enter** and type in the number you want, and then press **Return/Enter** again. If there are multiple fields, you can tab between them.

Magic Wand

The **Magic Wand** can be used to select areas of color. The sensitivity is driven by the Tolerance control. The larger the number, the more Photoshop will accept similar pixels (based on brightness and color level). The sample size setting in the **Eyedropper** Tool (**Point Sample,** 3×3 average or 5×5 average) also affects the **Magic Wand**. So if the wand is acting oddly, check your **Eyedropper** settings.

For more accurate control, most users select the contiguous option from the Options bar. This forces the **Magic Wand** to only make selections of adjacent pixels. This is particularly useful when trying to select background objects, such as the sky. This way, only adjacent pixels would be chosen, not similar blues in the clothes or foreground. With this option deselected, Photoshop chooses all of the similar pixels throughout the entire document.

Another option is to **Use All Layers**. This will ignore which layer you are currently using. Instead, all visible layers become part of the selection. You still must switch layers to manipulate data not on your current layer. However, you can make a selection based on several layers using this method.

Magic Wand selections tend to be very fragmented with rough edges. This happens because selections are based on pixels and tolerance settings. Essentially, the **Magic Wand** is a bitmap tool; pixels are either on or off. This is the primary disadvantage of this tool: it leads to pixelated edges. To minimize this, choose the **Anti-aliased** option.

It is possible to further smooth out the selection's edges to generate a usable selection. The first step is to grow the selection to fill in gaps. You can choose to add to the selection by **Shift**+clicking in adjacent areas. This will add to the primary selection based on the **Magic Wand**'s setting. It is better to use a lower tolerance and click multiple times than it is to use a high-tolerance setting. This is because more control is possible. Think of it as the difference between a hatchet and a pocketknife. If you want detail, it's better to take several shorter strokes and maintain finer control.

The lower third for this commercial harnesses Photoshop's alpha channel capabilities. It is possible to build complex effects that are impossible or time consuming in an NLE title tool. (Courtesy American Red Cross.)

It is often easier to select what you don't want, such as the sky, first. You can then invert your selection.

Want a better Magic Wand? The sample size of the wand is driven by the Eyedropper Tool. Switch to the Eyedropper Tool, and then choose 3×3 or 5×5 average. You'll get better selections now.

When you have most of your desired pixels, you can pick up little stray pockets by using the **Select** menu and **Modify** submenu. There are seven additional options that are useful. They are available for *all* selection tools and methods.

Grow. Expands your selection by choosing pixels that are both adjacent to the current selection and resemble the colors in the current selection. The selection will grow based on the tolerance setting you have in the Options bar for the **Magic Wand**.

Similar. This command works like **Grow**, except pixels need not be adjacent to the current selection.

Contract. This pulls the active selection inward a specified number of pixels.

Expand. This pushes the active selection outward a specified number of pixels.

Smooth. This useful command rounds out selections and gets rid of sharp corners. Specify an amount as a Sample Radius (larger numbers mean smoother edges).

Border. This command uses the current selection to create a new area of a user-specified thickness that borders the previous selection. It is limited in its practical applications, but can be useful for video makers to "de-fringe" an object. If your object has rough edges, you can load the object, then use the border selection to specify a thin two- or three-pixel border. This area can then be deleted or blurred. (Think of this as "choking the matte.")

Feather. The final step of most selections is feathering. This generates a graduated edge. Think of feathering as the difference between a ballpoint and felt-tip pen.

Lasso Tool

Think of the **Lasso** as a freehand selection tool. Draw around the area you want, and it is selected. This is much like a football sportscaster drawing on the screen. The better you are with the mouse or pen and tablet, the better you will be at making a selection. The regular **Lasso** Tool has only two options: **Feathering** and **Anti-alias**. A feathered edge will generate a soft edge. You can feather up to 250 pixels, but you'll rarely need to use that much on a low-resolution source. The **Anti-alias** option will smooth out your line to cut down on *jaggies* that will produce poor results on screen.

Rough Edges? If you have the jaggies, try running the median filter on your quick mask (Filter>Noise> Median). This will allow you to smooth over selections made with the **Lasso** or **Wand** Tools.

You can feather your selections first by selecting a feathering width in the **Options** bar. Feathering produces a gradual edge, which is often desirable.

Polygonal Lasso Tool

This tool is a favorite amongst broadcasters. It is frequently employed as the quick way to extract a headshot for producing on-air graphics. The advantage of the **Polygonal Lasso** is that you can release the mouse button as you draw. You simply click to add the first anchor point, then move the mouse to the next anchor and click again. Proceed to draw around the subject until you return to your starting point. If you make a mistake, press the **Delete/Backspace** key to delete one point back (you can delete multiple points). At any time, you can double-click, and Photoshop will close the loop for you. The Polygonal Lasso Tool works well for areas with large amounts of straight lines. Smoothing and feathering are particularly useful in avoiding an X-acto-blade look.

Magnetic Lasso Tool

The **Magnetic Lasso** Tool contains many options. By adjusting parameters based on your source image, Photoshop can use edge detection to help you in making a selection. To preview the brush size of the **Magnetic Lasso**, depress the **Caps Lock** key. (Note that this is directly opposite of what you would do with any other tool.)

Step 1   To start, specify the width that Photoshop will look for edges. The **Magnetic Lasso** will detect edges only a specified distance from the pointer. You can adjust the size of the brush by using the left and right bracket keys (**[** for smaller, **]** for larger).

Step 2   Next, specify the Edge Contrast to determine sensitivity to edges in the composition. You can choose a value between 1% and 100%. High values sense sharply contrasting edges; low values detect lower-contrast edges.

Step 3   The final option is Frequency, which specifies how often Photoshop sets fastening points. You can enter a value between 0 and 100. Higher values draw the selection quicker, with greater accuracy, but may cause aliasing problems (because the tool is now acting more like the **Magic Wand**). Make sure to smooth or feather your edge before using the selection.

For images with soft edges, use a lower width and edge contrast, and take your time when tracing the border. Images with well-defined borders can be traced more quickly. You can use higher width and edge contrast settings to generate good results. For pen and tablet users, you may choose to use the Stylus Pressure option to dynamically adjust the edge width based upon pen pressure.

Want to use both the Standard and Polygonal Lasso Tools? You can toggle Lasso Tools in midselection. Hold down the Option (Alt) key and drag. *(Photo by James Ball)*

Accidentally deselected what you were working on? Want to go back to your last selection? Photoshop stores your last selection in RAM. As long as the current document is open, you can choose Select> Reselect or press Shift+Cmd+D (Shift+Ctrl+D).

Extract Tool

The **Extract** Tool is very labor intensive, requiring you to draw around the edges and fill the areas you want to keep. This tool takes as much (or more!) time than layer masking. It also uses destructive-editing techniques that permanently discard pixel data. I'd recommend skipping ahead to layer masking. However, many users like to try *all* the tools, so I will attempt to make this tool useable.

The **Extract** Tool can be found under the **Filter** menu. It requires you to paint around the edges of your subject with a "highlighter." It is a good idea to zoom in when drawing your edge, and then use the **Hand** Tool to pan around. Common keyboard shortcuts that work well here Cmd++ or – (Ctrl++ or –) to zoom and the spacebar to access the **Hand** Tool. After drawing your edge, you fill in the areas you want to keep, with the **Paint Bucket** Tool. You can adjust smoothing controls to get better edges.

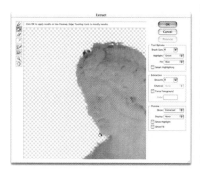

The **Extract** Tool will provide good results when used with a subject that has a high contrast background. It is prone to eating away at the edges of your subject, however, if there is a similar luminance or color in the foreground and background. When you can accept the preview, click **OK**. Again, the primary disadvantages are that the **Extract** Tool is destructive and that it does not offer the flexibility of layer masking.

Layer masking

Layer masking is the best way to extract an image. It is extremely flexible in that it supports multiple levels of transparency. You can continue to touch up your mask throughout the postproduction process. Change your mind, and you can restore any part or even all of the background.

To encapsulate the technology, a grayscale image is attached to the layer, which then masks part of the layer. The term *mask* is very appropriate because parts of the layer are *hidden*, not erased. You can add or subtract to a layer mask by simply painting on the mask. Masks are stored with the document when you save it and can be modified at any point.

Let's explore layer masks by building one.

New and Improved. The **Extract** Tool has moved to the Filter menu in version 7. It also received a tune up. It works a lot better than previously, but is no substitute for layer masking.

Step 1   Open up *CH03Chain Start.tif* from the chapter folder. This document contains no layers.

Step 2   You cannot mask the *background* of an image, because it is not a layer. You must convert it to a layer by double-clicking, and naming the layer. You can also use Option+double-click (Alt+double-click) to float the layer without naming it.

If possible, work with a higher dpi source image. This way you can zoom in farther without pixelization. This is helpful when building the layer mask. You can always downsample later.

Step 3   It is best to start a layer mask with a rough selection. Once you have the *Background* layer unlocked (*floating*), make a rough selection with the **Polygonal Lasso** Tool. With the selection active, click on the **Add Layer Mask** button at the bottom of the **Layers** palette. A black-and-white matte is now added to the layer. Black areas are 100% transparent; white areas are 100% opaque. These layer masks can also be blurred for soft edges, or contain gray values for partial transparency.

Step 4   When you are ready to clean up the layer mask, select your **Paintbrush** Tool and load the default colors by pressing the **D** key. White will be used for areas that are opaque (solid), and black will be used for areas that are transparent. You can now toggle between black and white by pressing the X key. A good mnemonic for this short cut is Devil's Xylophone. For large areas, use a large brush. You can quickly change brush size using the [and] keys. You can change brush softness with **Shift+[** or **]**.

Step 5   Zoom into the document so that you can easily see what you are working on. Start to paint, using a soft-edge brush. Make sure you are working on the mask by looking for the **Mask** icon next to the layer name. Click on the layer thumbnail to paint on the layer (**Paintbrush** icon) or the mask thumbnail to work on the mask (**Mask** icon). If you are working on a tough area, you may want to switch to a smaller brush or reduce the opacity of your working brush. Less opacity will require more strokes to build your mask. (Think of them as coats of paint.)

Don't worry about "perfect"; you can clean things up later.

Step 6   You can use the **Paintbrush** Tool to draw straight lines. Click for the starting point, and hold down the **Shift** key and click for the second point. Photoshop will draw the straight line.

There are a couple of special tricks you can use to make a "perfect" layer mask:

Contrasting. For the first, place a high-contrast, solid color directly behind the masked layer. This is a temporary step, but it makes it easier to see stray pixels. In our case, go to the **Create New Fill Or Adjustment Layer** icon at the bottom of the **Layers** palette and choose **Solid Color**. At any time, you can change the solid's color by double-clicking on the **Layer** icon.

Smudging. By using blending modes, the **Smudge** Tool becomes a great way to touch up your layer mask. There are two additional modes available to the **Smudge** Tool when in the **Mask** mode: **Lighten** and **Darken**. You can quickly shift between these modes by using the Shift++ and Shift+– key combo. Use the **Darken** mode to push the dark edges of the mask in; use the **Lighten** mode to push the white pixels out. Set the **Smudge** Tool to a low-pressure setting, and use short strokes to push the pixels around and fill up your layer mask. As always, the [and] keys change brush size, and the spacebar will give you the **Hand** Tool to pan around.

Blurring. You can use the Blur Tool to control the blurring directly or use a filter. Remember: you are blurring the layer mask only, not the image. The more blur you use, the more the edges will feather. Experiment with blurring until you get a realistic edge. If you ever go too far, you can always paint detail back in by painting with white.

Once you have the perfect layer mask, you can use it in different ways. If you keep it inside of Photoshop, the transparency is preserved. To use it in applications that do not recognize .psd layers, you must create an alpha channel (more on that beginning on page 60). At any time, you can choose to enable, disable, or permanently apply the layer mask. You access these advanced options by **Ctrl**+clicking/right-clicking on the **Mask** icon.

Use the **Smudge Tool** or **Blur Tool** to touch up your mask, At low pressure settings, it is easy to feather your edges.

Color Range is a quick way to select large areas of color or color ranges. You can specify any of the RGB or CMYK colors, as well as shadows, midtones, or highlights.

Color Range

A very powerful but overlooked tool can be found under the **Select** menu. **Color Range** makes it easy to select large areas of color or color ranges. To begin, use the **Eyedropper** on the desired color or area. To add to the selection, use the **Plus Eyedropper;** to subtract, the **Minus Eyedropper**. The **Fuzziness** control will soften your selection by increasing tolerance for stray pixels. It is also possible to preview the selection as a mask by using the Selection Preview pulldown menu. The **Color Range** command can also be accessed with the contextual menu.

Important keyboard commands for selections

There are three standard modifier key combos used when building selections:

- Holding down the Shift key, before making a second selection, adds to the initial selection.
- The Option (Alt) key lets you subtract from an item.
- Holding down Shift+Option (Alt) creates the intersection of the two selections.

By employing these three modifiers, it is possible to use the basic tools and build up a selection. But don't try and build your selection all at once.

You can add the **Shift** key after you have begun drawing with the **Marquee** Tool to constrain the selection to a perfect square or circle. Holding down the Option (Alt) key will enable you to draw from the center with the **Selection** Tool. This is particularly useful when selecting a circular area. It is possible to combine the previous key combinations.

Complex Selections with the Quick Mask Mode

The **Quick Mask** mode is another one of those overlooked features that really should make its way into your skill set. In **Quick Mask** mode, you can use **Paintbrush** Tools and the **Smudge** and **Blur** Tools to generate an accurate selection. Enter this mode from a button near the bottom of the toolbox. It is a good idea to build a rough selection first.

 Masks are very dependent on your paintbrush skills. Remember to practice free-drawing with the mouse or tablet to improve your ability to create brushstrokes.

Open up the image *CH03Hannah.psd* from the chapter folder. Use your selection tools to build a rough selection. When you are satisfied, click on the **Quick Mask** icon or press Q. Depending on user preference, either the masked or selected areas will be covered with a color overlay signifying the masked areas. By default, this is a 50% rubylith mask. This is customizable: just double-click on the **Quick Mask** icon. You may find it helpful to pick another color that is higher contrast or to make the mask more opaque.

 Hold down the spacebar to temporarily switch to the Hand Tool.

As you work your way in to the finer parts of the mask, particularly in areas of hair, it is a good idea to zoom in. If you are scanning your own images, scan at a higher dpi so that you can zoom in farther before the image begins to degrade. You can always resize the image after you perform the extraction or mask. While painting, holding down the spacebar will temporarily switch you to the Hand Tool. This makes it easier to move around the work area without having to slow down.

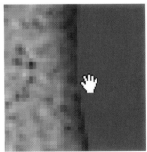

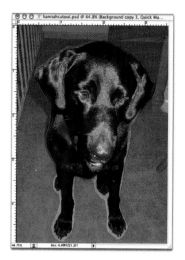

Don't like red? The mask color and transparency can be changed. Just double-click on the **Quick Mask** icon.

Use the **Smudge Tool** or **Blur Tool** (R) to touch up your mask. At low-pressure settings, it is easy to feather your edges.

Some people will also place the **Navigator** palette in plain view. The red box signifies the current view area and can be dragged around easily. The Navigator gives you a visual interface to the work area.

Now you need to clean up the quick mask. To start, press the D key to load the default colors, pure black and white. When you create the quick mask (or any mask), using black will add to the mask, white will subtract. If you use the brush at less than 100% opacity, you will generate feathered edges. It is a good idea to paint as close as you can with a large, soft brush. You can make your active brush larger by pressing the right bracket key (]); the left bracket ([) will reduce the brush size. To soften the edges of your brush, use the Shift and [or] keys.

The final touches to a quick mask come from the **Smudge** and **Blur** Tools. Adjust the pressure setting to a low value. Zoom in so you can clearly see your edges. By employing a series of short strokes, you can touch up the soft edges of your mask. When you are satisfied with the quick mask, click on the icon or press Q to turn the quick mask into a selection. The quick mask is a temporary mask. When you close the document or deselect the current selection, you will lose the mask. If you want to save the mask permanently, use a layer mask or alpha channel.

The Navigator serves two purposes. (1) It's a great way to quickly zoom and pan around a large image and (2) It gives you a large reference image when you are zoomed in making small corrections.

Better Edges Through Feathering

Feathered edges are important to creating believable composites. A feathered edge uses graduated steps to go between selected and unselected. Think of it as the difference between a ballpoint pen and a felt-tip marker.

You can feather after making a selection by going to the **Select** menu and choosing **Feather**. You can feather up to 250 pixels, but the amount will vary based upon the resolution of the source image. You can also modify the **Marquee** Tools to have feathered edges. Experiment with feathering to improve your selections.

Most high-end stock photos come with paths, not channels. You will have to convert these for video use.

• Cmd+click (Ctrl+click) on the path's name in the Paths palette.

• (Optional) You can choose to feather the selection.

• Then switch to the Channels palette and click on the Save Selection as Channel icon at the bottom.

Masking Versus Erasing

Once you have built a good selection, you have an important decision to make. You can add transparency in a destructive or nondestructive way. Many users will choose to cut and paste the selected object—or invert their selection and press the **Delete** key.

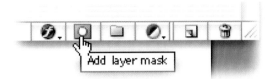

A better choice is the layer mask. Once you have made a selection, click on the Add Layer Mask button at the bottom of the **Layers** palette. This will generate a grayscale matte attached to the layer. Editing the mask is easy and allows plenty of fine adjustments. First, click on the **Layer Mask** icon. A new icon replaces the paintbrush in the **Layers** palette. The process is now identical to editing a quick mask. Use your **Paintbrush** Tools and touch up your edges with the **Blur** and **Smudge** Tools.

When finished, you can click on the layer thumbnail and edit the picture. It may be helpful to place a blank layer behind your masked layer and fill it with a high-contrast color. This will let you see any stray pixels. By Shift+clicking on the layer's mask, you can temporarily disable masks.

When using a layer mask, look closely at the icon next to the thumbnails. Clicking on the Mask thumbnail enables mask editing. Click on the Layer thumbnail to edit the layer's pixels.

Saving Selections as Paths

Paths do not allow soft edges, and generally find the most use in print applications. However, creating a path from an existing mask or channel is *easy*.

Step 1   Make an active selection. If you are in **Quick Mask** mode, exit. If you have an alpha channel or layer mask, hold down the Cmd (Ctrl) key and click on the layer's thumbnail.

Step 2   Switch over to the **Paths** palette, which is usually docked with the **Layers** palette.

Step 3   Click on the Make Work Path from Selection button at the bottom of the palette. You should see a path appear with the title *Work Path*.

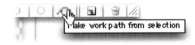

Step 4   Italicized paths or masks are temporary. It is necessary to double-click on these and assign a name.

Step 5 The path can now be exported out to Adobe Illustrator, where it can be cleaned up or sized. Vector graphics have the advantage of unlimited scaling, with no quality loss.

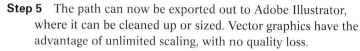

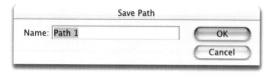

You may need to go the other direction when using stock images. Because paths are vector-based, they take up much less room in file size. These savings make it much more likely to find clipping paths with stock photos collections on CD-ROM. You can Cmd+click (Ctrl+click) on the path's icon, and then switch over to the **Channels** palette. Click on the **Save Selection as Channel** icon, and you are set.

Converting Channels into Masks

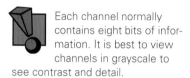

Each channel normally contains eight bits of information. It is best to view channels in grayscale to see contrast and detail.

Sculptors often say that the figures are already in the stone; they just release them. The same is often true with alpha channels. Look at each channel independently until you find the ones with highest contrast. We will use an advanced procedure called Calculations to combine two channels into a new channel, which will function as the alpha. Depending on the source photo, you will generate anything from a perfect mask to a great start.

Step 1 Open up the document *CH03Munster.tif* from the chapter's folder.

Step 2 Call up the **Channels** palette and look for the highest contrasting channels. Because you want to remove the background, look for the highest contrast between foreground and background. The red channel should stand out the most.

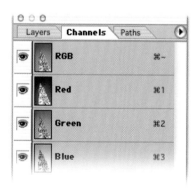

We will now use an advanced command to merge channels together. Before Photoshop had layers, it had calculations. The name scares most people off—math is not a favorite course at most journalism and art schools. Relax. The computer does the math. All you have to do is enable the **Preview** function and tweak a few dropdown menus. This feature is designed to combine channels from the same document or documents of an identical size.

Step 3 Call up the Calculations command from the **Image** menu. Make sure the **Preview** box is active.

Step 4 You can now combine the red, blue, green, or grayscale composite channels to form a new channel. With this image, use the red channel as your first source.

Step 5   Combine it with the blue channel, using the Subtract blending mode. The resulting image should show a high-contrast image, a dark shape for the church tower, and a gray image for the sky.

Step 6   Click OK and generate the new alpha channel.

Step 7   Now make a Levels adjustment to clean up the matte. You want a high-contrast black-and-white matte. Adjust the midpoint and white point until a clean matte is generated.

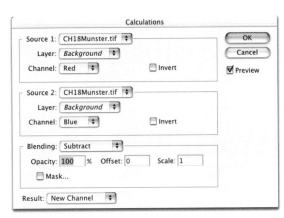

With a little bit of experimentation, a perfect matte can be generated. This alpha channel can be kept and used in a video application, or it can be loaded and turned into a layer mask. Calculations aren't a solution all the time, but they are worth a try when you have high-contrast channels.

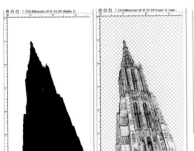

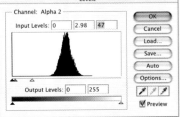

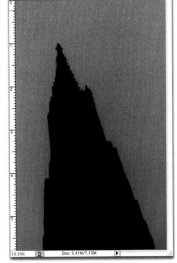

A high contrast matte is key to generating clean edges. Notice how the finest details, including the windows, have perfect edges.

Advice on Selections

There is no single technique that is perfect for making the ultimate selection. It is the situation that dictates the technique, not your comfort level. It is important to get comfortable with all of the methods discussed in this book so you can begin to unlock Photoshop's power.

Garbage mattes

Garbage matte is a compositing term. It means using a simple matte to block out the complex noise or garbage in the image that would otherwise interfere with a more elaborate matte. In other words, we chop the object out and then refine it.

When making selections, move quickly but effectively. I don't imagine you have time to spend 30 minutes generating the perfect selection. By making a broad selection with the Wand, Lasso, or Color Range method, you have less to worry about. Then start to refine things down inside of Quick Mask mode. Finish it off with some touchups and feathering using the Blur and Smudge Tools or the Median and Gaussian Blur filters. You also may find the Minimum and Maximum filters useful for "choking" the matte.

Along the way, you can employ intermediate alpha channels so that you can save your selection. If you mess up, some quick painting of the matte will get you back on track. Most intermediate users try to make the entire selection in one step, but they soon realize that a good selection involves several short (and quick) steps. Don't try to do too much with one click. Use all the methods as needs arise, and you will be fine.

Paths and channels

If a photo comes with a path or channel, use it. Many editors are so deadline driven that they forget to check if someone has already created a channel or path. There are a few ways to handle embedded data; all of them are far quicker than starting from scratch. As they say, there's no need to reinvent the wheel. Always check your **Channels** palette for an included alpha channel and the Paths palette for an included path or clipping path.

Always check your stock images to see if they contain an embedded path or channel. A path or channel can be converted into a selection by holding down the Cmd (Ctrl) key and clicking on it.

If you have a path or clipping path, simply Cmd+click (Ctrl+click) on the path thumbnail in the Paths palette. Then switch over to the Channels palette and click on the Save Selection as Channel icon. If you'd like a softer edge, run a Gaussian Blur filter on the alpha channel.

If you have multiple paths or channels that you'd like to combine, load the first one by Cmd+clicking (Ctrl+clicking) on the path/channel thumbnail. To load additional items, use the same key combo, but add the **Shift** key. When you have loaded all the selections, click on the Save Selection as Channel icon. It is a good idea to throw away any unused alpha channels before saving for your NLE. Most systems do not correctly interpret multiple alpha channels.

Unlike layers, you cannot merge channels, but Photoshop does have two helpful techniques for this situation. The Load Selection command (Select>Load Selection) allows you to load the first channel, and then add the second one. This creates a new selection, which then must be saved as a channel.

With the **Calculations** command (Image>Calculations), you can add two channels together. If you have two existing alpha channels, launch Calculations. You can then specify both alpha channels, tell them to add together, and form a new channel. This process sounds tougher than it is. Calculations can also be used to form an alpha channel based on color channel information.

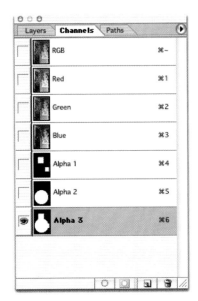

When to Make an Alpha Channel (and how to create it in 10 seconds)

When do you make an alpha channel? Whenever you want to embed the transparency data into the flattened file. You worked hard for that transparency. Why throw it away? Think of an alpha channel as a stencil or mask. Most nonlinear editing systems support some form of real-time alpha keying. It's a good idea to use it.

While many nonlinear editing systems support Photoshop layers, it is still a good idea to save flattened files with alpha channels. A PICT or TARGA file with an embedded alpha channel gives predictable, consistent results. *(Courtesy of the American Red Cross.)*

For Best Results:
• Have only one alpha channel per document, delete unused channels before saving.

• Choose a 32-bits-per-pixel alpha channel.

• Do not use any compression when saving your file.

Now you're probably thinking, "My NLE supports Photoshop layers and transparency. I don't need an alpha channel." Wrong. Support for layers and transparency is great, but you will not get a perfect import. Even if your layer effects, grouping, and blend modes make it in (they won't, by the way), do you really want a five-layer title bar? Talk about hogging tracks in the timeline. I'm happy to have layer support, but I still pick a single, streamlined file 90% of the time. Sometimes you will want to animate or manipulate layers within the NLE, but that's why you always keep a layered design file to go back to. Proper use of alpha channels lets you change part of a composition without having to redo all of your work.

Alpha channels grew out of work done at the New York Institute of Technology back in 1977. The goal was to embed transparency data directly into each file, to cut down on rendering. The name alpha was chosen because it is the part of a mathematical equation that represents blending between composited images. The embedded alpha channel eliminated the need for a separate traveling matte. After Effects users should consider embedding alpha channels like Photoshop users do. Embedded mattes reduce the need for two-step rendering and eliminate the possibility of a misaligned matte.

Step 1   Making a perfect alpha channel starts with having an active selection loaded. To load a layer, Cmd+click (Ctrl+click) on the layer's icon in the **Layers** palette until you see the marching ants. If you need to load multiple layers, then add the **Shift** key to the Cmd+click (Ctrl+click) step.

A good alpha channel starts with a good selection. With the selection active, click on the **Save Selection as Channel** button in the channels palette. Save your flattened file with the alpha channel attached and you're done!

Photoshop 7.0 changed the way TARGA files save an alpha channel. This new method made a lot of folks unhappy. The 7.0.1 update changed it back. Be sure to download the update from Adobe Online. (Click on the eyeball graphic at the top of the toolbox.)

If you've already extracted everything to multiple layers, leave those on and make everything else invisible.

Create a new layer, highlight it, hold down the Option key (Alt) and choose **Merge Visible** from the **Layers** palette submenu. Now you have only one layer to load.

Step 2   Once you have a selection, it gets easy. Switch to the **Channels** palette. Locate the **Save Selection as Channel** icon (second from left). Make sure you have only one alpha channel for your document (if you have more than four channels in an RGB+alpha image, you have more than one alpha channel).

Step 3   Save your native .psd file. Then pick Save As, and choose a format supported by your NLE. The most common formats are PICT and TARGA. Make sure the Alpha Channels and As a Copy boxes are checked.

Photoshop used to have the **Save a Copy** menu option. This is actually the preferred method for saving a flattened file, and still saving and preserving your .psd file. The keyboard command still works. Choose Cmd+Option+S (Ctrl+Alt+S) and you will automatically be in **Save a Copy** mode. **Save a Copy** is the preferred method because it allows you to save any changes you make, first into the flattened production file, and then in the layered .psd design file (upon closing the document). Save the flattened file to the appropriate location. Then, when you close your layered .psd file, tell it to save changes.

That's it; no voodoo magic. Have a selection made, switch to the Channels palette, and save it. Really, that's it.

Preserving transparency

A common problem with alpha channels is fringe; this is especially true with drop shadows and glows. To avoid this problem, place a solid color adjustment layer on the bottom of your layer stack. Choose a color that is identical to your glow. You can leave this layer off when working in Photoshop. Remember to turn it on before saving off your file with an embedded alpha channel. For more on straight versus premultiplied alpha channels, see Chapter 4, "Why Layers?".

Layer styles must be flattened to load correctly (for more info, see **Chapter 4**, "Why Layers?").

Profile: Johnathon Amayo

If you ever go to an Avid event, you'll likely meet Johnathon Amayo. As Senior Instructor for Avid, Amayo frequently travels to trade shows and training events to demonstrate Avid editing. Some even call him "Mr. Xpress DV" because he was picked to be a poster child for Avid's marketing campaign.

Amayo is an accomplished video professional as well. He served four years in the Air Force as Combat Camera. Amayo joined Avid shortly after, but continues to keep his editing feet wet to stay in touch with the craft.

"I work on several entertainment and independent projects in the Boston area. I've worked on 35mm and 16mm film projects, as well as some digital video features," said Amayo. "Recently, I've been doing a lot of DV editing."

Early in his professional career, Amayo decided to expand his editing skills. The first complementary program he decided to learn was Adobe Photoshop (v2.5). This was a natural extension that let him better control the use of graphic and still images with his videos. "Photoshop is the most complementary software program for an editor using an Avid system or any other NLE. When you add After Effects, it becomes one of the best value programs. Any user can run them on almost any computer," said Amayo. "An experienced guy can take a $1,000 application and compete with million-dollar graphic systems."

Amayo stressed the importance of editors to branch out: "Learning Photoshop and After Effects can increase your value to a company," said Amayo. "We now have to work with DVD, the web, and CD-ROMs. Editing is changing because we now have to wear so many hats."

Amayo stressed that experienced pros and even newcomers should not let these demands overwhelm them. Powerful editing tools such as

Xpress DV and graphic tools like Photoshop and After Effects are easy to access.

"We're expected to be a jack-of-all-trades and master-of-none. But that doesn't have to be. These programs are available to us early on, and they are affordable."

Amayo has relied heavily on Photoshop's powerful tools for matte creation. "I seem to have a flair for creating mattes. I find it cleaner and easier to do it in Photoshop." He suggests cutting a logo or title up into several pieces and then animating it within Avid's timeline. "When I create a title or an effect, I'll often lay it down four or five times. I can then introduce moving fills and other effects."

Despite his personal comfort level, Amayo said that improvements in Avid's support for Photoshop layers has let him do more and worry less about creating mattes and alpha channels. These improvements were made to make things easier for the editor. He still turns to Photoshop for titling effects, however.

"I really use it for advanced titles, especially since I can import layers into my Avid," said Amayo. "You get more control and dynamic editing. You can really adjust things with greater control. When I was learning Avid, I decided that Photoshop was the most complementary tool. It's flexible and it's quick, a very easy program to use."

For DV editors, Amayo says that Photoshop can be useful for fixing tough problems. "Healing and cloning can be very useful for cleaning up frames. It's slow, but a good alternative if you are working on a DV system."

Amayo is a firm believer that most editors need to expand their skill set. "When you go to big places, like LA, especially to a studio, you're likely expected to only know one application and be the best," said Amayo. "But not everybody is going to be able to work there. Most of us are at shops where we are expected to do it all."

Why Layers?

When Photoshop was created, it did not have layers. It was an application that worked extremely well for touching up photos, frames of film, or video stills. The introduction of layers moved Photoshop from image touch-up program to robust graphic tool. The key to being fast in Photoshop is understanding the **Layers** palette.

Think of layers as tracks from a video timeline. The way you build and organize the show affects your end results. With proper organization, you can come back later and quickly make changes. Clear labels make it easier to move the project into After Effects or your nonlinear edit system. Mastering layers is your first step to becoming a Photoshop power user.

What Are Layers?

One view of layers is that they are like cells in animation. You place objects on clear pieces of acetate and begin to stack them up. As you build your composition, the stacking order affects depth perception.

Video folks usually find the basic interface of the **Layers** palette similar to most NLEs. Not taking sides on who's copied whom, it's safe to say that Photoshop and most popular video applications share a similar interface. Just as it's hard to edit with your **Timeline** window closed, you really should leave the **Layers** palette open at all times. If you need to hide it temporarily, press the **Tab** key.

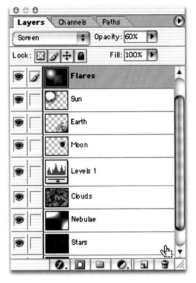

Layers can contain objects, text, effects, or image adjustments. Good naming and organization is crucial in a fast-paced production environment.

There are many controls tied to the **Layers** palette. This chapter will cover layer creation, navigation, blending, and organization.

- For Layer Styles, see page 81 of this chapter.
- For Layer Masks, see page 54 of **Chapter 3**.
- For Adjustment Layers, see page 152 of **Chapter 8**.

How Layers Work; Understanding Composite Images

Layers are much more than a storage bin. They can contain text, image adjustments, special effects, and annotations about your work. After Effects users will feel right at home; Photoshop's **Layers** palette is a close sibling to AE's timeline. From the **Layers** palette, you can control visibility, opacity, blending modes, naming, and stacking order.

New and Improved!
Photoshop 7 dramatically reorganized the **Layers** palette into logical groupings by function. It also introduced new modes for increased compatibility with Adobe After Effects.

With most NLEs beginning to support Photoshop layered files, you can keep similar elements for one show, such as all the lower thirds, in a single document. By consolidating, you have fewer files to keep track of. Updates are easier too; change the color of the bar in one document, and you can quickly update in your timeline (Final Cut Pro users, this is automatic. Avid users must select Batch Import). By turning layers off and on, you can generate all of your namebars. You also won't need to worry about small shifts in the bar or logo, a common problem with multiple versions.

I use Photoshop to complete 75% of my After Effects and DVD menu work. The superb alignment tools, text controls, and quick-rendering filters allow me to prebuild my work. I can then import layered documents into Adobe After Effects and Apple's DVD Studio Pro. It is then easy to swap in some moving elements. It is far faster to render text and shadows in Photoshop whenever possible. I also find it far easier to do on-screen layout in Adobe Photoshop. Be sure to look at the great tutorials on using Photoshop for Motion Graphics and DVD work.

Working with the Layers Palette

As a common starting point, open up the file *CH4PLANETS.psd* from the book's disc. This 10-layer document is a good example of using the general features of the **Layers** palette. To start, all layers are turned off; don't be surprised to see an empty screen or checkerboard pattern. (The checkerboard is Photoshop's default way of showing transparency.)

Step 1   Begin turning layers on from the bottom up, starting with Warp.

The bottommost layer is a simple pattern that adds a sense of energy to the piece. This pattern was made using Harry's Filters, a freeware set from the PlugIn Site, and is included on the disc.

Step 2   Turn on the next layer, Stars.

Notice that the layer is set to 70% opacity. Opacity is the opposite of transparency. Something that is 70% opaque is 30% transparent.

There's a great shortcut for changing opacity of a layer, but you must have a tool selected that does not have its own transparency settings (such as the **Move** or **Marquee** Tools). To change the opacity of a layer, type the corresponding number on the numeric keypad. For example, press the **2** key for 20%, the **5** key for 50%, and so on. If you want to be really specific, you can quickly type a number such as 23, and Photoshop will adjust the layer accordingly. This only works when you have a tool selected without its own transparency settings.

Step 3   Turning on the third layer, Nebulae, introduces another layer feature: *blending modes*.

If you look in the top left corner of the **Layers** palette, you'll see this layer is set to **Linear Light**. Here I'm using a high-contrast matte (a grayscale file) to add highlights. Blending modes are the most underused, least understood part of Photoshop. They are the foundation of my design work and a useful tool in digital video (see "Blending Modes" on page 74 for more info).

Step 4   Turn on the fourth layer, Clouds, and you'll see a similar technique employed to add a little texture to the image.

For more on patterns, see Chapter 10, "Creating Backgrounds for Video."

A good technique is to try changing the blending mode *before* you make an opacity change. This subtle change to your working style will give you dramatic results.

Step 5   Turn on the fifth layer, which looks different than the rest. It is an adjustment layer.

Here I have applied a Levels adjustment to multiple layers simultaneously. A Levels adjustment affects the overall balance of lights and darks in an image. It is similar to a gamma adjustment in video. The key benefit of the adjustment layer is that it is nondestructive; the effect is "live," in that you can alter or disable it at any time.

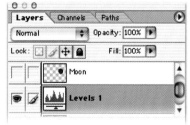

Now, double-click on the **Layers** icon, and the controls pop up. Try adjusting the middle slider and see the resulting changes.

You should make a Levels adjustment on every composition; it is the key to maintaining video-safe levels and attaining proper lighting and contrast. Levels adjustments are covered in greater detail in Chapter 8, "Color Correction: How to Get It Right."

Step 6   Turn on the next three layers, Earth, Moon, and Sun, to fill out the scene.

These three objects were created with some great filters from Flaming Pear (http://www.flamingpear.com). You'll find a full-featured demo on the disc.

Notice how Moon falls on top of Earth? I've improperly stacked the layers.

Step 7   Click on the Moon layer in the **Layers** palette and drag it below Earth. Or, use the left and right bracket keys instead of all that clicking and dragging.

Cmd+[(Ctrl+[)	Move current layer down one spot
Cmd+] (Ctrl+])	Move current layer up one spot
Shift+Cmd+[(Shift+Ctrl+[)	Move current layer to the bottom of **Layers** palette
Shift+Cmd+] (Shift+Ctrl+])	Move current layer to the top of **Layers** palette.

Step 8   Turn on the next layer, Flares, to add highlights to the composition.

Here I'm using Photoshop's versatile **Lens Flare** filter. Filters cannot be applied to empty layers, so I had to create a new layer and fill it. I chose black because it is easy to "luma key" this part out. After applying the filter to the solid, I set the layer to **Screen** mode, thus leaving the lens flare perfectly composited on the lower layers. Adjustment to the layer's opacity will further refine the effect.

Step 9   Turn on the top layer, Ship, to see a 3D object with a motion trail.

The 3D object was created using the defunct KPT5 Frax4D filter. This package can still be found at places like e-Bay or the bargain bin at computer stores. Unfortunately, it does not run under OSX on the Mac. I hope to see all of my old favorites updated for modern operating systems. The key here is that I used a layer mask to "blend" the vapor trail. Layer masks are a great way to apply transparency or erase portions of a layer in a nondestructive fashion (see Chapter 3, "What About Transparency?").

By employing proper use of layers, I have generated a photorealistic piece that I can use as is or import the layers into another application to animate. Proper naming makes it easy to find each layer. To name a layer, double-click on the name in the **Layers** palette. Note that old versions of Photoshop require you to Option+double-click (Alt+double-click) on the name.

Layer Organization Techniques

Layer organization starts with naming, but does not end there. A lot of effort has gone into developing technology for improved layer management. Intermediate steps include linking, aligning, distributing, locking, merging, and flattening layers. Advanced options include grouping, color coding, and use of layer sets. For this lesson, open *Ch4organization.psd*.

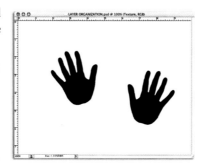
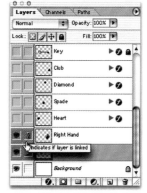

Linking. Multiple layers can be linked together. Linking enables you to move multiple objects together.

Step 1   Make the Right Hand and Left Hand layers visible.

Step 2   Select the Move tool by pressing the letter V.

Step 3   Now click on one of the red layers, and link the other one to it by clicking on the space next to the eyeball on the second layer.

You can now move the two layers as one. With the **Move** tool selected, you can click and drag. You can also use the arrow keys to move the image one pixel. Add the **Shift** key and you can supershift 10 pixels at a time.

Align and Distribute. It is possible to have precise alignment in Photoshop. You can align or distribute objects in relationship to one another.

Step 1   Hide the hand layers by clicking on their visibility switches.

Step 2   Now turn the green layers on. You should see the four playing card symbols randomly arranged on the screen.

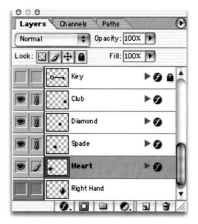

Step 3   Select the heart symbol and position it where you'd like it to fall on the screen.

Step 4   The first step to aligning or distributing is to link the objects together.

Step 5   Now link the other three symbols to the heart.

The **Alignment** tools are tied to the **Move** tool. If you have the layers linked together and the **Move** tool selected, you should see them at the top of the **Options** bar. It takes two or more objects to perform an alignment. The alignment is based upon the object you have selected. In this case, when you choose **Align Bottom**, the other three will move while the heart remains stationary.

The misalignment problem is solved, but things still aren't right. The viewer's eye expects these objects to be evenly spaced; this is called distribution. You must have at least three items to perform a distribution. In this case, four is more than enough. The second set of boxes in the **Options** bar is for distribution. Choose the second-to-last box to distribute horizontal centers. Notice how the objects snap to place perfectly.

Locking a layer only does so in Photoshop. This is a useful way to avoid accidental edits or movement on a layer.

Locking. Photoshop offers great flexibility in locking layers. It is possible to lock the transparent areas of an image, lock the pixels to avoid changing color, lock position to prevent accidental shifting, or any combination of the three. These features are enabled by highlighting the layer and then picking from the **Lock** icons at the top of the palette. This is a good way to avoid accidental changes. If you do need to make a change, unlock the layer. Take a look at the key layer; you should see a **Lock** icon. If you try to use the **Move** tool, Photoshop will warn you that the layer is locked.

Merging and Flattening Layers. Sometimes, you know that you'd like to *permanently* join two objects together. This is called *merging;* it is the Photoshop equivalent of a video mixdown.

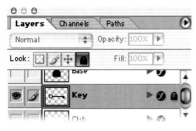

Step 1 Turn off all layers except the yellow Base and People layers.

Step 2 Highlight the Base layer and link these two layers together.

Step 3 From the **Layers** palette submenu (the triangle in the right corner), pick **Merge Linked**.

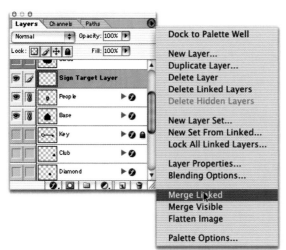

The two layers are now permanently joined. This is a useful way to cut down on layers and simplify your project.

Another technique is to merge linked layers to an empty target layer. Think of this as a selective merge. Highlight the Sign Target layer and link the other yellow layers to it. Now hold down the **Option (Alt)** key and select **Merge Linked**. Notice how a flattened copy appears on the new target layer, while the originals are left behind. This is a useful technique for simplifying your project, while still preserving source layers.

There are times when you want to merge all of the visible layers in the document. Simply choose **Merge Visible**. One step further is to **Flatten** your composition. This discards all non-visible layers and merges all visible layers into a single background layer. It is

Targeted Flattening. You can merge multiple layers into one layer to make it easier to manipulate. This is also a necessary step for creating alpha channels from layer styles.

1. Link the source layers to a blank target layer. Make sure that none of the layers are a locked *background* layer. Otherwise, double-click on the background layer and name it.

2. Highlight the target layer.

3. Hold down the Option (Alt) key.

4. Choose **Merged Linked** from the Layers palette submenu.

This flattened copy will now import cleanly into your NLE, Compositing application, or DVD authoring application. The editable version is left as well for future changes. For more on Layer Styles, see page 81.

very rare that you will need to perform this step. There is a myth that you must flatten your artwork before sending it to some NLEs. This is inaccurate; you should choose **Save a Copy** in a format that does not support layers (such as PICT or TARGA) in order to import into some NLEs. This saves an additional flattened copy to the specified location. It does not get rid of your layers in the .psd file. Layers are key to future changes; preserve them or regret it later.

Grouping. Grouping in Photoshop has a completely different meaning than in any other computer application. A grouped layer will only apply its pixels to the opaque areas of the layer it is grouped to. This is very similar to using a track matte in After Effects. Turn on the Cloud and Texture layers. To map the Texture layer, highlight and press Cmd+G (Ctrl+G). You should notice that the layer indents. To ungroup layers, add the **Shift** key to the combo. Other ways to perform the same task include accessing the **Layer** menu or **Option**-clicking (**Alt**-clicking) *between* two layers in the **Layers** palette. Grouping is a great replacement for Paste Into because it takes one step instead of five.

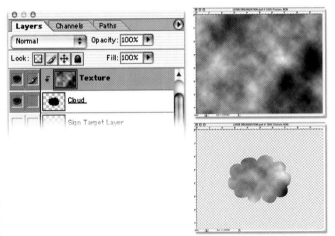

Color-coding. Throughout this lesson, the layers have been color-coded. This is a great way to identify items, and helps to mentally organize a complex composition. These colors only appear in the **Layers** palette and do not affect your final output. To assign a color to a layer, you must access the **Layer Properties** command. With a two-button mouse, you can right-click on the desired layer. One-button mouse users should hold down the **Control** key when clicking.

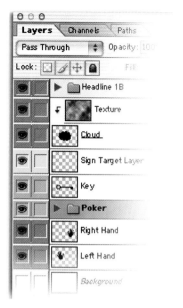

Use of layer sets and color coding is an essential part of gaining speed.

Layer sets. An incredibly useful feature is layer sets. Think of these as folders in a file cabinet. Instead of throwing everything in a drawer, you can make life easier and put similar things together. This makes it easier to work with layers. This is a great way to prepare options to show the client. For example, you can prepare the same headline two different ways. Headline 1A has a serif font, while Headline 1B uses a sans-serif typeface. It is easy to turn entire sets off and on as a group. Layer sets can also have their blending modes and opacity changes as a group.

There are several ways to create a set. You can click on the **New Set** icon and drag the layer into the set. An easier method involves linking.

Step 1   Go back to the Heart layer; the other three symbol layers should still be linked.

Step 2   Now choose **New Set From Linked** from the Layers palette submenu and name the set "Poker." By employing a layer set, you can align a group of objects.

Step 3   Highlight the Background layer and link it to the new layer set Poker.

Step 4   Select the Move tool.

You now have the **Align** tools available and can choose to center the symbols as a single unit. Centering objects on a page is as simple as linking the layers or layer sets to the highlighted Background layer and using the **Align** tools.

Blending Modes

Photoshop's least-used feature is also its most powerful. Nothing is as mysterious as Photoshop's blending modes. I have read many convoluted attempts at explaining these 22 different options, but there are few absolutes when it comes to blending modes. Ask 10 knowledgeable users what they do and you'll get at least 10 answers. When pressed for more explanation as to what blending modes actually do, the common answer is "It depends."

Your next logical question is likely "Depends on what?" Simply put, the effect achieved by blending two layers varies with the contents of those two layers. A blending mode compares the content of two layers and enacts changes based on the contents of both layers. In real-world terms, you can put milk, strawberries, and vanilla ice cream in a blender and get a great milkshake. Use the same blender with other ingredients—say, tomatoes, onions, jalapeños, and cilantro—and you've got salsa. The same appliance gives different results depending on the ingredients.

Blending modes appear in virtually every tool, can be combined with every filter, and show up at every turn. Blending modes are the final exam on the Photoshop Guru test. So please, read on, and I promise to let you in on all the secrets.

Step 1   Open the file named *Ch4Solar.psd*.

In this five-layered document, I have used four different blending modes. I have applied these modes for artistic effect, although there are *many* postproduction-oriented uses as well. Let's dissect this document and see how modes are used.

Step 2   Turn each layer off, starting at the top, and notice how things change.

Layer blending modes offer a lot of variety. The first secret is "Don't try to memorize what they all do." The good news is that they are grouped by similar traits. As you make your way through the list, you will notice a gradual progression through styles. The first group darkens your underlying image, while the second will lighten it. The third set adds contrast, while the last two generate dramatic results by comparing or mapping values. Depending on your sources, some blending modes will generate little or no results. Sound confusing? Keep reading.

The second secret is "Experiment." The best way to use blending modes is to try them out. Clicking through a long dropdown menu is boring. A much better alternative is the keyboard shortcut.

Step 3   Turn off all but the two bottommost layers in our test file. Select the layer Globes; then pick the **Move** tool.

These are four of the many combinations possible by employing blending modes. Most users never explore the flexibility offered by these great layer options.

Step 4   You can cycle forward using **Shift**+; you can cycle backwards with **Shift**+-. This shortcut works as long as you have a tool selected that does not have its own blending modes (such as the **Move** or **Marquee** tools). Cycle through until you find a look that you like.

Step 5   Then switch to higher levels and repeat. It is possible to generate many different looks by changing the blending modes on multiple layers.

The third secret is "Exploit them." Need a quick visual pop? Try blending a blurred image on top of itself. Need to tint something? Place a solid or gradient on top and change to hue or color mode. Need to quickly luma key an item? **Multiply** knocks out whites; **Screen** knocks out the blacks. You'll find blending modes in virtually every filter (choose Fade Filter from the Edit menu) and all of your brush tools. Blending modes rock, and they can be our little secret.

Export Issues with Layers

While other applications and NLEs are beginning to recognize Photoshop layers, at this time, it's not a seamless exchange.

The best advice is to have things clearly labeled. The default naming scheme of Layer 1, Layer 2, Layer 3 will not help you make your deadline. Use descriptive, *unique* names per layer. Photoshop will allow you to have identical names, but your editing application will become confused by the duplication. Here are some other points to consider.

Saving a flattened copy for your NLE

It is common to need to save a flattened version for your editing system. If this is the case, *do not* flatten your .psd file. Choose Save As or use Shift+Cmd+S (Shift+Ctrl+S). Select a flat file format that your edit system recognizes. The two most common formats will be PICT and TARGA. When you pick these formats, the Layers box will automatically gray out and the As a Copy box is checked, but grayed out. If you want to save a flattened file, Photoshop will make it easy and preserve your layers at the same time. You worked hard for those layers. Keep them.

Layer styles will not load or affect an alpha channel. To work around this, it is necessary to merge a blank layer with the affected layer. This will create a flattened copy of the layer that will properly load transparency information.

Blending Modes (adapted from Photoshop 7 Help file)

Original

Overlay

Dissolve

Random replacement of the pixels with the base or blend color.

Darken

Pixels lighter than blend are replace; darker ones are not.

Multiply

Similar to drawing strokes on the image with magic markers.

Color Burn

Evaluates each channel; darkens base by increasing contrast.

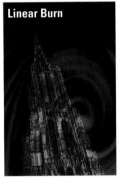
Linear Burn

Evaluates each channel; darkens base by decreasing brightness.

Lighten

Evaluates each channel; uses base or blend color (whichever is lighter).

Screen

Results in a lighter color. Useful for 'knocking' black out of a layer.

Color Dodge

Evaluates color information and brightens base by decreasing contrast.

Linear Dodge

Evaluates color information and brightens base by increasing brightness.

Overlay

Overlays existing pixels while preserving highlights and shadows of base.

Blending Modes continued (adapted from Photoshop 7 Help file)

Soft Light

The effect is similar to shining a diffused spotlight on the image.

Hard Light

The effect is similar to shining a harsh spotlight on the image.

Vivid Light

Burns or dodges by increasing or decreasing the contrast.

Linear Light

Burns or dodges by decreasing or increasing the brightness.

Pin Light

Useful for adding special effects to an image.

Difference

Evaluates each channel and subtracts depending on greater brightness.

Exclusion

Similar to, but lower in contrast than the Difference mode.

Hue

Uses luminance and saturation of the base and the hue of the blend.

Saturation

Creates color with luminance and hue of base and saturation of blend.

Color

Preserves gray levels. Useful for coloring and tinting.

Luminosity

Inverse effect from that of the Color mode.

© **2002**

Blending Modes continued (adapted from Photoshop 7 Help file)

Original

Blurred

Dissolve

Darken

Multiply

Color Burn

Linear Burn

Lighten

Screen

Color Dodge

Linear Dodge

Overlay

Soft Light

Hard Light

Vivid Light

Linear Light

Pin Light

Difference

Exclusion

Hue

Saturation

Color

Luminosity

© 2002

R H E D

P I X E L

Using a Glow or Drop Shadow? Make sure your background color is the same as the soft edge. This will create a straight alpha. This will give you a cleaner edge (with no fringe) when the image is composited in your NLE.

The star on the left is premultiplied; the glow is composited over black. The star on the right cannot be seen without enabling the alpha channel. The right star will generate better results when keyed over a video source.

Pre-multiplied alpha channels will often pick up noise from the background layer. This is evident in the left star by the black fringe in the outer glow.

Alpha Channels Revisited

You have to make some choices in Photoshop if you are saving out flattened files with alpha channels. It's important to decide between premultiplied or straight. This becomes an issue when you have edge effects, especially drop shadows and glows. The alpha channel stored the transparency information as an 8-bit file. This grayscale file contains levels of opacity. The stars in the accompanying figure have a yellow glow applied to them. The star on the left is over black, a common background color used by video pros when building graphics. The star on the right (it's really there) has been placed over a background that is the same color as the glow.

When we create an alpha channel for these files (Chapter 3, "What About Transparency?"), the shape is identical. The star over black, however, is considered premultiplied, a benefit

when working in Photoshop so that we can see our work. The star on the right contains a straight alpha—that is, the alpha contains the glow info, but the background is a solid color that will become the glow when the image is keyed.

Notice how the premultiplied alpha picks up black around the edges? This is a subtle but nasty problem. It will show up when you have light-colored glows or drop shadows. The second star, with a straight alpha, keys perfectly with no color contamination. This is an extra step, but one worth doing when you save flattened files for video. If you plan on importing your .psd file with layers into your NLE, this extra step should not be an issue.

Exporting with Layers for Animation

Be sure your layers have unique names. Also, it is a good idea to rasterize your type before sending things out. You can access this from the contextual menu or go to Layer>Rasterize>Type. While you're there, you can also choose to Rasterize All Layers. You should rasterize if there is a concern that the other machine may not have the font loaded. This is a good extra precaution, but it's only needed if you intended to import the *layered* file into your NLE. Flattened files (such as PICT or TARGA) already rasterize type when you save. If you are going to rasterize, make sure to make the changes to a *copy* of the original. This way, you can go back and make changes.

Other things that may not travel well include layer styles and adjustment layers. It's a good idea to flatten your layer styles because they will be ignored by your NLE. Adjustment layers should be avoided as well if you are going to import the layers. Unfortunately, our NLE manufacturers are still trying to catch up and offer better support for the .psd format.

To avoid future problems, consider a version of your file with the text layers rasterized. This production file will reduce the chance of problems arising from not having the same fonts on all machines.

Layer Styles

Many graphics are clear to read at high-print resolutions, but become lost in the frame when keyed over moving video at lower resolutions. Common techniques include adding bevels, glows, or contrasting drop shadows. While there are many excellent techniques and products developed over the years, nothing is better suited for the video world than proper use of layer styles.

Imagine effects that never need rendering. Did I mention that they are infinitely customizable? Oh, and if you make a change on the layer, they instantly update. Layer styles are the perfect tools for video deadlines. They are fast. They can be embedded into the document or easily transported, eliminating the need for identical plug-ins and cross-platform issues. Better yet, there are thousands available online for free. (Check out the incredible adobexchange.com site and you will find a generous community offering free layer styles.) And best of all, the effects are "live" (much like After Effects), which gives you the ability to apply, stack, undo, or remove as many times as you (or the producer) wants.

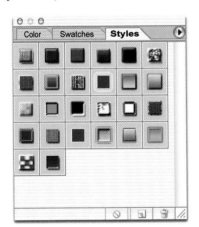

The best way to understand layer styles is to simply apply them. Of course, there are a few gotchas— it wouldn't be a computer application if there weren't. Layer styles are designed to work inside of Photoshop, which means they aren't particularly friendly when you import layered files into a video application. They also don't work perfectly with alpha channels. However, both problems can be solved in 15 seconds, still leaving layer styles well ahead of the race against the clock. There are four major ways to apply styles.

Layer styles used to be called *layer effects*. Do not get confused if looking at older articles or tutorials.

You'll find the layer styles shown in this chapter on the book's disc, as well as 55 styles from Action FX.

- The Add a Layer Style pop-up menu at the bottom of the **Layers** palette
- The Style palette
- The Layer Style dialog box
- The Layer menu (Layer>Layer Style)

Each provides unique advantages, depending upon your situation. We will cover all four in this chapter, but let's start with the pop-up menu.

Step 1   To begin with, create a new document sized 500 pixels by 250 pixels.

Step 2   Place an element such as text on an empty layer. Choose a thick, sans-serif font and type a short word.

Step 3   Go to the bottom of the **Layers** palette, click on the circular *f*, and choose the first effect, Drop Shadow.

Step 4   The **Layer Style** dialog box appears, and you have the chance to tweak your effect.

Drop Shadow

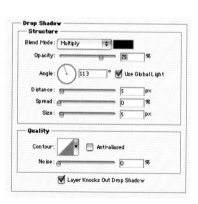

The drop shadow is a straightforward effect that will serve well as an introduction to the other layer styles. Many of the options presented will reoccur in other layer styles. One of the first things you'll notice is that it asks for the blending mode for the shadow (see "Blending Modes" on page 74). This setting enables your shadow to more realistically blend with lower layers. Different colors and modes will produce very different results. Remember, shadows aren't always black; they often pick up the color of the light source or background on which they are cast. To change the color of the shadow, click on the colored rectangle. You can also pick a contrasting color to help offset your type or logo on a busy background. You may want to experiment with the opacity controls as well.

The next controls affect the shadow position and size. You can change the angle manually or use the **Global Light** option to set a consistent light source to be used by all layer styles. It is a good idea to keep the **Global Light** box checked so that your designs appear to have realistic lighting. You can affect how far the shadow is cast with distance, and then use **Spread** and **Size** to affect the dispersion and softness aspects respectively.

The next field contains the **Contour** settings. These are generally overlooked or avoided. The contour is a curve; it represents how Photoshop fades transparency. We'll explore this powerful option later in this chapter. If you'd like, you can explore it at any time to generate dramatically different effects.

Don't forget to check the **Anti-aliased** box. Anti-aliasing will give you smoother on-screen results, especially at video resolutions. While at the bottom of the window, you can adjust noise in the shadow. Noise can add random dispersion to your style.

Inner Shadow

Inner shadows cause a shadow to be cast in front of your layer. This effect can be used to create a "punch-out" or recessed look. Inner shadows look best when they are soft. Play with the distance and size sliders to get a desirable effect. Inner shadows work well with other layer styles, but look distracting when overused.

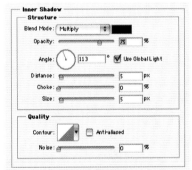

Outer Glow and Inner Glow

These effects offer similar controls. Both enable you to set color, amount, and shape of the glow. The key difference is that the inner glow lets you set where the glow emanates, the edges of the layer or the center of the layer. Inner glows signify light coming from behind the layer. It is unlikely that you would need to apply a drop shadow and a glow simultaneously. Tweak the contour and quality for a variety of shapes to your glows.

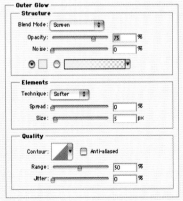

Be sure to try out the many contour settings for great effects.

Bevel and Emboss

This versatile effect enables you to access five different types of edge effects. These work very well for offsetting a layer. Bevels complement inner and outer glows to produce a realistic depth effect. Outer Bevel adds a three-dimensional beveled edge around the outside of a layer; this is generated by adding a clear edge. Inner Bevel generates a similar effect inside the edge but uses the layer's own pixels. The Emboss effect combines inner and outer bevels. Pillow Emboss combines the inner and outer bevel, but reverses the outer bevel, causing the image to appear stamped into the composition. The last effect, Stroke Emboss, must be used in combination with the Stroke layer style. These two combine to create a colored, beveled edge along the outside of a layer.

Don't overbevel. A subtle bevel helps a text or logo element lift off the screen and adds subtle depth. Overuse, however, looks amateurish.

The beveled edges allow a great deal of control. It is possible to change the lighting source and direction of the bevel, as well as thickness, softness, and depth. It is also possible to use the power of blending modes to create extremely photorealistic effects, such as plastic or chrome. The flexibility of the **Contour** controls is the bevel effects' best feature. There are many presets to try. Or create your own. There are two contour settings: the first pane affects the lighting of the bevel, and the **Specialized Contour** pane alters the shape of the edge.

Soft-Edged Stroke? Sure—it's called Outer Glow. Adjust the size and spread for better appearance.

The final option is **Texture**, which can be applied to the bevel or entire surface. Many presets can be used by clicking on the triangular menus. Additional patterns can be loaded or created. Many textures exist at online creative sites; you'll also find a variety of textures included on the bundled disc. Creating unique textures is also easy, as we'll see.

Satin

Satin is used to add regular ripples or waves in your layer style. With a little practice, you can create liquid effects and subtle highlights. This style requires some experimentation because its controls are very sensitive.

Choosing different colors, contour settings, and blending modes will produce widely different results. Satin works very well in combination with other effects.

 Satin is an underused effect that can add soft highlights to a layer.

Color, Gradient, and Pattern Overlays

These three styles all serve a similar purpose: to replace the contents of your layer with new fill colors or textures. A great time-saver is the ability to quickly

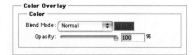

swap colors on a group of layers without having to repaint or edit each layer. It is possible to switch the color of text by applying a new color in the layer style. This same style can be applied to multiple layers simultaneously.

Step 1   Copy the layer style by Ctrl+clicking (right-clicking) on the small *f* icon.

Step 2   Link all of the layers together

Step 3   Then Ctrl+click (right-click) and choose Paste Layer Style to Linked.

Gradient and pattern overlays are useful in creating new looks, especially when using photorealistic patterns or seamless tiles. To create more believable effects, be sure to combine pattern usage with blending modes. All three of these overlay effects are useful in creating your own layer styles.

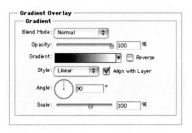 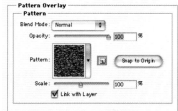

Stroke

The **Stroke** effect places a colored border around the outside edge of a layer. This is a great replacement for using the **Stroke** command under the **Edit** menu. It is now possible to keep the stroke as an easy-to-update effect without needing to place it on its own layer. All of the needed controls are here: you can choose from inner, outer, or center strokes, as well as advanced controls such as

 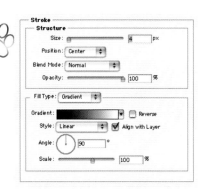

blending modes, textures, and gradients. The **Stroke** style can be further enhanced by combining it with the **Stroke Emboss** effect.

Loading prebuilt styles

Sometimes the best way to start is with a preset. Photoshop includes some good styles to work with. The easiest way to work with styles is to call up the **Styles** palette, which by default is docked with the **Color** and **Swa**tches tabs. If you've closed that window, look under the **Window** menu and call up the **Styles** palette.

You'll notice a small swatch that represents each style. To apply a style, highlight any layer (other than the Background layer or a locked layer) and click on a swatch. You can view these presets in many ways. You can click on the triangular sub-menu icon in the upper right corner of the **Styles** window. For the visually minded, I recommend the thumbnail view. If you have many presets to choose from, the large list view is helpful because it combines a name and thumbnail.

When you need more, simply pick from the dropdown list. Photoshop comes with 10 styles to choose from, although you can ignore any with the word "rollover" in the title because they are intended for Internet design. When you select a new set of styles from the **Preset** list, you are presented a choice. You can:

• Append (add these new styles to the bottom of the current list)
• Cancel (not load anything new)
• Select OK (which replaces the current list with new presets)

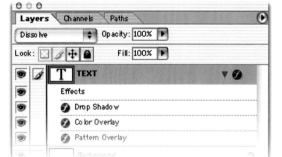

Let's try these out.

Step 1 Open up the *CH4Start.psd* file in the chapter's folder. If you do not have access to this file, create a new document with a floating text layer.

Step 2 Select the Text layer so that the layer is highlighted. Call up your **Styles** palette. From the submenu, choose Text Effects 2.

Step 3 Click on each preset, pausing to study the end results.

See how quickly the simple text layer changes from organic effects, to shiny metal, to jelly-like letters? This is just the beginning.

Action FX

Known best for its many action files, Action FX has an impressive collection of layer styles as well. What started as a site for Photoshop hobbyists has quickly become a popular stop for Actions, Layer Styles, Brush Sets, and Textures.

There are many tutorials and articles created by Photoshop author Al Ward. Al calls himself a certified Photoshop addict and is the webmaster of Action FX Photoshop Resources. He also contributes to the official NAPP Web site as the Actions area coordinator (www.photoshopuser.com).

Action FX has included 55 Layer Styles on the book's disc. You'll find these a great timesaver in your upcoming projects. There are many more styles and resources available at the Web site as well. Action FX offers tons of free downloads that will generate fast results. If you like what you find, there are over 4,000 other great things to be had by joining. A one-year membership is less than $50—far cheaper than a plug-in package.

Besides creating cool software, Al is an accomplished author and is worth looking up the next time you are in the market for a book on special effects. You can count on more great things from Al Ward, as he lists coffee as his favorite food group and sleep as the one pastime he'd like to take up some day.

To fully appreciate the power of layer styles, have your **Layers** palette open. As you change styles on a layer, the palette updates. Double-click on each component to call up the dialog window. You'll discover how the effect was made. Better yet, these presets are merely starting points! You can modify them and save them for later use or sharing with others.

If you'd like to load new styles that don't appear in the preset list, choose Load Styles from the Styles window submenu. For inspiration, we've included a large collection of styles on the disc. If you'd like these to appear in your preset list, find the *Presets* folder inside your Photoshop application folder and look for the *Styles* folder. Any layer styles copied into the *Styles* folder will appear as a preset the next time you launch the program.

Technology is only as good as it is customizable. Fortunately, layer styles are infinitely tweakable. You can create your own entirely from scratch, or build off an existing style. The practice of building styles is booming in Photoshop user groups. One of the best places to look is Adobe Studio's Xchange (www.adobexchange.com). This popular site is free. (Don't be thrown off when it asks you to register.) Here you will find tons of content available for all Adobe products. On first visit, stick to Photoshop and look at the styles available. You will find many users have been busy posting their own creations. Download a few styles to help on your next project and see what's possible with layer styles.

Your own styles

Creating a style is a straightforward process. You can apply any combination of the previously mentioned 10 styles. Change the options, use a new texture, apply gradients and blending modes, etc. If you are unsure how each layer style is applied, flip back to "Layer Styles" on page 81. Styles are quick to learn and easy to master; just continue to experiment with many options. Advanced customization through contours, gradients, and textures will be covered later on in this chapter.

If you add new styles to a library, you must *resave* the .asl file to update it. Otherwise, the new styles will be cleared when you load another library.

Saving styles. Once you've created an original style (or even modified an existing one), you will probably want to save it. There are two ways to save a style; both are easy. The first way is to do nothing; Photoshop automatically embeds the layer style information into the layered files. As long as you save the document in a layered format (such as Photoshop Document, Layered TIFF, or Photoshop PDF), you can call this information back up at a later time. So six months from now, when your project comes back, when you open up your source files and start making changes, the layer styles will automatically update as you edit the layer.

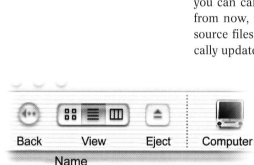

The second method is really a two-step process. After creating a style, you can add it to the existing style swatches by clicking on an empty space in the **Styles** window. A new swatch is created, and you are prompted to name the swatch. It is now available to you until you load another style library. This can be helpful if you want to temporarily save a style so you can apply it to other layers or to other open documents. However, it doesn't allow you to keep a copy to reload or share.

To save your styles *permanently*, you must create a style library or set from the loaded swatches. A good idea is to create a personal set in which to store your styles. There is no "new set" option. Simply create new styles as you did in the previous paragraph. You can delete any styles you don't want by dragging them into the **Trashcan** at the bottom of the palette. **Option**+clicking (**Alt**+clicking) an unwanted style is also a quick way to remove it. When you are ready to save, go to the submenu of the **Styles** palette and choose Save Styles.

Updating your presets. A good place to store styles is in Application folder>Presets>Styles. Styles stored in this default location will appear in your pop-up menu after restarting.

Step 1   When you create a style worth sharing, load the library where you want to save it.

Step 2   Select the affected layer in the **Layers** palette, and then click on an empty space in the **Styles** palette.

Step 3   Now choose Save Styles; name the file with the same name it had before and save it to the same location.

The power of Contour settings

Perhaps the least understood option of the **Layer Styles** dialog boxes is the **Contour** settings. Most users leave it set to the default linear slope setting. The easiest way to understand the contour is to think of it as a cross-section of the bevel. The contour represents the shape of the bevel from a parallel point of view. A simple linear contour reflects light with predictable results. Irregularly shaped contours can generate metallic highlights or multiple rings to the bevel. When you think you've tried every option, the contour settings will unlock *many* more. Just make sure to pick the **Anti-aliased** option.

To modify a contour, you can click on the dropdown menu and select a preset. If you don't like the 12 included, feel free to load some or make your own. Loading contours is similar to loading styles: just click on the submenu triangle. Making your own involves defining the shape of the curve. Click on the curve and add points. If the **Preview** box is selected, your curve will update in near real time. This is the best way to learn how the contour controls work. Contour controls are available on glows, shadows, and bevels.

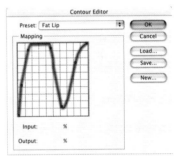

Textures and Gradients

Another way to create a unique look is to use custom overlays for your layer. These can be a gradient or a texture. You have precise control of how the overlay is blended and scaled to the layer. These tools behave exactly the same way throughout Photoshop, so if you are experienced with gradients or textures, this will be easy!

Think of the contour as a cross-section of the bevel. It represents the shape of the bevel from a parallel point of view.

Contours to try out! You'll find a collection of contour settings to try out on the disc.

Gradients.   A gradient is simply a gradual blend between two or more colors. Photoshop offers many gradient libraries in the **Presets** menu. To access these, follow the triangles. Try different styles of gradients (radial, linear, angle, reflected, or diamond) for a new look. The angle setting will also change the gradient's appearance. To go even further, change the blend mode.

Creating your own gradients is a simple process. Clicking on the image of the gradient will bring up the **Gradient Editor**, where the color stops and opacity stops define the color and opacity throughout the gradient. The midpoint can also be adjusted to favor one color over the other. To add new stops, click in an empty space above (for opacity) or below (for color). You can also create copies of existing stops by holding down the **Option** key and dragging left or right. Gradients are useful for adding depth and life to an image. Be careful to avoid extreme contrast between stops, or you will get visible banding or patterns on your video output.

Look for *Cole Patterns.pat* on the disc to try out some pre-made patterns.

(Photo by Susan Cole.)

Patterns. The introduction of photorealistic patterns goes a long way towards adding life to your layers. Patterns can be created from any scan or digital photo. You may also choose to paint your own. There is an abundance of patterns available online and from third-party vendors. The trick is to use a seamless pattern that tiles smoothly.

Creating a seamless pattern is now simple, thanks to the Pattern Maker filter in Photoshop 7. There are five steps to creating and saving a seamless pattern. In total, the process should take you less than two minutes.

Step 1 Activate the desired layer and select the pattern with the **Crop** tool. Apply the crop.

Step 2 Choose **Select All** and then run the **Pattern Maker** filter. The Smoothness and Sample Details should be adjusted to produce best results. Be sure to click on the Use Image Size button to generate a large texture.

Step 3 Click on the **Generate** button to create the first pattern. Repeated clicks will generate multiple results, all of which are tracked in the lower right corner.

Step 4 When you are happy with the results, click OK.

Step 5 With the entire layer selected, choose Edit>Define Pattern.

Choose the pattern from any pop-up list, such as the one included in the **Texture Overlay** layer style. If you'd like, you can access the sub-menu in the **Layer Styles** palette and choose to save your currently loaded textures. (This process is identical to saving contours.)

Creating duotones and sepia tones with layer styles

The Color, Gradient, and Pattern overlays are useful when working with photos. If working with groups of historical sources or grayscale photos, you can use layer styles for consistent tinting effects. Often it is far easier to strip all of the color data out of a historical photo before restoring it. Add the duotone or sepia tone effect back in as the last step. I've included a handful of tint effects for you to try out called *PhotoStyles.asl*.

Final advice when working with layer styles

Shortcuts

How do you add shortcuts to a technology based on shortcuts? The designers at Adobe managed to squeeze a few in. Here's the most useful shortcuts related to layer styles.

- Double-click on a layer in the layer's palette (except on the name), and you will be in the Layer Style dialog box.
- To edit a specific effect, double-click that effect's name in the Layers palette.
- Turn effects off temporarily by clicking on the eyeball icon next to it.
- Copy and paste layer styles by Ctrl+clicking or right-clicking on the effect icon in the Layers palette and choose Copy layer style.
- You can also paste a copied effect to multiple layers that are linked. Just Ctrl+click or right-click on the Effect icon and select Paste Layer Style to Linked.

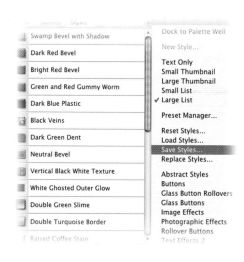

Sharing styles

Layer styles offer a convenient way to share effects within the Photoshop Community. In that spirit, you will find many layer styles on the disc. Sharing styles can be accomplished two ways:

- First, you can give someone the project that you used the style in. The styles remain attached to the layered document.
- The second method is more efficient for the web. You can save the styles as self-contained .asl files.

Whatever items currently appear in the **Styles** palette will be included in the style library. It is a good idea to remove unwanted or preset styles from the palette first. You can drag these into the palette's **Trashcan**, or **Option**+click (**Alt**+click) on the ones you wish to delete. When ready, choose Save Styles from the Style palettes submenu. The resulting file is small and can easily be e-mailed to others. To prevent the file being garbled in e-mail, make sure that you include the .asl extension.

Alpha channels and import issues

"Marching ants" don't lie... the light bulb on the left is loading incorrectly as it does not recognize the outer glow layer effect. It is important to flatten layer effects before sending them out to other video applications.

You'd think alpha channels would be a snap with layer styles as such a perfect timesaver. Despite my lobbying efforts, layer styles do not affect how a layer loads; this is a crucial step in creating the alpha channel. Simply put: loading a layer with a drop shadow or glow will ignore any pixels outside the initial shape. This makes generating an alpha channel nearly impossible. Adobe has yet to generate an effective solution.

To add to this problem, other applications have difficulty with layer styles. Both Final Cut Pro and Avid systems incorrectly interpret effects. Even After Effects imports them as multiple layers and pre-compositions with some features not fully supported. While the Create Layers command is often recommended as a solution, it is not a perfect fix. It generates messy results with grouped layers and some effects displaying incorrectly.

Targeted flattening. Many designers I know have given up on layer styles and reverted back to using filters. But you can keep using layer styles without problems. The solution is simple: Flatten them! It is simple to flatten the contents of an individual layer so that it loads perfectly and travels easily. Better yet, through a little **Layers** palette trickery, we can make a portable copy while still preserving an editable layer. This technique, which I call *targeted flattening*, is similar to a video mixdown or a nested composition.

Step 1   Save your document under a different name by using Save
As. This is an extra precaution against accidentally deleting your
work. (I usually rename it Document Name for *AE.psd* or
Document Name for FCP.psd, etc.)

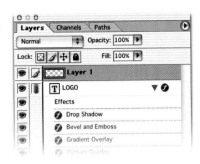

Step 2   Double-click on the background and give it a new name,
thus creating a floating layer. This procedure will not work
correctly if the background layer is part of your linked set.

Step 3   Create a new (empty) layer and link it to the layer(s) that
needs processing.

Step 4   Leave the empty layer highlighted. While holding down the
Option (Alt) key, click on the submenu and select **Merge
Linked**. This merges the layers to the target layer, but leaves the
originals behind.

You should have a flattened copy on the target layer. Repeat for all
layers and save your work. This method will produce a layered document, which can be cleanly imported into other editing applications
that support layers.

Update. You can easily jump into the Photoshop document to make
updates. After Effects users can choose **Edit Original** (Cmd+E/Ctrl+E).

Step 1   Select the flattened layer, choose **Select All**, and press
Delete.

Step 2   Then pick the original (unflattened) layer and make your
changes.

Step 3   Repeat the Option (Alt) **Merge Linked** procedure.

This process works well with the **Edit Original** command in After
Effects or Final Cut Pro's External Editor. It can also work with
Avid's batch import command and support for Photoshop layers as
well on newer systems.

Create the alpha channel. If needed, you can now Cmd+click
(Ctrl+click) on each layer to load it. Creating an alpha channel is just
one click away.

Step 1   With the "marching ants" circling, go to the Channels
palette.

Step 2   Click on the **Save Selection as Channel** button (second
from the left). You have now created the needed alpha channel.

Step 3   Choose **Save As** and pick a format that your edit system
recognizes and that will support an alpha channel. Be sure to
only have one alpha channel in your **Channels** palette (visible
or invisible). Additional channels will cause problems when you
save your files out for video.

Profile: Rachel Max

Rachel Max is Irish, born and raised in Dublin, but has considered herself fully assimilated to American culture since watching *Pee-Wee's Big Adventure* on video in 1997. Perhaps drawing inspiration from that unlikely source, Max is a professional animator and has been screening her work in festivals since 1999. Her films have won several awards and recognition. In fact, she has an animated series on **Hypnotic.com**.

Awards don't pay bills, so Max also combines her love for animation and video into her day jobs. She designs motion graphics and DVDs for GEICO (but is not responsible for the gecko commercials). She is also a teacher of Photoshop and After Effects at Washington, D.C.'s Corcoran College of Art and Design.

Max is well known in the After Effects community. She has been a trainer for several companies, including the Discovery Channel. Max is also quite fluent in Avid and Final Cut Pro systems. Despite all of the motion programs, however, Photoshop holds an important role for her.

"I use Photoshop for 90% of my design work. I use it to design menus and slideshows in DVD Studio Pro, as well as to draw my characters for my series, and to do initial design and storyboarding for my motion graphics."

Max harnesses Photoshop's speed to cut down on her rendering times for her motion work as well. She uses it as her primary titling tool and for effects work.

"I do a lot of preliminary compositing in Photoshop. Also, when I don't have to animate my drop shadows, I use the Photoshop drop shadows as opposed to applying drop shadows in After Effects. The Photoshop drop shadows render much faster and look slightly more realistic, I think."

Max has a few of her own favorite tricks to make Photoshop easier:

- Scroll through blending modes with the Shift++ or – key combo.
- Use the **Smudge** Tool for blending.
- Use actions for huge time savings (go to **http://www.AdobeXchange.com**).
- Complete as many tutorials that you can (even if you are a power user).

The key to success for Max is continuous learning.

"You can feel very overwhelmed by graphics and digital media programs," said Max. "I've worked with top professionals who admit that although they use Photoshop 8 hours a day, 5–6 days a week, they still don't know all the ins and outs. Never stop wanting to learn."

To find out more about her and see her work, visit **http://www.rachelmax.com**.

Some Words on Words, Logos, and Symbols

Proper use of type is crucial in designing effective graphics for video. Designing motion graphics (or even graphics that must be keyed over a moving source) is an extremely challenging task. It becomes necessary to balance legibility with style, fitting enough information on the screen, but not crowding it. Despite the importance of good typography, this is one of the weakest areas of the video industry.

Vector Type

The key to Photoshop's flexibility is its use of vector-based type. Vectors are mathematically defined shapes that describe all of the characters in a typeface. These fonts can then be scaled to whatever size is needed, producing clean results at almost any size. Fonts are often available in multiple formats including Type 1 (PostScript), TrueType, and the newer OpenType. You will need to check the manuals of your operating system and nonlinear editing software to see which are supported. Nearly all font foundries provide you with multiple formats, but some of the cheapie packages ($29 for 1,000 fonts) often provide only PC-compatible TrueType. I am not saying that fonts need to be expensive—many of my favorite foundries give away freebies—but make sure that you buy compatible fonts.

When you add type to Photoshop, it adds it as pixels, or *raster information.* The rendered type layer is written at the resolution of the composition. However, the link to the original font is preserved, and you can modify the type layer (provided the font is loaded on the system) at any point in time. This is extremely helpful for fixing spelling problems or for scaling the size of text. You must save your design files as Photoshop, Photoshop PDF, or layered TIFF to preserve this flexibility. If the font is not loaded on the system, the font layers will be marked with an exclamation point (!) icon. The font will display correctly, unless you attempt to edit the type layer.

The right font helps set the mood for your show. Thymesans was chosen for its prestige. *(Images courtesy National Association of Home Builders.)*

Type in Photoshop is vector-based. This allows you to easily resize or edit it at any time (as long as the correct font is loaded). "Old timers" will remember the pains suffered with the old **Type** tool.

Selecting the right font

Extensis Suitcase helps you track all of the fonts on your system. You can create sets by client as well as preview fonts before loading them. For more information, visit **www.extensis.com**.

Whenever I visit a postproduction facility or television station, I am amazed at how many fonts are loaded on the system. I often carry 2,000 fonts or so on my system, but rarely have more than 75 active at any time. If you have active hundreds (or even thousands!) of fonts on your system, you could have an unmanageable mess on your hands. Too many fonts loaded may make it difficult to find the right font. It also can lead to serious performance issues such as an unstable operating system and slow launch times.

Here's a common scenario that I see repeated far too often. The editor will randomly pick a font and ask the client if they like it. If the answer is "no," they go to the next one on the list. Eventually, out of exasperation, all parties decide on a font, usually somewhere in the Hs of the list. Instead of scrolling all day long, interview your client about the style and mood they want to invoke. If they suggest a boring font, steer them towards an alternative that looks similar, but may be better optimized for video.

Serif versus sans serif. There are two major distinctions when dealing with fonts: *serif* or *sans serif*. For instant clarity, serif fonts (such as Times, Garamond, or Concorde, the text font of this book), have small strokes at the end of the larger strokes of the text. The alternative is sans-serif fonts (such as Helvetica, Arial, or Univers, used for this book's chapter headings), which have a cleaner style comprised of generally even-weighted lines.

SERIF
VS.
SANS-SERIF

The clearest distinction between fonts is serif and sans serif. Featured are two faces from the Chank Company: BrainGelt and Mingler.

When working with serif fonts, be careful with the thickness of each character. Because serifs often come to small points, it is essential that the type is thick enough, or you will get shimmer. Serif fonts are much more likely to vibrate on video, especially at light weights and small sizes. Many clients prefer serif fonts because they are more traditional and are considered by many as easier to read in print. There are often more serif fonts to pick from because serif type has a long history. Serif fonts are modeled after many handwritten texts as well as the initial type used in printing presses.

Sans-serif fonts are a more modern development. It is often possible to compress more text into a smaller space by using a sans-serif font. These fonts are also more likely to be optimized for on-screen viewing. For video purposes, sans-serif fonts are often easier for an audience to quickly comprehend, and they read better in smaller point sizes.

ascender
x-height   **descender**   baseline

X-Height. The *x*-height is the distance from the top to bottom of a lowercase *x*. The *x* is measured because it is a clean letter with a distinct top and bottom. The height of the *x* does a lot to define the character of a font. The visual distinctiveness of a font is a combination of its *x*-height and the ascenders and descenders that grow from that center space. This height is perhaps the second most distinctive aspect when comparing two fonts.

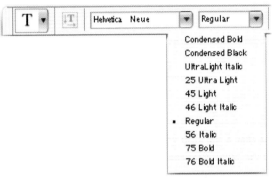

Font Weight. The most useful fonts are those that have multiple weights. A font will generally have a book (or roman) weight. A font family may also include Light, Medium, Bold, Black, Italic, and more alternates. These alternates are helpful in designing effective screen graphics because you can cut down on the number for fonts used and stick with one font family.

Appearance on Screen. Some fonts are meant to be printed only. This fact is easier to accept if you remember that the print industry has been around a heck of a lot longer than the television. Test your fonts. If they are too busy or have too many elaborate serifs, make them inactive or remove them from your system.

Many modern fonts look particularly good on screen. Some recent additions include Georgia, Verdana, Myriad, Impact, Trebuchet, Gill Sans, Helvetica Neue, and Futura. These are just a few of the fonts that have been optimized for viewing at 72 dpi. Any font marked as optimized for web output is also well suited for video work.

Style. Ask your client to describe the video. I generally ask for 10–20 adjectives that describe the company or product being featured. I then dig deeper and ask what the new video is supposed to accomplish. With this knowledge, you can make sound aesthetic decisions and impress your client with your good taste. Remember to use a distinctive display font for titles or headlines. Text or body fonts should be used for bullets or smaller copy.

Check out the interview with Chank Diesel at the end of this chapter (page 122) for great advice on how to make style decisions, as well as to get a better perspective on what goes into making a font.

Different goals need different fonts to communicate.

Using the Character Palette

The **Character** palette provides you with total control over the appearance of text in your graphics. To get started, call up the **Character** palette by selecting it from the **Windows** menu or by clicking on the palette's button in the **Options** bar when you have the **Text** tool selected. Next, select the **Type** tool and click in your document to add a type layer. Single-clicking will enable point type, or you can click and drag to define a block for paragraph type.

There are many fields in the **Character** palette. The easiest way to understand them is to quickly run through each field's function. Feel free to jump ahead if you are comfortable with a particular area. I will mention shortcuts wherever possible.

Field 1: Set the font family. Here's where you pick the font to use. You can quickly cycle through fonts by clicking in this field and using the up and down arrows. Add the **Shift** key and you will jump to the top or bottom of your font list. Press the Tab key to move to the next (and subsequent) fields.

Faux Bold? That's just another way of saying Fake Bold. Always choose a true bold or italic typeface from the font menu before invoking the faux options of the Character palette. The true bold and italic versions created by the font's designer will *always* look better.

Field 2: Set the font style. If a font has multiple styles, such as a bold, italic, or black version available, this will make it quickly available. These too can be cycled with the arrow keys. It is *always* more desirable to use the actually bold or italic version of a font rather than the **Faux Bold** or **Faux Italic** buttons.

Field 3: Set the font size. It is possible to set the font size to any unit of measure. The standard is points, but you can type in a number followed by *px* (for pixels) if that is easier for you. The up and down arrow keys will increase one point each; add the **Shift** key and you will jump 10 points. For an additional shortcut, press **Cmd+Shift+<** or **>** (**Ctrl+Shift+<** or **>**) to decrease or increase font size.

Field 4: Set the leading. *Leading* (pronounced "ledding") is a term derived from the days of a printing press when the printers inserted actual pieces of lead between the typeset characters. It refers to the space between the two lines of type measured in points. It is measured from the baseline, which is where the lowercase *x* sits in a line of type (see the previously mentioned *x*-height).

You can click on this toggle button to open and close the **Character** and **Paragraph** palettes.

You can generally trust the auto setting for standard leading. Type is usually set with leading being 120% of the point size. For example, 24-point type would have 28.8 point leading. You can choose to adjust this manually, or pick from a dropdown preset list. If you haven't noticed the pattern, the arrow and **Tab** keys work here too.

A problem often arises with setting the leading for lines of text at different point sizes. Often descenders from the top line will cross ascenders from the lower line. These occurrences are called *tangents*. They are usually undesirable if they form accidentally. A tangent will draw your viewer's eye to the intersection. Since video graphics are often visible for only a short time, you don't want your viewer getting stuck. Adjust the leading or kerning to avoid tangents.

Field 5: Set the kerning between two characters. The space between two letters is called kerning. This is the most subjective area of typography. You'll need to develop a sense of visual balance. The goal is to have the text appear evenly weighted. Proper kerning allows the reader to easily recognize word shapes and lets them keep reading without having to pause on a word.

While you can edit kerning from the field, it is far easier to use the keyboard. Move your cursor using the arrow keys. When the blinking I-bar is between the two letters in question, hold down the **Option (Alt)** key and use your arrow keys. The left arrow will pull the text closer; the right arrow will push it further apart.

The most common complaint is that this is a time-consuming process. It is, but it is critical that you kern your text. People always ask why they don't have to kern in a word-processing program. The difference is that the gaps don't stand out at 12-point. However, when the text blows up significantly larger in Photoshop, minor flaws become gaping holes. If you skip this step, it's the equivalent to forgoing scene-to-scene color correction or a final audio mix. This is the professional polishing of graphics.

If you have worked on Avid editing systems, the **Title Tool** incorrectly identifies kerning as the space between all characters on a line. That is called *tracking*, which is our next field.

Field 6: Set the tracking for selected characters. *Tracking* refers to the looseness or tightness of text, the space between the letters. Photoshop provides a handy list of dropdown presets. Tracking is how you can get that pesky *Executive Vice-President of External Communications and Community Affairs* title to fit on one line. You can also adjust the tracking by highlighting the desired words, holding down the **Option (Alt)** key, and using your left and right arrow keys.

The space between two lines of type is the leading. This term dates back to the traditional printing press days, when strips of lead were inserted between lines for proper spacing.

President
improper kerning

President
proper kerning

tracking
loose tracking

tracking
tight tracking

$$H_2O$$

negative baseline shift

Photoshop provides support for several languages in its spell-checker.

Fields 7 and 8: Vertically and Horizontally scale. These two fields enable you to stretch your text to force it to fit. Horizontal scaling set at 75–95% is another useful way to compress a line of text that cannot wrap to another line. Use **Scaling** as a last resort, but don't forget that it's there to help you out of a jam.

Field 9: Set the baseline shift. If you write out scientific expressions or mathematical notations, you'll need to shift the baseline. Highlight the text in question; enter a positive number to shift it up and a negative number to shift it down.

Field 10: Set the text color. Click and you're in the standard color picker. No surprises here.

Type Enhancement Buttons. These buttons pull out type modifications that used to be buried in menus. The first two, Faux Bold and Faux Italic, add a false bold and italic. These just thicken or skew the standard font. Use them only if a bold or italic version does not exist for the font you are using. True bold and italic fonts are better optimized for optical recognition by the viewer.

The other six buttons provide quick access to All Caps and Small Caps. It is also possible to pull text up or down using superscript or subscript. Finally, **Underline** and **Strikethrough** provide common word-processing text effects. Do not overuse them in video (or print).

Language selection menu. To harness the power of Photoshop's spell-checker, you must set the language on the selected characters. This also drives the automatic hyphenation.

Anti-alias menu. These are the same controls available from the **Options** bar. Photoshop 7 has added additional anti-aliasing options. Very small text (under 16 points) should not be anti-aliased. To improve anti-aliasing on small type, deselect the **Fractional Width** option in the **Character** palette menu. This will improve the spacing between letters at small sizes.

Larger font sizes often benefit from anti-aliasing, however, because it gently blurs the edges of the type, making it appear smoothly composited with the background layers. You will need to experiment with anti-aliasing because it will vary with fonts chosen and user's taste. There are five levels of anti-aliasing to choose from:

- **None** applies zero anti-aliasing.
- **Sharp** makes type appear the sharpest.
- **Crisp** makes type appear somewhat sharp.
- **Strong** makes type appear heavier.
- **Smooth** makes type appear smoother.

Using the Paragraph Palette

The **Paragraph** palette is generally docked with the **Character** palette. You can call it up individually, or tear it free from the **Character** tab. The Paragraph palette works on a limited basis for point text. To access full control over type, you must click and drag with the **Type** tool to add a text box.

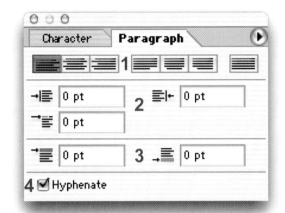

Field 1: Alignment Buttons. You can specify alignment, as well as justification. Left justification is the easiest alignment to read. However, you may choose other alignment options for style reasons.

Field 2: Indent Fields. You can specify how much to indent a particular paragraph or the first line of a paragraph. These controls will enable you to have fewer text blocks by giving you better control.

Field 3: Spacing Fields. Tell Photoshop how much space you want after each hard return. This will enable you to space paragraphs out without needing to insert blank lines.

Field 4: Enable Hyphenation. In order to fill more horizontal space, words are often broken across lines at a suitable point within the word. If you want it, check it. Photoshop will use the installed dictionary for the language you specify in the Character palette. This will ensure that words are *properly* hyphenated.

Color

Broadcast safe colors

While they get boring quickly, only a few colors look good for text and remain clear to the viewer. The #1 color for text in video is white. (But don't exceed 235 brightness value, an off-white.) The second most popular color is video black (above 16 on the RGB scale, a really dark gray).

Not happy with these two colors? Then feel free to pick another hue, but make sure to use very light or very dark shades. Lighter colors that work well include light blue, yellow, and tan. Darker colors that hold up include navy and forest green.

Type sets the mood. An aggressive trailer needs a matching typeface. *(Trailer by Raymond Soto.)*

Pantone colors

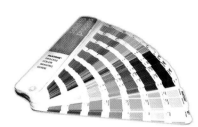

Coca-Cola Red, AT&T Blue, The Golden Arches. The colors are distinct. Companies keep consistent colors by specifying Pantone colors. The Pantone Matching System (PMS) is the mostly widely accepted color standard in the printing industry (http://www.pantone.com). Each color is assigned a PMS number, which corresponds to a specific ink or mixing standard, thus ensuring that a client will get consistent printing results.

So what does this aspect of printing technology mean to you? Everything. Clients will expect consistent colors through all media outlets, print, web, and video. Each TV is set up differently, though they all probably have the reds overcranked (hence the Never Twice the Same Color concept). But if you stay consistent at least during the creation stage, you have ground to stand on if the client ever questions the colors you've used.

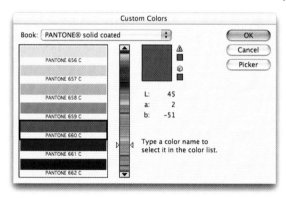

Accessing Pantone colors within Photoshop is easy.

Step 1   Double-click on the foreground or background color swatch.

Step 2   Click the Custom button.

Step 3   From the **Book** menu, you must choose between several options. Always ask your clients if they are using coated or uncoated printing. Also check which library they used—solid is the most common, but you will find separate libraries for metallic and pastels.

Step 4   To speed up your search, type the number of the color.

Step 5   Double-check yourself. Show the client your Pantone book and what comes on screen. You can also save off a square and e-mail it. An uncompressed format such as TIFF works best.

Step 6   Click in your **Swatches** palette and add the color so it's readily available. Be sure to name it with the PMS Color name or number.

Testing and Improving Readability

The most common problem with video graphics is that small type is used without any visual assists for contrast. When we are building our graphics, we are likely 1–4 feet away from the computer monitor. Virtually no one in your audience is sitting that close to the television set. (And if they were, their mothers would be aghast.)

Readability is best tested on a true video monitor, but you can make a reasonably informed decision on your computer's monitor. To check your graphics for readability, you need to put some distance between you and the computer. I recommend putting the graphic into full-screen mode. Press the Tab key to hide your palettes, and then press the letter F to go to full-screen mode. If you need to, use the keyboard to zoom in with Cmd++ (Ctrl++). Your computer monitor should now resemble a television set. Stand up, pry your hands off of the mouse and keyboard, and walk to the opposite side of your office or edit suite. When you are at least 10 feet away, look back at your monitor. Can you still read everything?

You have been viewing graphics on a relatively high-resolution device at short focal distances. Imagine how much different those graphics will look on low-resolution televisions, dubbed to VHS tape, and viewed from 10–30 feet? Repeat after me: "I will design for the back of the room."

Special Typographic Effects

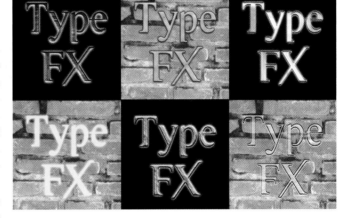

Photoshop has a number of ways to specially set off text. By employing layer styles, it is possible to quickly generate impressive type effects. All of these techniques were created using layer styles. The two primary advantages of using styles is no render times and editability. By using photos for texture maps, extremely unique type effects are possible

For more on layer styles, see Chapter 4's "Layer Styles" on page 81. Also check the *Chapter 5 Goodies* folder, where many styles can be found. You'll also find a sample document called *CH5TypeFX.psd*. Use these as starting points for your own text effects. All of these can be easily modified by changing the individual layer styles. Reserve heavily stylized effects such as these for titles and header graphics. For body text, use simpler drop shadows to help counteract the type on pattern problems associated with video and text.

Free Transform Tool

One of the quickest ways to resize and reposition text is the **Free Transform** Tool. Because text is vector, you can modify it indefinitely, and it will link back to the installed font and redraw. Your text layer must be in a committed (nonediting) state before accessing

You can Ctrl+click (right-click) to access specific transformations when you are in the **Free Transform** mode.

the transformation commands. If you have been modifying text (or adding it for the first time), you must click the **Commit** button in the **Options** bar, or press Enter on the numeric keyboard.

When you are ready to resize or reposition the text, press Cmd+T (Ctrl+T) to access the **Free Transform** command most quickly. Free Transform lets you rotate, scale, skew, distort, and change perspective in one continuous adjustment. Instead of choosing many different commands, you hold down modifier keys to switch transformation types.

To scale, grab a handle and pull. Add the **Shift** key while pulling to constrain proportions. Hold down the **Option** key (Alt) to scale from the center point. You can combine these keys for quick text sizing. To rotate, place your arrow outside one of the corners. When the cursor changes to a curved arrow, you can drag the item to rotate. Add the **Shift** key to constrain rotation to 15 increments. For free distortion, press Cmd key (Ctrl), and drag a handle. For skewing, press Cmd+Shift (Ctrl+Shift), and drag a side handle. When positioned by a side handle, the pointer becomes a white arrowhead with a double arrow. To apply a perspective change, press Cmd+Option+Shift (Ctrl+Alt+Shift), and drag a corner handle.

All of these options can also be accessed with precise numerical controls from the **Options** bar. To constrain proportions numerically, click on the **Link** icon. The reference (or anchor) point can be modified from the **Options** bar by clicking on the miniature grid in the upper left corner. It is possible to drag the anchor point manually as well. To move an item, enter new values into the **x-** and **y-axis** boxes. You can also choose to move the item manually, adding the **Shift** key to constrain movement to one direction.

To apply the transformations, press the Return (Enter) key, click the **Commit** button, or double-click inside the transformation marquee. To cancel, press **Esc** or click the **Cancel** button in the **Options** bar. Before committing or escaping, you can go back one transformation by pressing your **Undo** key Cmd+Z (Ctrl+Z) or selecting **Undo** from the **Edit** menu.

Warped Text

Warped text is one of those cool features that you should reserve for special occasions like show or segment titles. The **Warped Text** command allows you to distort text to a variety of shapes, including Arc, Bulge, Flag, Fisheye, Squeeze, and Twist.

Step 1   To access these features, highlight your type layer, and select the **Type** tool.

Step 2   Click on the **Create Warped Text** button (a T above an arc) in the **Options** bar.

Step 3   Choose a style from the dropdown menu, and then adjust the options for a more precise effect.

Step 4   To apply, click the OK button.

To remove a warp, double-click on the type layer; then click on the **Create Warped Text** button, and choose **None** from the **Style** menu. Note that you cannot warp text that has the Faux Bold formatting applied or if the font is only a bitmap font.

Just a few possibilities using the **Distort Text** Feature. You can continue to modify the text with no quality loss, as it stays vector throughout the process.

Video Type Details

Help, I have diffikultie speling

This may sound obvious, but the best way to avoid mistakes is to copy and paste from the script. Ask your client or producer to provide you a .txt or .rtf file, and open it with your computer's text editor. You can now copy and paste titles directly. While this is not a foolproof solution, it does make it easy to figure out where the error occurred (and it usually will not be with you).

Spell-checker

Photoshop has become a freestanding graphic creation tool. It is now possible to proof your text in a number of different languages. If you are familiar with a word processor's spell-checker, Photoshop's will seem completely standard. Remember, you must set the language for a text field by using the dropdown menu in the **Character** palette.

New and Improved!
Spell-check? You bet! Version 7 added a spell-check feature to the **Edit** menu.

To launch the spell-checker, choose it from the **Edit** menu (Edit >Check Spelling). If it flags a word that you know is right, you can choose to ignore it or add it to your dictionary. There's no earth-shattering technology here, but the cries of web and video designers have been answered.

Related to the spell-checker is a **Find-and-Replace** command. This allows you to go through all of your text layers and swap out words. Say that you've listed Williamstown Resort throughout your full-screen graphics. A few days later, the client calls and says it's actually Williamsburg Resort. You can have Photoshop scan through and replace all instances of the improper name throughout your composition. Again, the technology is standard, but it can be a time saver.

Safe title area

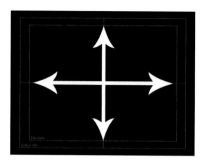

All type must fall within the inside box (safe title area) for traditional video. This region is approximately 80% of the full screen size. *(Original template from Tools for Television.)*

Even though the first image looks too loose, you must still follow safe title area. When the video is viewed on a television, the outermost edges are lost.

If you put a computer screen next to a television screen, one distinction should stand out. Computer monitors have black borders around the viewable areas, while televisions provide edge-to-edge viewing. On any given television set, up to 10% of the viewable signal is lost because the tube is recessed into a case. This viewable area is called the action safe area.

We must move all text elements in an additional 10% (or 20% from the edge.) By placing text within the safe title area, we ensure that it is readable. Unlike Adobe After Effects, Photoshop does not have a safe title area overlay. It is necessary for us to use a template, run an action, or manually create safe title area markers.

Several alternatives to creating a safe title area were discussed in Chapter 2, "Pixels: Time for Tech." Here is one additional method using Photoshop's built-in features: create an action for this item so that you can recall it for later use. There are several steps involved, so if you have a good template, use that. I present this so that if you are ever in a jam, you can build your own safe area overlay document. We are going to build a safe title document for a D1 system, sized 720×540.

Step 1 Create a new document, and pick the 720×540 Std. NTSC 601 preset from the dropdown menu. Set the document to RGB mode.

Step 2 Choose Select All by pressing Cmd+A (Ctrl+A). Then, choose Edit>Fill and fill with black.

Step 3 Create a new (empty) layer, and then name it Safe Area Overlay. You should still have an active selection.

Step 4 Scale the active selection to 90% by choosing Select>Transform Selection, and then typing in 90% in the **Options** bar for width and height. Press Return (Enter).

Step 5 Load a red swatch as the foreground color. Then choose Edit>Stroke and specify four pixels centered. This is the action safe area.

Step 6 Choose Select All by pressing Cmd+A (Ctrl+A), and scale the active selection to 80% by choosing Select>Transform Selection.

Step 7 Type in 80% in the **Options** bar for width and height. Press Return (Enter).

Step 8   Choose Edit>Stroke and specify four pixels centered. This is the Safe Title Area.

Step 9   Lock the Safe Area Overlay layer by clicking on the **Lock** icon in the layer's palette.

Step 10   Save your work.

Anti-aliasing revisited

In the case of type, anti-aliasing is the process of blending the edges to produce a smoother image. Anti-aliased text is less likely to "buzz" or "shake" on screen. You have five choices under Photoshop 7. These can be accessed easily through the **Options** bar or **Character** palette. You can change the anti-aliasing at any point in time, provided the fonts used in your composition are loaded on your computer.

You can access anti-aliasing from the options bar or character palette.

Larger font sizes generally benefit from anti-aliasing because it gently blurs the edges of the type, making it appear smoothly composited with the background layers. You will need to experiment with anti-aliasing because it will vary with fonts chosen and user's taste. Remember, many serif fonts will produce unsatisfactory results with or without anti-aliasing. There are five levels of anti-aliasing to choose from:

If you look closely at the smooth version, it is possible to see the impact of anti-aliasing. Anti-aliasing dramatically cuts down on "flicker" in video work.

- None applies zero anti-aliasing.
- Sharp makes type appear the sharpest.
- Crisp makes type appear somewhat sharp.
- Strong makes type appear heavier.
- Smooth makes type appear smoother.

Type on pattern

Unlike most print designers, video artists must design type over diverse canvases. Often this background contains a full spectrum of color. Achieving sufficient contrast is the key to preserving legibility.

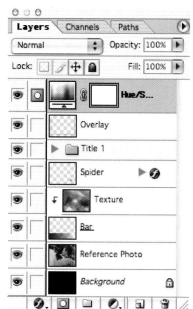

A Hue/Saturation adjustment layer offers a nondestructive way to check contrast of type over a patterned background.

When using light-colored type, it is essential to make it larger than if it were dark type. Don't be tempted to use all uppercase to make the letters stand out. Unfortunately, uppercase letters take more time for the viewer to recognize word shapes and process what they are seeing. This is generally time they don't have.

Applying a stroke, outer glow, or tight drop shadow is an effective way to getting a contrasting edge. The biggest problem with type and video is that there will always be light and dark elements in your scene. It is crucial to add a contrasting edge to any type that is going to be keyed over a full-chroma, moving background.

One way to test your contrast is to convert the file to grayscale. This can be achieved with several methods:
- You can print it out, add a saturation adjustment layer, and desaturate (set to **0% Saturation**).
- You can use the History palette to create a duplicate document that you flatten and desaturate.

Adequate separation between foreground and background elements will make for better viewing for your audience. Think of color as tonal value. Some combinations show very low contrast when desaturated.

Composition, space, and alignment

Give careful attention to how your text fills up the page. The screen is not a box that must be packed edge to edge, with as many words as possible. White space is that area around the text, which is empty, and helps focus the viewer's eyes on the text. Think of white space in terms of the printed page. Don't cram, or you will cause information overload. Think of white space as visual breathing room for your composition.

In terms of alignment, Western civilizations are most used to left-justified text. Look at the proliferation of newspapers, magazines, and books that follow this practice. It is okay to rock the boat, but be prepared to allow more time for your audience to read and comprehend the information.

Pay close attention to your first, second, and third read points. Where is the viewer's eye attracted to first? Then what brings them to the second point, followed by what motivates them to go to the next focal point? These read points are primarily formed due to scaling, composition, and color. Remember: design first, and add effects later.

Be careful with tangents, the places where ascenders and descenders overlap. A tangent adds a focal point to your text, but accidental tangents are undesirable because they make the viewer work harder. Tangents are an unintentional effect when different point-size lines are mixed together. A good way to check for tangents is to take a flattened copy of your composition and apply a 30-pixel Gaussian Blur. Look for dark areas that signify high-density, and adjust leading and kerning to correct them.

Logo standards

Despite your personal experience, logo standards do not exist to make your life difficult. A company places a lot on that little piece of art. A logo helps a company stand out; it stands for quality and uniqueness. For large companies, a fortune is invested in developing that logo and promoting it to the world. Companies want to have that logo and brand identity moving in the same direction.

Of course, problems do arise. Logos may contain serifs or fine design elements that don't hold up at low resolutions. Often arguments will pop up in the edit suite about drop shadows or glows. Other times it will be over the need to keep the ®, ©, or ™ symbols, which turn to little blobs on the television monitor. A great place to start is the company's web site. Look at how the logo has been simplified to work on the "little" screen. You'll find that several of your battles will have already been decided. Every company that takes its brand seriously will have a style guide. Here you will find precise details on fonts, colors, size, and placement. You *must* get a copy of this. Ask your clients. If they are unsure, start making phone calls. Try the in-house graphics department, the marketing group, the creative department, or the company's ad agency. If the group is small, you might even ask who created the logo and follow up with the designer.

Creating Lower Thirds

Most video editors choose to build their title graphics (or lower thirds) within the title tool of their nonlinear edit system. These built-in character generators are *very* limited and do not give the precise control over text and graphical elements that Photoshop provides. I recommend that you use Photoshop as a supporting player, or let it assume the role of character generator entirely.

As a supporting player, Photoshop is quite effective at making complex gradients for use in bars. Let's create a lower-third bar from scratch.

By blurring the text, it is easier to see the tangent. Unintentional tangents will likely distract from your layout and impact your viewer's focus.

An Adobe Illustrator or Vector EPS file is the best format to get a logo in.

Keep it Legal (the other way). Often a scanned logo will have its legal symbol become illegible. You may choose to insert these special characters using the Key Caps on a Mac or the Character Map on a PC. The following keyboard shortcuts are also available on a Mac:

™ (Option+2)

© (Option+G)

® (Option+R)

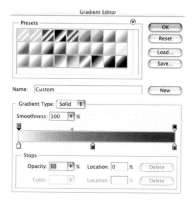

Photoshop's **Gradient Editor** outperforms all other gradient tools (even those in other Adobe applications). Choose from complex shapes, multiple colors or hues, and advanced blending options for superior results.

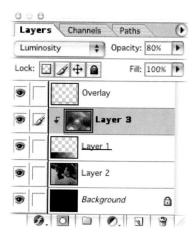

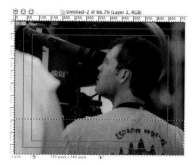

Step 1   Open a safe title document. Use the one created earlier in this chapter, or try out the Tools for Television Safe Grid Action found on the DVD.

Step 2   Grab the corner and expand the document so that you can see some of the empty space around the canvas. It is a good idea to place a photo or freeze frame in the background for reference purposes.

Step 3   With the **Rectangular Marquee** tool, draw a box across the lower fifth of the screen. You may choose to have the box extend to the bottom or have it stop around the action safe area.

Step 4   Select the **Gradient** tool. Click on the gradient in the Options bar to edit the gradient to your choice. You may load gradients from the submenu or create your own from scratch. You may want to adjust the opacity stops for a ramp effect.

Step 5   Draw the gradient within the selection. Experiment with different gradient shapes, as well as point of origin and length of gradient.

Step 6   Deselect the gradient, and apply a Gaussian blur filter on the layer to soften the edge.

Title Tools vs. Photoshop. There are still a few reasons to use the title tool that came with your editing application.

• Rolls   • Crawls   • Animated Character Effects   • Embedding titles in Sequence file

Photoshop, however, has its own benefits that push it over for standard titles and lower-thirds work.

• Layer Styles   • Speed   • Spell-checker   • Advanced Character Control   • Advanced Paragraph Control
• Texture Mapping and Fill Effects

Step 7 If you'd like to introduce some texture, place a grayscale photo or pattern directly above the layer and group it with the bar with Cmd+G (Ctrl+G). You may also choose to adjust the blend mode (luminosity works well) and the opacity to achieve the desired effect.

Step 8 Add the logo. If the file is an Adobe Illustrator file, choose Place from the File menu. Otherwise, you can open the document, and copy and paste the logo. Or better yet, just drag it in with the Move tool (V). You may want to use layer styles, such as a drop shadow or glow to offset the logo from the bar. See Chapter 4,"Why Layers?" for more details on layer styles.

Step 9 Draw the text block for the name, I recommend using Paragraph text so you have better control over the characters.

Step 10 Duplicate the text layer, shift it down, and modify the text and font. Choose a smaller point size and different font or style for the title, which is generally longer than the name.

Step 11 Apply a contrasting edge effect such as a glow, drop shadow, or stroke.

Step 12 Link the two text fields together and choose new set from the submenu of the layer's palette. You can now duplicate this set by choosing Duplicate Layer Set from the Layer menu (or drag its layer onto the **Layer Set** icon in the layer's palette) as many times as needed. Turn off the **Visibility** icons and work with one copy at a time for each title.

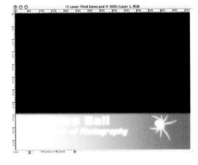

Targeted flattening revisited

When you are ready to save for your NLE, you must save the composition out as a flattened file (generally PICT or TARGA) with an alpha channel. There are several approaches to flattening a file. Targeted flattening, introduced in Chapter 4, is one technique that works well.

Step 1 Turn off all elements you do not want flattened (including the background or placement image). Create a new (empty layer) and highlight it.

Step 2 While holding down the Option (Alt) key, choose Merge Visible. All layers are now flattened to a single layer.

Step 3 Turn this layer off by clicking on the **Eye** icon.

Step 4 Hold down the Cmd (Ctrl) key and click on the layer name in the layer's palette. The marching ants should encircle the layer.

Step 5   Switch to the **Channels** palette and click on the **Save Selection as Channel** button. Choose **Save As** from the file menu and **Save A Copy** as a PICT or TARGA with an alpha channel included.

Step 6   If you have multiple titles, discard the alpha channel (NLEs get confused if there are multiple alpha channels) and repeat for each lower third.

While this process may seem time consuming, you'll become quick at it with a little practice. The quality you can achieve is superior to any standalone character generator or built-in title tool. The time savings really add up for multiple titles. Remember to always save a layered file so that you can make changes.

Prepping a Logo for Animation

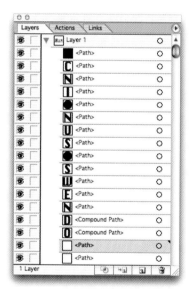

Drag the layers to "un-nest" them.

By using Adobe Illustrator, an Illustrator or vector EPS file can be easily split into layers. These layers can then be saved out into a layered Photoshop file, which can be tweaked in Photoshop and easily imported into After Effects or your NLE. Once there, you can animate and render. See? That's only six degrees of separation. Let's try it out.

Step 1   Open the file *Ch5NSI.ai* or another vector logo in Adobe Illustrator.

Step 2   Call up the layer's palette and flip down the twirl-down menu. You should see every item in the logo listed separately.

Step 3   It is necessary to consolidate items a bit to make them more manageable. Press A to activate the **Direct Selection** tool.

Step 4   Lasso around the newspaper, and choose Object>Group or press Cmd+G (Ctrl+G).

Step 5   Repeat for the microphone, copyright symbol, and corporate name, grouping each one individually. Your layer's palette should be much cleaner.

Step 6   Highlight layer #1. Go to the palette's submenu and choose **Release to Layers** (Sequence). This will put each group on a new layer. The **Build** option would do a progressive build where each layer would contain all of the previous items, plus one additional.

Step 7   If you would like to name a layer, double-click on its name. You can also drag the layers to change their stacking order. For predictable results, it is a good idea to "un-nest" the layers by dragging them out of the layer set.

Step 8   Choose File>Export; then name the file and select Photoshop (.psd) as the format.

Step 9   Specify resolution, and choose to write layers. Do not change the color model during export. It may affect the on-screen appearance (especially with gradients and transparency). Allow Photoshop to do your color conversions instead.

Step 10   Open up the file in Photoshop. All your layers should be intact. Feel free to filter or process the image with layer styles (if you use styles, be sure to flatten them).

Step 11   Import into your editing or compositing application. It is a good idea to add the end keyframes first before moving layers. This way, all of the elements will return into proper registration.

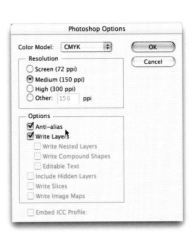

Design Ideas

The two most common techniques to help a logo stand out are a glowing edge or a drop shadow. This is based on the principle of type on pattern, which says that a contrasting edge makes it far easier to see something when it is positioned over a busy or moving back-ground. Use *Ch5LogoPractice.psd* to get started, or grab a copy of your own logo.

Reflections

By employing the **Free Transform** Tool, we can cause a logo to reflect off a flat surface. This effect can be keyed, but looks particularly effec-tive when positioned over a background created with a reflected gra-dient.

Step 1   Scale the logo to about 60% screen size, positioning it near the top of safe title.

Step 2   Duplicate the logo layer by pressing Cmd+J (Ctrl+J).

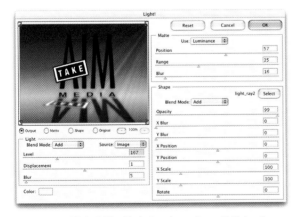

Light! from Digital Film Tools has lots of possibilities for both design and production.

Special thanks to Take Aim Media for letting us play with their logo. (http://www.takeaimedia.com)

Access distortion controls by Ctrl+clicking with a one-button mouse or right-clicking.

Step 3   Free Transform that layer again. Flip vertically by Ctrl+clicking or right-clicking and selecting Flip Vertical. Nudge the logo down using the arrow keys so that the bottom edges line up. You can add the Shift key for a power nudge.

Step 4   Scale the logo to make it shorter by grabbing the bottom edge and pulling up.

Step 5   Access the perspective distortion by Ctrl+clicking or right-clicking. Spread the logo out to simulate a cast reflection. Click the apply transformations box, or press Return (Enter).

Step 6   Reduce the opacity and blur the layer to achieve the desired look.

Step 7   You may choose to add some lighting effects for an additional effect. Make a new empty layer, select all and choose Copy Merged (Edit>Copy Merged), or press Shift+Cmd+C (Shift+Ctrl+C). Render out the lighting effects using the excellent plug-in from Digital Film Tools called Light! (You'll find the demo on this book's DVD.)

Step 8   It is likely that the © symbol will need to be replaced. Add a new type layer and insert the needed symbol.

3D Perspective

Sometimes you will want your shadow to have a little depth. This effect is simple, but extremely popular because it dramatically improves readability.

Step 1   Position your logo on the screen.

Step 2   Make a copy of the logo by duplicating the layer. The fastest way is Cmd+J (Ctrl+J).

Step 3   Place the copy behind the original by dragging it in the layer's palette.

Dynamotion is a kids fitness show; to find out more, visit http://www.dynamotion.com

Step 4   Load your default colors by pressing the D key. Black should now be loaded as the foreground color.

Step 5   Load the duplicate layer by holding down the Cmd key (Ctrl key) and clicking on the layer's thumbnail. Press Option+Delete (Alt+Delete) to fill with the black foreground color.

Step 6   Leave the layer active, and select the **Move** tool by pressing V.

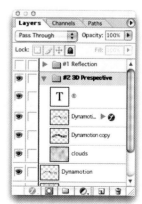

Step 7   You are now going to nudge a copy. Hold down the Option key (Alt key) and quickly tap the down and right arrow back to back. Repeat until the desired edge appears.

Step 8   To further enhance the effect, you can apply a beveled edge to the original logo on top.

Step 9   It is likely that the © symbol will need to be replaced. Add a new type layer and insert the needed symbol.

Fill with a pattern (group)

You will often be asked to place a pattern or image inside the letters. In the past, I would have suggested the Paste Into Command. However, now a much more flexible solution called *grouping* exists. This effect is similar to a track matte. To make this effect easier to show, use the items in the layer set called #3 Group. The font used is Mingler Snowy by Chank.

Step 1   Position the logo where you want it.

Step 2   Add a texture layer above.

Step 3   Select the texture layer and group it by pressing Cmd+G (Ctrl+G).

Step 4   Adjust the blending mode and opacity to isolate the effect.

Step 5   You may choose to add an outer glow or drop shadow to the logo layer to help it stand out more.

Step 6   Any changes to the logo layer will automatically update with the new texture.

Lightblast

One technique to offset a logo is to "light" it from behind. This technique is easy to accomplish. The background in this example was made with Glitterato from Flaming Pear.

A similar color background will help complement this effect. I used the Glitterato filter from Flaming Pear.

Step 1   Position the logo where you want it.

Step 2   Make a copy of the logo by duplicating the layer. The fastest way is Cmd+J (Ctrl+J).

Step 3   Run the Radial Blur on the duplicate layer. Choose the Zoom option, set to Maximum Blur, and use the **Good** option. (**Best** takes forever to render.)

Step 4   Press D to load the default colors.

Step 5   Load the duplicate layer by Cmd+clicking (Ctrl+click) on it. Fill the selection by pressing Option+Delete (Alt+Delete). Deselect the layer by pressing Cmd+D (Ctrl+D).

Step 6   Repeat the blur, load, fill cycle until your rays are the desired length.

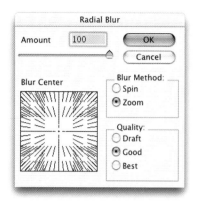

Step 7   On the blurred layer, apply the color overlay layer style. Select the desired color and adjust opacity to taste. You should get a real-time preview of your work if the Preview box is checked. Click OK.

Step 8   Place the glow layer behind so the beams shoot past.

Step 9   Optionally, you may also choose to place an additional copy of the beam layer on top. Adjust the opacity to make the color look like it has wrapped around the logo.

Cast shadows

This technique is similar to the reflected type treatment. It allows you to cast a shadow in any direction.

Step 1   Position the logo where you want it.

Step 2   Make a copy of the logo by duplicating the layer. The fastest way is Cmd+J (Ctrl+J).

Step 3   Press D to load the default colors.

Step 4   Load the duplicate layer by Cmd+clicking on it (Ctrl+click). Fill the selection by pressing Option+Delete (Alt+delete).

Step 5   Apply Free Transform to the layer and select the Perspective Transformation. Access the perspective distortion by Ctrl+clicking or right-clicking. Be sure to grab the transform handle in the middle of the top edge. Put it to the right or left, depending on your "light" source.

Step 6   Next, access the scale command by Ctrl+clicking or right-clicking. Adjust the length of the shadow to taste. Click the Apply Transformations box, or press Return (Enter).

Step 7   Blur the shadow and change its blending mode to multiply.

Step 8   You may want to add a contrasting edge depending upon your background layer.

Step 9   It is likely that the ® symbol will need to be replaced. Add a new type layer and insert the needed symbol.

Subway

Need some energy? Setting a type layer into motion can help create a sense of movement. By employing multiple blurs, this effect can be quickly built.

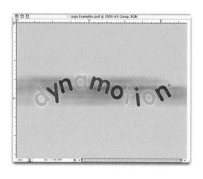

Step 1   Position the logo where you want it.

Step 2   Make *three* copies of the logo by duplicating the layer. The fastest way is Cmd+J (Ctrl+J).

Step 3   On the bottom copy, apply a Motion Blur filter. I set the angle to 0 and chose a high amount. Adjust the blur to taste. Repeat this step on layer #2, creating a sandwich effect.

Step 4   On the top-most layer, apply a Gaussian Blur filter. Change the blending mode until the logo "pops" a little more. I used the Screen mode here.

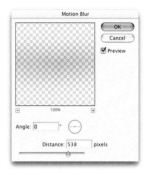

Those Other Programs

Sometimes there's no way around it: you have to work with programs other than Photoshop—or at least you have to know how to make another program's output cooperate with Photoshop. Here are a few tips from the trenches on handling the usual suspects.

PowerPoint

While in business school, I finally worked closely with those "other" people who make all of the awful speaker support slides we get. You know, the "I need to use this PowerPoint presentation in my video" kind of folks. I was amazed at the decisions (or lack thereof) that went into making a presentation.

In response, I developed a list of "deadly sins." I shared this list with my classmates and offered it to the world on my personal Web site (http://www.richardharringtonvideo.com). Now I'd like to bring a concentrated version to you.

Seven Deadly Sins

1. **Too few slides/screens.** There is no per-screen charge.

2. **Too many words.** You are not creating "open captions for the thinking impaired." Just a key phrase or few words to reinforce the current point.

3. **No road signs (where are you going?).** Use several titles slides for each section so that it is clear where you are. Make it clear where you are in the video.

4. **Reliance on gimmicks.** If you have to use a Kiki wipe to keep your audience's attention, your full screens aren't working.

5. **Ignoring design.** Just because the client says it all has to fit on one slide doesn't mean you shouldn't suggest alternatives. You are being hired because of your good taste and technical skill. Use it.

6. **Not proofing.** Many little mistakes sneak in. Changing tenses for verbs, first or third person writing, small spelling errors such as *your* versus *you're*. Don't assume that any presentation you are given has actually been proofread.

Keep your slides as uncluttered as possible. Also, maintain proper contrast between video and background sources,

Use an AE Plug-In

I am embarrassed to admit how long it took me to figure out that you could use After Effects plug-ins on Photoshop files. How you ask? It just involves a slight "road trip." You may know that importing a layered Photoshop file into After Effects is easy. You might not have realized that you can make changes and save them back out. I've included a simple, two-layer file called *For AE.psd* in the chapter folder. We're going to take it into After Effects to use an awesome, third-party effect created by Trapcode called Shine.

Step 1   Launch After Effects (install Shine if you'd like or use any other effect in AE).

Step 2   Import the file *For AE.psd* as a composition.

Step 3   To avoid cutting of the edges of our effect, we must pre-compose the logo layer. Highlight RP and choose Layer>Pre-Compose and leave all attributes.

Step 4   Double-click on the Pre-compositions icon in the Project Window.

Step 5   Change the file size to 720×540 by accessing Composition>Composition Settings.

Step 6   Close the Pre-Comp and return to the *For AE.psd* comp.

Step 7   Highlight layer 1, the pre-comp, and duplicate it by pressing Cmd+D (Ctrl+D).

Step 8   Select layer #2 and apply the desired AE Effect, in this case Effect>Trapcode>Shine. You may want to turn off layer 1 so it is easier to see your work.

Step 9   Play with the different Options. I added a 3-Color Gradient based on the alpha channel for the layer.

Step 10   This step is critical. Make sure all layers have their quality switches set to *final* quality (/). Then ensure that your Comp Window is set to Full Quality.

Step 11   Save the file out to the PSD format by choosing Composition>Save Frame As>Photocells Layers. If you receive a warning about unsupported blending modes you can ignore it. After Effects 5.5 was released before Photoshop 7, and was first to offer the new blending modes such as Vivid Light.

Step 12   When you open up the file into Photoshop, the new effect is visible. All opacity changes, blending modes, or additional layers are accessible.

This is an excellent way to harness powerful After Effects plug-ins that have no Photoshop equivalent.

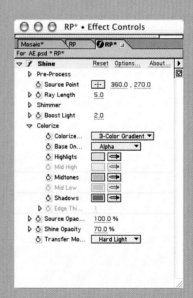

7. **Forgetting your audience.** Remember, you want the audience to actually be able to read the slides *and* comprehend them. Keep them uncluttered and the point size readable.

Rules of good presentation design

1. **Limit fonts used.** No more than three; aim for two. Stick with a font family, if possible, to keep it looking clean.

2. **Use a heavy font.** Make sure it is readable on screen. Use a medium-to-black weight if possible.

3. **Avoid stock templates.** Do you want an engineer in Seattle designing graphics for your video? Build new backgrounds that complement your client's message; then offer them JPEGs so they can use them in their real presentations in the future.

4. **Use 3-7 bullets per page.** Any more is "death by bullets."

5. **A bullet is 1–5 words.** You are giving the audience a key word or phrase to help them encode the information. You are not placing the script on the screen. That's what closed captioning is for.

6. **Readability test (Design for the back of the room).** It may look big from your chair, but stand back and test it.

7. **Use builds or simple animations to bring bullets on line by line.** Reveal the information to keep your audience paying attention. Every time something moves, your viewer is likely to look at the screen.

8. **Be consistent with justification and capitalization.** This one is tough. Decide in advance. Are you going for sentence case or title case? Establish a style guide per project and follow it. Share it with others working on the project as well.

9. **Use transparency.** Ramp effects, partial transparency, and soft drop shadows/glows help to make the presentation seem more "organic."

10. **Easy to change.** Create a template and use it. Always keep layered files around, even after the project is done. If you have full-screen graphics in your video, they are the most likely things to be changed in the future.

EPS and Illustrator files

Earlier we solved the color problems with client files, but we're not done yet. If you are ever asked how you want a client's logo, answer, "An Encapsulated PostScript or Adobe Illustrator file would be best, please." Even though we are working in a primarily raster program, the flexibility in scaling a vector file will prove invaluable.

An Adobe Illustrator or Vector EPS file is the best format to get a logo in.

Be careful, however. Not all EPS files are vector. Always ask for a vector file. If the client tells you to get it from their Web site, it is likely that they didn't understand what you were asking for. It's worth the extra effort to get the right file from the get-go. If a raster file is the only available option, check out the little-known Adobe Streamline, which proves invaluable when converting between raster and vector.

One important gotcha: you don't open a vector file in Photoshop, you place it (File>Place). You will be presented with a bounding box identical to the **Free Transform** tool. Remember, holding down the Option (Alt) key will scale from the center. The Shift key constrains the width and height scaling. You can also rotate the image by moving your cursor to the outside edge.

WordArt

I bring this up only because I have to. Every once in a while, you will come across a logo created in Microsoft Word. Microsoft pushes its Office Suite as an all-in-one solution to business owners. Don't be surprised to find simple logos being created inside the word processor. Your clients may be telling you the truth when they say that a Word document is the only version they know of.

Generally speaking, these logos are vector. Your first reaction would be to take it into Adobe Illustrator. While this preserves the vector data, the image's appearance will likely be distorted because it does not copy and paste cleanly into Illustrator. The trick is to size the logo inside Word.

Step 1 If you have Microsoft Word, open the file *Ch5WordArtdemo.doc*.

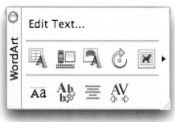

Step 2 Copy the logo to your clipboard.

Step 3 Create a New document.

Step 4 Paste the logo.

Step 5 Click on the logo. The WordArt formatting palette should appear.

Step 6 Click on the format WordArt button to access scale controls. You should be able to enlarge the logo to the required size. Be sure to click the lock aspect ratio check box.

Step 7 Copy the item to your clipboard. Word works at 300 dpi, so this should provide plenty of pixels to work with.

Step 8 Create a new document in Photoshop. The new document will automatically be sized to the clipboard's contents.

Step 9 Paste, save, and start working.

Need to know more? If you feel like searching the web, here are some great starting points.

- http://www.chank.com
- http://www.chankarmy.com
- http://www.fonthead.com
- http:// www.myfonts.com
- http://www.t26.com
- http://www.acidfonts.com
- http://www.fontalicious.com
- ttp://www.microsoft.com/typography/
- http://www.adobe.com/type/main.html
- http://www.fontlab.com/
- http://graphicdesign.about.com/cs/typography/

Profile: Chank Diesel; Spotlight on Type

Whenever my projects have needed a unique twist, I find myself turning to the Chank Company. This Minneapolis-based, full-service design firm specializes in fonts. Their sources of inspiration include historical signs from industrial districts, distinctive handwriting, and playful display fonts.

Mr. Chank Diesel, president and CEO, began making fonts in 1992, when he worked as creative director of the alternative music magazine, *Cake*. The first font he created, Mister Frisky, remains his most popular.

Compared to most foundries, you'll think the cold has gotten to the Chank Company when you see how affordable their fonts are. My favorite is the Font-of-the-Month club, which drops a new creative font (and idea or two) in my e-mail box each month. The web site also contains several free fonts as well that are works-in-progress. Be sure to link to the Chank Army web site, where you will find yourself plugged into the vibrant world of typographic design practiced by many affiliated artists.

Chank Diesel took the time to answer some of my questions on type. I think the interview has some great stuff that will make you think differently when designing type-based graphics such as lower thirds and full-screen titles.

Harrington: How is a font created? What software is used, what skills are needed?

Diesel: Fonts can be drawn on paper or in the computer. Use Adobe Photoshop to scan your artwork in and clean it up if you want. Adobe Streamline converts your grayscale scan into an EPS (Encapsulated PostScript) file, which you can open and edit in Illustrator. Use Adobe Illustrator as a clipboard for importing your outlines into Fontographer. You can also use Illustrator as the original drawing board for your characters. Macromedia Fontographer is the program that makes fonts. You can also draw characters directly in this program if that is best.

Harrington: What issues exist when working cross-platform?

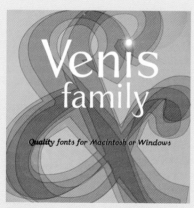

Chank's Venis family, featured on a limited-edition CD packaging.

Chank's Top Ten Fonts are conveniently packaged in one CD. Liquorstore is used for the packaging display.

Chank Army's site is a great launching pad to find fonts from affiliated designers. Start here as a portal site into the world of contemporary typographic design.

In 1996, Taco Bell used Mister Frisky for their Halloween campaign.

Diesel: Most Mac users prefer PostScript fonts, and most PC users prefer TrueType. TrueType is becoming more popular for Mac, though. If you design something on a Mac and a PC user has that same font installed, ideally, they should have no problem seeing that font. A new system called Open Type is supposed to become the industry standard, used by both Mac and PC (www.microsoft.com/typography).

Harrington: What is the difference between free fonts on the web and professional fonts that you must purchase?

Diesel: The Chank free fonts are experimental in nature and do not typically have complete character sets. The Chank fonts that I sell have full character sets, including foreign symbols and some ligatures. A lot more design time goes into the professional fonts, and they are more useful overall.

There are other free fonts on the web that are similarly experimental. However, there are also some pirates out there who illegally distribute free and professional fonts. Watch out for those because they are not legally licensed, and there can be problems with the files.

Harrington: How do you come up with the inspiration for a font?

Diesel: Sometimes I like the letters in an old hand-painted or neon sign. Using a few letters as the basis, I will interpret the entire character set in that style. Other times, a functional or aesthetic design need will inspire a font's creation. For example, Futura Condensed Extrabold is an extremely useful font for legible bold text displays, but I decided there needed to be an alternative design that functioned similarly, so I created the Mingler Fonts.

Harrington: What advice would you give when picking a font?

Diesel: A font is a great way to reinforce an image or message. Think of the image you want your words to portray. Try two or three different fonts for each project. Plug 'em in and see how they work. Choose fonts that complement your design work. Don't force fonts into a design. If you need a font that dances, pick one with a little bounce instead of forcing a straight font to jump up and down. If you're working on a cowboy piece, for example, look for letterpress-style fonts to reflect the time period.

Harrington: Any general guidelines about using fonts in a composition? What's the total number of fonts I should to use? What about using font families?

Chank also distributes fonts by other designers. Joseph Churchward of New Zealand has more than a dozen fonts in Chank's library.

Chank's painting of Dizzy Gillespie and handwriting font Corndog grace the cover of a CD by Minneapolis jazz ensemble GST.

Diesel: Make sure they are legible! Don't use display fonts for massive amounts of text. They're intended for headlines and such. Text fonts are made to be legible at small point sizes; display fonts are not.

You usually don't need more than three or four fonts for a project. Sticking with a family of fonts is a good way to have clean design. Use an extrabold version for headlines and lighter versions for text or captions.

The best tip I can offer is that you should not use the automatic Bold and Italic buttons to change your fonts for design work. If you compare letters created with those functions to a true bold or italic of the font, you'll notice that characters have spacing problems and may be awkwardly shaped. When font designers create true bold and italic versions of a font, they carefully create each character to avoid those problems.

Harrington: If you are on a budget, where should you invest first?

Diesel: Fonts are an inexpensive way to make a difference in design. Fonts can easily be changed. Fonts visually reinforce the message of the words they display. Fonts can often carry an entire design, and also tie together a campaign. I offer fonts at an affordable rate so that freelance designers can have easy access to them.

Be sure to look on the disc for some freebies and a special offer from the Chank Company.

1-877-GO-CHANK
www.chank.com
www.chankarmy.com

Profile: Jayse Hansen

Jayse Hansen started his career with a Bell and Howell Super-8 camera when he was nine years old. This hobby was short lived, because $18 for three minutes of silent film is hard to come by on an allowance.

"I started in photography, migrated to print and web design, and now combine all of that background into my motion design and visual effects," said Jayse. "I knew from age 10, when I fell in love with *Return of the Jedi*, that I wanted to work in film and video. So in a way, I'm fulfilling my life-long dream."

Jayse makes a living in Las Vegas designing show intros, bumpers, special effects, web pages, and print work. Jayse's work is known internationally with clients in Europe, South Africa, and Canada. He is a master at combining After Effects and Combustion with Flash, Illustrator, Photoshop, and anything else that works. Visitors to Creative Cow's forums and tutorial pages appreciate his motion graphics work. He also is the creator of VTC's Adobe After Effects 5/5.5 Essentials, a nine-and-a-half-hour training program available on CD (http://www.e-lysian.com/vtc/).

"In motion, I like to do stuff that's like my digital still art. I create emotional imagery. I usually use tons of layers, duplicates, blending/transfer modes, and strong typography to create a final piece that I hope has enough emotion in it that it provokes the audience to feel something powerful."

At its core, motion graphics are a series of still images. To support his motion habit, Jayse relies on a still program, Photoshop.

"Photoshop is my number-one program. For video work, I find it much more efficient to work with layer masks and layer styles than to try to recreate that (and render each frame) in After Effects. Even if I need to recreate the text in AE, I'll often design in Photoshop because of its superior capabilities and layout finesse."

After a short conversation with Jayse, it is clear that he is all about digital. His work is on the cutting edge, and he helps develop tutorials for leading plug-ins. Despite this love for digital, he warns against the fast-and-cheap aspect often associated with modern video production.

"Most video editing software has a very distinct look to its graphics. I call it the 'DV' look. It's downright cheap looking. If you surf through local TV ads, you'll see evidence of this all too often. Buzzing-Awkward-Text that just looks thrown on last minute. For backgrounds and titles, Photoshop is invaluable," said Jayse. "If someone's still using marble or gradient backgrounds in pink or blue with big beveled boxes just because that's what comes built into their video editing program—they *need* to invest in Photoshop and create something a bit more modern and different. Respect yourself and your work enough to take it up a notch."

Many editors and motion graphic artists find it difficult to master all of Photoshop. This is not because they are incapable; time is just in such short supply.

"In my opinion, there is *absolutely* no substitute for learning Photoshop. Even advocates of competing art and photo programs are very well versed in Photoshop. If you want to have that extra edge, gain that extra respect, and free your creative genius, learning Photoshop is an absolute *must*."

To get you started, Jayse stresses that the key to his successful designs is the combination of layer masks, adjustment layers, and transfer modes.

"For most of my work," said Jayse, "I find myself using Gaussian Blur, Motion Blur, or Radial Blur (zoom) on layers—or on duplicated layers with their transfer modes set to Lighten, Soft Light, or Overlay. Sometimes I'll also use Filter>Texture>Grain to blend things or add depth. That's about it for filters."

The key is not how many filters you have, but how fast you can move through Photoshop. Learning the keyboard shortcuts will allow you more time to be creative.

"If you focus on learning shortcuts, you can really master a program—and people who watch you work will *know* you know the program. These are my *all-time* superfavs:

- Cmd+spacebar (Ctrl+spacebar) while dragging a marquee box to zoom in on a very specific area of

my image. Clients' mouths drop whenever I do that. Add Option (Alt) and click to zoom out. Then I keep the spacebar held down and click and drag to move my image to just where I want it.

- [and] while using the brush to enlarge and decrease its size.

- Cmd+Shift+< or > (Ctrl+Shift+< or >) to increase or decrease the font size. Love that. Add Option (Alt) to supercharge it!

- Cmd+T (Ctrl+T) for **Free Transform**—access to all your transformation needs!"

Jayse admits that creating graphics in front of a client can be intimidating. "Know that, whatever a client asks of you, anything *can* be done in Photoshop. I've proven it many times, when even I questioned it at first."

Jayse also said that Photoshop can set you apart from others in the digital video world. "Wherever you work—make it your goal to be indispensable—you'll be set. Take the extra step of learning or even mastering Photoshop."

Jayse has several great tutorials and tips, as well as an impressive portfolio, which you can browse for inspiration. Be sure to drop in for a visit at http://www.jayse.us.

A Sense of History

A true test of how powerful a computer application is lies not in the ability to "do," but rather to "undo." Having the ability to create with a safety net is a liberating experience. By harnessing the power of the History palette, an editor can manage to try new things without having the pressure of a missed deadline.

By default, you have 20 history states. A history state is simply a level of undo. If 20 is not enough for you, activate **General Preferences** with Cmd+K (Ctrl+K). You can increase this number, but keep in mind that you are tying up your computer's RAM for each level of undo. Fortunately, Photoshop is very efficient in tracking changes. History states are stored in RAM, where you can access them quickly. If you run out of RAM, they are written to the available scratch disk.

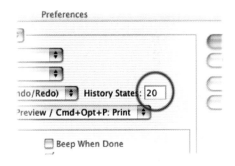

Photoshop currently supports up to 1,000 levels of undo. It would take some very fast mouse clicks to use those up. Since you are generally working with small file sizes, RAM requirements are low. I recommend 100 history states as a starting point. Go up or down as needed.

While you are looking at your **General Preferences**, you may want to change your Redo key settings. Most nonlinear editing systems will "walk backwards" when the **Undo** key is pressed. By default, Photoshop will dance a two-step: undo/redo, undo/redo. To change this, simply pick one of the other two options under the Redo key settings. This will speed up your access to multiple undos and make Photoshop act more like your NLE.

 History States are stored only in RAM. If you close a document or your computer crashes, you lose your multiple undos. Be sure to save your work frequently.

The **History** palette is not the most visible window. Most users have it shrunk down to just a few lines; some have it hidden completely. To make this wonderful palette more accessible, dock it in the palette well. Drag the tab to the upper right corner of your screen. The **History** palette will dock itself in the **Options** bar, always ready, never in the way.

History states = multiple undos. Photoshop supports up to 1,000 levels of undo. These history states eat up RAM, however. Set yours to taste, but I recommend a number less than 50 for better performance.

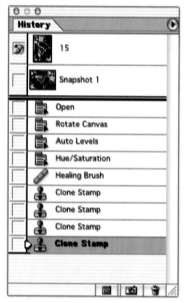

Think of the **History** palette as an edit assistant that tracks your every move. As you move forward through your project, you can instantly jump back as many steps as you need. If you are decisive, set your history state number lower. If you are experimental, leave this number high. Every time you click and make a change that affects your canvas, that change is recorded. You can now access this list visually with the mouse, or through keyboard shortcuts. Take a deep breath, and jump in the pool of creative thinking.

Performing Multiple Undos

Let's try out the **History** palette. Create a new document sized 720×540 pixels at 72 pixels per inch. Regress a little and finger paint. This is a great opportunity to try out the flexibility of Photoshop's **Brushes** palette. Start painting a background that you could use in your next video. Combine different brush strokes and colors. Don't hold back, just create.

After you've finished painting, look at what you've created. Select the **History** palette tab, and you will see a comprehensive list of every step you took. Your final step is highlighted at the bottom of the list. To go backwards, click on the state you wish to return to. The change is instant. The speed and flexibility of the **History** palette will let you explore different approaches without having to keep multiple copies of an image open. For those who prefer keyboard shortcuts, cycling through your undos will take you backwards through the **History** palette. Earlier you changed the **Redo** key to Cmd+Y (Ctrl+Y) under the General Preferences tab; this is a faster way to access previous history states.

For now, make sure you are working in the linear mode. This is the standard mode for the **History** palette; it can be accessed by going to the palette's submenu. Click on the small triangle next to the word "History" on the palette's tab. Choose **History Options** and make certain the **Allow Nonlinear History** box is unchecked. Notice how states become grayed out and italicized? This is letting you know that you are working in the linear mode. As you move backwards, Photoshop is alerting you that these steps are undone. Moving forward, by

 I want my NLE! By default, hitting Undo will toggle back and forth between your last modification and the previous state. However, you can make Photoshop more like your NLE by modifying its preferences. From the General Preferences pane, you can specify that you want Photoshop to use Cmd+Y (Ctrl+Y) as the Redo key. This way, invoking undo will continue to step back through all available history states.

applying a change to the image, will result in these grayed items being dropped off the list. Once an item has been removed from the History palette, it is gone.

It is very important to remember that the **History** palette is tied to RAM. Power failures, computer crashes, kicked power strips will all interrupt your computer's power supply and, therefore, your RAM data. Do not think of the **History** palette as a replacement for saving your work. And note that the history information is not stored with the document when you save it. The **History** palette for a specific document resets each time you open that document. However, you can toggle between open documents, and each will retain its own

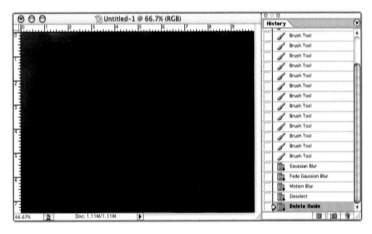

History palette information and levels of undo. Program-wide changes to palettes, user preferences, actions, or color settings are not recorded to the **History** palette.

Using Snapshots

A snapshot is exactly as its name implies, a captured moment in time. Making a snapshot creates a point that you can quickly jump to. Proper use of snapshots will expand flexibility. Since the changes are stored in RAM, you can jump from one point to another very quickly.

Making a snapshot is easy. At the bottom of the **History** palette, click on the **Create New Snapshot** icon. In earlier versions of Photoshop, this icon was identical to the **Create A New Layer** icon. In Photoshop 7, the icon was updated to the more logical camera icon. Option-clicking on this icon will give you advanced options, including the ability to name the state when you create it.

Snapshots appear at the top of the History palette. Photoshop will create the first snapshot by default when you open the document. This gives you a very quick return path to revert to the original document; this is significantly faster than reloading the file back from disk. You can add new snapshots whenever you want a milestone to return to. Photoshop supports more than 1,000 snapshots, depending upon available RAM and scratch disk space.

It is possible to create your own time-stamped backups. Photoshop can automatically create a snapshot each time you save. Snapshots are useful, but are only temporary, because they are stored in RAM.

Don't Panic! If you get a scratch disk warning, it's not the end of the world. Photoshop uses RAM to store open documents; when RAM fills up, it switches to disk space. It is a cosmic law that hard drives will eventually fill to capacity. If this happens to you, there are four possible solutions.

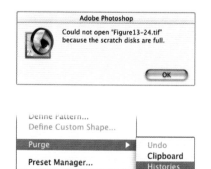

1. Purge your history states, undo memory, and clipboard to finish the current task.

2. Buy more RAM.

3. Back up old files and erase.

4. If you have multiple drives or partitions, specify them as additional scratch disks (Preferences>Plug-Ins and Scratch Disks).

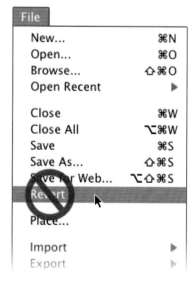

Revert is slow and painful. Your computer has to reload the original file into memory. Instead, use the first snapshot for an instant "go back to start" jump.

One particularly helpful option for snapshots is to have Photoshop create a new snapshot every time you save. This is similar to the "attic" or "vault" features of many nonlinear editing systems. To access this feature, access the triangular submenu in the **History** palette. Choose **History Options** and enable the Automatically Create New Snapshot When Saving check box. Now each time you save your document, a new snapshot will be generated. Jumping between different versions is as simple as clicking on the icon. Photoshop names the new state with the exact time it was created. This feature is invaluable when the client or producer is sitting next to you and wants to make "just a few" changes. It now becomes possible to jump through numerous hoops, yet always return to any given point in a near instant.

On the subject of frequent changes, you can generate a new document from any history point by clicking the **Create New Document** icon at the bottom of the palette. This will  open a new document (with its own **History** palette) based upon your current history state. Dragging a snapshot on the Create New Document icon will create a new document based on that state. This is identical to a common editing practice of making a duplicate sequence before undertaking significant revisions.

Linear versus nonlinear mode

You may be surprised to hear an editor say he does not prefer a tool to work in a nonlinear fashion. By default, this option is disabled, for good reason. The nonlinear mode opens up an incredible amount of increased flexibility, but making sense of that flexibility often becomes a brain teaser not worth solving.

The **Nonlinear History** mode can be accessed from the **History palette** submenu. When enabled, a user can go back in time and make changes without losing the subsequent history states. In practice, this can be seen as branching. You can jump back to step 3 and design in a new direction. Your old steps still appear at the bottom of your list; they do not drop off.

While editing video in a nonlinear fashion may seem natural, most users (rightfully) avoid this option in the **History** palette.

The editor eventually needs to make a choice: return to the bottom of the list, abandoning the side-tracked design, or manually remove the unwanted items at the bottom of the list by dragging them onto the **Delete** (trash can) icon. Sound confusing? It is. A more logical approach that does not involve organizing "alternative realties" would be employing the previously mentioned **Create New Document** feature. Other users prefer using multiple snapshots to simplify this process.

What Are Those Weird Brushes?

Your toolbox contains two tools with the word *history* in their titles: the **History** brush and the **Art History** brush. These tools require you to use snapshots. The first tool lets you paint backwards in time. The best way to understand these tools is to see them in action.

These two brushes have very little to do with multiple undos. But you can create a nice, painterly look with them.

Step 1   Open any source photo with a single subject. You may use the photo called *Becha.psd*, which can be found in the Chapter 6 folder on the DVD. Ensure that Photoshop created a new snapshot when the document was opened.

Step 2   Now you will filter the image using the **Crosshatch** filter (Filter>Brush Strokes>Crosshatch). You may use the shown values or create your own. Notice how the photo is now filtered evenly, including facial details. By employing the **History** brush, you can restore this missing information.

Step 3   Click next to the desired snapshot in the **History** palette so the **Paintbrush** icon becomes visible. By default, the icon will already appear next to the original snapshot. Using the **History** brush, you can paint back the unfiltered photo.

This is a good idea for restoring missing facial detail. Before the **History** brush, designers would often duplicate the photo, filter the top copy, and then erase back down to the unfiltered version below. The **History** brush is essentially giving you the same results without the need for extraneous layers.

But what about that other one? The **Art History** brush is an attempt to simulate natural media effects. You deploy it in an identical way to the **History** brush. You will notice advanced features in

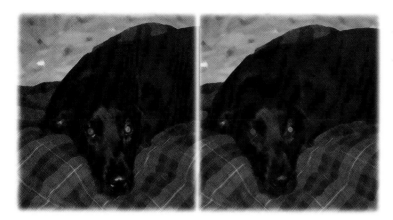

Using the **History** brush, it is possible to "paint backwards in time." Here I restored facial details that were lost when I ran the filter.

the **Options** bar that affect the shape of the strokes, as well as tolerance and style. The end result will vary, but the official answer is that you can create paintings from photos. This is often useful for backgrounds, but the **Art History** brush is not always a practical tool for a deadline-focused environment. Getting good results will often take a lot of time. Other alternatives would include filters or third-party applications like Synthetik Software's Studio Artist or Procreate's Painter. This is an interesting area to explore, but not an essential skill for use in digital video.

Profile: Greg Mitchell

Greg Mitchell is a well-established creative director who has completed Avid's Master Editor Workshop. Not content to just cut and dissolve his way through a timeline, Mitchell is a big fan of graphic-rich videos. Before he co-founded his own company, Greg worked as a producer/editor for a full-service production facility.

"It's funny to think how I used to long for the green grass over at the big post houses in town. Hearing about those cool boxes with names like Flame, Smoke, Flint, etc., used to make me all warm and fuzzy inside," said Mitchell. "I *love* compositing—*going vertical,* as I like to call it—stacking track upon track, layer upon layer. Using all sorts of crazy plug-ins, transfer modes, and processors to rack focus back and forth through gooey glowing layers of all sorts of what-have-you… yum. I often felt compelled to outsource stuff just to get that high-end look that my clients expected because that's what they saw on TV every night."

Fortunately, the current crop of digital tools allows Mitchell to produce a high-end look right from his desktop.

"I have always been fairly comfortable mixing it up (Photoshop and Avid have always been a match made in heaven). But it has not been until the past few years that a technology has existed that really allows the two worlds to integrate so seamlessly (and affordably!)," said Mitchell. "With the advent of the 'Holy Trinity' (Photoshop, After Effects, and Avid or similar NLE), all of a sudden I've got my *own* little incendiary device that's warming me up just fine. Photoshop is no longer just a high-end title generator for my NLE. It's now the springboard for some pretty wild creativity in the edit suite."

Although most of Mitchell's work is only for the small screen, he cautions against building graphics at low-resolution. He says that higher-resolution graphics allow more flexibility in compositing and for dealing with client requests.

"I develop all graphics using Illustrator and Photoshop, making sure that the art is vector or at least very big (e.g., 300 dpi). Even if you're only creating some elements for video that don't need to be any bigger than 720×540 pixels, you would be surprised how often your client will ask you to 'send me those graphics you made for the video so I can make an 8×6-ft banner out of it.'" said Mitchell. "Once you're happy with your design, just make some copies and dumb them down for video—720×540, 72 dpi, flatten the image with an alpha channel—and you're ready to import and edit."

Mitchell say he relies heavily on Avid's ability to import layered Photoshop files with transparency intact. He will frequently animate right within the Avid to take advantage of its ability to sync audio. He says his emphasis on graphics to complement his stories is essential to meet clients' demands.

"If you are not interested in expanding your craft beyond classic video editing, you may soon be facing some fierce competition in the marketplace (if you're not already)," said Mitchell. "Though forever a staple of video editing, cuts and dissolves alone just don't cut and dissolve it anymore. At least not with the clients I've been working with. The most successful editors these days are the ones who are just as comfortable working in a graphics program as they are in their NLE."

Greg co-founded JuiceBox Design Communications Inc., in 2001 (http://www.juiceboxdc.com). It's a company operated by creatives; just like an agency, only without all the suits.

Filters

Filters are one of Photoshop's most popular features, specialized add-ons that boost performance. Some people collect them, entire books are written on them, and the variety available is overwhelming. They are also completely overused and underutilized.

How can that be? A look becomes popular, and everyone wants to use it. Because people don't fully understand Photoshop, they rush out and buy add-on after add-on. Don't get me wrong—I'm always happy to try out new filters, and I'm amazed at what wonderfully creative software designers come up with. However, you can do a lot with a little, and a better understanding of how to use filters will help you maximize your investment of time and dollars.

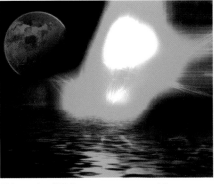

This entire "3D" scene was created in Photoshop using a variety of filters from Flaming Pear (**www.flamingpear.com**).

Filters Defined

Proper application of filters significantly extends the abilities of Photoshop. It is possible to achieve results quickly that are time consuming (or even impossible) otherwise. By definition, a filter must reside in your Photoshop *Plug-Ins* folder. Other options such as actions and styles should not be confused with filters.

When buying filters, be sure to check compatibility. Many filters have yet to be updated for OSX or Windows XP. Many old favorites have been retired as developers move on to the next new thing. Some filters will never be revised because their publishers no longer exist. Why bring this up? Because many catalogs and stores will continue to sell old products that don't work with the new operating systems, always check a manufacturer's web site for compatibility before purchase. *Caveat emptor.*

Many filters are incompatible with OSX or Windows XP. "Photoshop 7 compatible" does not mean OSX or Windows XP compatible. Always check a manufacturer's site for compatibility before purchase.

The Guide to Standard Filters

So you say you know filters? I've included a full-color guide on the DVD-ROM. You'll find a video-friendly intro to each filter with hidden features that most users don't touch, such as the Fade command—the key to unlocking a filter's power.

Be sure to see *The Guide to Standard Photoshop Filters* on the DVD-ROM. Print the guide and place it into your edit suite.

Essential filters

Add Noise

Charcoal

Clouds

Dark Strokes

De-Interlace

Diffuse Glow

Dust & Scratches

Emboss

Film Grain

Find Edges

Gaussian Blur

Grain

Lighting Effects

Maximum

Median

Minimum

Motion Blur

Radial Blur

Sharpen Edges

Unsharp Mask

The guide presents filters in the order you'll find them. This is for ease of use for when you are trying to memorize where a filter can be found. Feel free to skip around; read the text when an image catches your eye. I guarantee you'll see a lot of new things.

Similar but not the same...

Many effects in Adobe After Effects have very similar names to Photoshop filters. You will find a lot in common with these two programs, but they have their own unique differences. Filters in AE with the PS+ extension are Photoshop filters. In fact, try copying your third-party filters from Photoshop into After Effects. Many of them make the leap just fine, giving you more bang for your buck!

Third-Party Filters

When looking for filters, two great starting places come to mind. The *Photoshop User* magazine frequently reviews plug-ins. Members of NAPP often get discounts as well. Go to their site and click on the Free Issue button to find out more.

The second resource is this book's disc, where you'll find free filters, trial versions, and time-limited demos. I've saved you the trouble of big downloads and have included the documentation packages as well.

The National Association for Photoshop Professionals (NAPP) is the most up-to-date source for information on Photoshop. You'll find tons of resources in their member's areas, as well as in their great magazine, *Photoshop User*, www.photoshopuser.com

Before Running a Filter

Before you rush in and try out every filter in the application and on the disc, you need to make sure the image is ready to be processed. If the image needs to be cropped, sized, or rotated, do that first. Many filters are render intensive; there's no reason to spend extra render time on pixels you were going to throw away.

An image should be color-corrected properly before filtering. Remember: Garbage In = Garbage Out (GIGO). For more on Image Adjustments, see **Chapter 8**.

Keyboard shortcuts

Repeat last filter	Cmd+F (Ctrl+F)
Re-open last filter with same settings	Cmd+Opt+F (Ctrl+Alt+F)
Fade last filter	Cmd+Shift+F (Ctrl+Shift+F)

If the image needs to be touched up, do that first. Filtering mistakes only seems to draw further attention to them. Most importantly, make sure the image is properly exposed. This can most easily be accomplished using a Levels adjustment (Image>Adjustments>Levels). For now, you can click Auto. Or if you've had previous experience, adjust the gamma (midpoint) for a proper exposure. For more on Levels, see Chapter 8, "Color Correction: How to Get It Right."

Many filters will produce pleasantly unexpected results when used in situations they weren't designed for.

Make sure you are working in RGB mode (Image>Mode>RGB). Many stock images come in CMYK mode; you'll need to convert them to RGB. The majority of filters only work in RGB mode. Only those filters that are meant for print work have been optimized to work in CMYK mode. You do not have to worry about color shift when converting from CMYK to RGB. Because CMYK has fewer colors than RGB, no information will be lost.

For best results, zoom into 100%. Double-click on the magnifying glass in the toolbox, or press Cmd+Option+0 (Ctrl+Alt+0.)

General Advice

Making time for "research and development" is tough in a production-driven world. The investment pays off, however, because you don't want to be sitting in the edit suite with the manual open trying to achieve the look your client is asking for. There are three key steps to maximizing your investment in filters.

Run them through a full test. Before you run out and buy more filters, discover what you already own. Filters are highly specialized miniprograms, and they can accomplish a lot! You need to try out every filter: pull every pull-down, slide every slider, try the presets that came with it, and don't forget to try blending modes with the Fade command (Edit>Fade Filter) immediately after running the filter. You can streamline this testing process by working on a small, low-resolution source image.

Filters run with a preset will often look "canned." Be sure to experiment with filter combinations and blending modes to achieve unique results.

For color images, run the **Unsharp Mask** in the **Lab** mode. Select the **Lightness** channel and adjust the sharpness. Be sure to switch the image back to the RGB mode when finished.

Put them into new environments. Sure, that **Unsharp Mask** filter is for sharpening, but what happens when I crank it all the way up on a flattened text layer? What would happen if I used the Wave filter on a gradient layer? What if I try the Minimum filter on an image? You might be surprised what happens when you try doing Western swing to heavy metal for a change.

Combine them in unlikely ways. The true power of filters is in the combinations. You will see several techniques used throughout this book. Be sure to check out the tutorials on the disc. (Refer to the "Guide to the DVD-ROM Tutorials" on page 6.) I also employ filters heavily in Chapters 5, 8, 9, and 10, so be sure to check those out.

While you are experimenting, don't forget other parameters, such as which colors are set, because the foreground and background will change the way many filters perform. The resolution of your source file will also impact how dramatically the input values affect the image. For example, a 20-pixel blur on a 72-dpi image will behave very differently than on a 300-dpi source. Keep this in mind when working with Photoshop cookbooks. Many are written for print audiences.

A little experimentation can go a long way. This German church is now ready for an episode of Science Fiction. When working with filters, try unusual combos, especially with filters being used for reasons other than their "official" purpose.

Understanding Filter Interfaces

Some filters have no user interface; for example, **Blur More** and **Despeckle**. These limited filters will quickly fall off your favorites list. Most filters will have some form of a user interface. When you launch, ensure that the **Preview** box option is checked; I know very few people who can make artistic decisions without previewing the edit. Generally, you can zoom in to the Preview window using Cmd++ and zoom out with Cmd+–. Panning through the preview area is also possible. Click in the **Preview** window and pull your view around. Photoshop 7 has significantly improved the size and quality of the preview image.

If there's a variable, change it. If there's a **Load** button, try loading presets that shipped with the product. Many manufacturers and web sites offer additional presets that you can download. The support of textures or bump maps allows you to load grayscale images as textures. There are many of these included on the Photoshop Install CD, and I've included an assortment on this book's disc as well.

Alien Skin's filters offer clear controls and large preview windows.

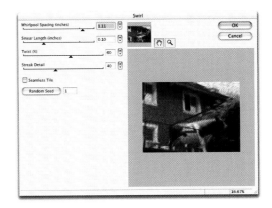

 Look for a huge collection of seamless textures from Auto FX on this book's disc. These can be used as bump maps for many filters that support loading textures.

Defining the Area to Be Affected

The key to achieving results with filters is accurately specifying the area to be affected. Depending on the desired outcome, filters may be run on the entire image, a small portion, or even a single channel. It is a good idea to test a filter by running it on a small area first.

 Good filtering requires good selections. Be sure to see **Chapter 3**.

With no selection made, a filter will process the entire image, even those parts that extend beyond the work area. Running a filter with no selection assures that you will filter all pixels on a layer, even those that are not currently visible.

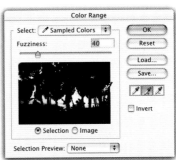

To affect only a portion of the image, you must make a selection with either the **Marquee**, **Lasso**, or **Wand** tools. For more details on additional selections, see Chapter 3, "What About Transparency?".

Step 1   The most useful selection technique for filters is the **Select Color Range** command from the **Select** menu. The key to making a good selection is to eyedropper on the initial area you'd like to use to build your selection.

Step 2   Next, with **Eyedropper Plus** and **Eyedropper Minus**, you can add or subtract to the new selection.

Step 3   Adjust the **Fuzziness** to be more tolerant and form a smoother selection.

Step 4   Finally, click **OK**, and you can start to work with your selection.

Smoothing out

One final piece of advice: soften your selections. There are two keys to achieving smoother edges.

Step 1   The first step is to smooth your selections. (Select>Modify>Smooth). This rounds out hard corners in your selection.

The Select Color Range tool is invaluable for selecting large areas of an image. It is significantly faster (and easier) to use.

I need to "render" a background. The render filters are a big help in creating backgrounds for video use. Here we employ two of them to create a nice "3D" look.

Step 1   Select a Foreground and Background color that are complementary.

Step 2   Open or create a safe-title document

Step 3   Run the Clouds filter; if you don't like the first pass, repeat.

Step 4   Go back to the **Distort** menu and access **Ripple**.

Step 5   You will likely need to soften your image with a Gaussian Blur.

Step 6   Now the cool part, access Lighting Effects and add a spotlight to the scene. Play with different settings. I chose to cast a light across the bottom corner.

Step 2   The second is to feather the edges with Select>Feather or Cmd+Option+D (Ctrl+Alt+D). This modification will produce a gradual edge. This is similar to the difference between a line drawn by a ballpoint pen and one by a felt-tip pen.

Step 3   Adjust your feathering to get a soft transition between filtered and unfiltered areas.

Fading and Blending

You will read about and see several examples of fading filters in the filter guide on the DVD-ROM. This is one of those little-known secrets about Photoshop. You can further modify filters by harnessing the power of blending modes (See Chapter 4, "Why Layers?").

You will not believe how much more life your filters will have with blend modes. Photoshop currently has 21 blend modes besides normal. That means your filter collection is 21 times bigger than you thought. The **Blend** command must be invoked immediately after the filter is run, even before you deselect the active selection. You can find it under the Edit menu (Edit>Fade [name of filter or image adjustment last run]). The quickest way to access this command is to use the shortcut Shift+Cmd+F (Shift+Ctrl+F). Think of it as you want to command (or control) the shifting (fading) of the filter. If you forget to invoke **Fade**, step backwards through your **History** palette until the filter is removed. Run the last filter with the same settings by pressing Cmd+F (Ctrl+F) and then fade it.

Now that you've had a taste of what filters can do, let's take a look at another Photoshop powerhouse: color correction.

Want 21 times more filters? Fade them and give a new look to your project.

The **Fade** command must be invoked immediately after the filter is run. Choose Edit>Fade (name of filter or image adjustment last run). You can also press Shift+Cmd+F (Shift+Ctrl +F).

Profile: Angie Taylor

European TV viewers will recognize Angie Taylor's animations, visual effects, and motion graphics. She's produced work for a broad range of clients, including the BBC and Channel 4 television. She is currently working on a series of music videos with Chris Cunningham, who is well known for his controversial music video directing. Angie is also involved in producing special effects and postproduction for Scotland's first science-fiction movie.

"I try to provide plenty of variety in terms of graphic style; I think that's a mark of a good designer. You need to always push forward and endeavor to improve on what you've already done, exploring new methods and techniques constantly."

One of those newer methods involved switching to a home-based studio. Taylor uses three Macs and an NT box to design and produce her animations. With these machines, she is capable of outputting component, DVCAM, mini-DV and uncompressed materials for broadcast and film.

"Most of the work I've undertaken has been for television, although I am now in the process of getting into film work," said Taylor. "My systems are fully capable of film work, and I can't wait to see the results on the big screen."

This flexibility has allowed her business to grow and adjust to economic change. "Working on desktop systems also opens up a lot in terms of being able to have more than one designer working on some of the bigger projects. Rather than having one person

working on a Henry or Flame, I can subcontract other freelancers and have two or three people working on the desktop systems."

Despite her mastery of everything desktop video has to offer, Angie Taylor took a roundabout path to the video industry. After earning a degree in sculpture and drawing, she set off for London to be a prop maker for the television and theatre industry.

"As a result, I visited various special effects departments and was fascinated by them. At that time, computers in that area were still in the very early stages. One thing led to another and, for a time, I became involved in producing original artwork for the music industry as well as deejaying in the London club scene. Then one day, one of the record companies took me to a graphic design workshop. From across a crowded room, I saw a guy using Photoshop on the Mac to composite my images together. It was love at first byte."

Angie is an expert at combining Photoshop and After Effects together to produce results. She has written a successful book entitled *Creative After Effects 5.0*, which contains several interactive tutorials. Angie is also a demo artist for Adobe and Apple, as well as a popular presenter on After Effects in Europe and the United States. If you ever get a chance to see Angie present, her creativity and expertise burst through.

"I'd used music sequencers when I was deejaying, which led me to think that surely you could sequence images in the same way. A friend then acquainted me with Photoshop and After Effects (working together) on an Apple Mac, and I've worked on them ever since."

Angie says that thinking about possibilities really opens up her video work.

"I like to learn the software inside out so that I really know what it's capable of," said Angie. "I have a natural inquisitiveness about how things work, and this takes me beyond the everyday functions of an application and into the nitty-gritty."

Angie puts Photoshop through its paces. She uses it to prepare images for TV broadcast. She also employs its powerful color correction and cloning abilities. She's quite adept at tiling images as well as creating backgrounds and textures for use on screen.

When asked to define a Photoshop power user, she replied: "It's somebody who understands how channels and paths work, and knows how to control an image without losing information."

Angie also offered a few tricks to speed up your Photoshop work:

- Use D to load default colors of black and white for masking.

- Use the X button to toggle between black and white when in Quick Mask mode.

- Hold down the spacebar when making a selection to move the selection.

Taylor stressed that the key to success in this field is to "Work bloody hard and love what you do." She also said that being comfortable with your tools would keep your clients coming back.

"Clients are encouraged to sit with me in the preliminary stages, experimenting and interjecting ideas here and there," said Angie. "I think it's important to deliver on time, especially when you're a one-stop-shop or a freelancer. People need to depend on you, and you need to prove yourself a little bit more than the big production companies do."

To see more of Angie's work, visit:

http://www.adobe.co.uk/motion/gallery/taylor/main.html

http://www.angie.abel.co.uk

  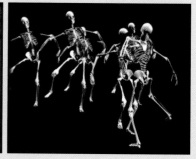

Color Correction:
How to Get It Right

When working in Photoshop, the most common type of color correction you will need to perform is *scene-to-scene* correction. That is to say, you will need to bring a variety of shots, from a variety of sources, closer together. They will need to seem as if the same photographer shot them under similar lighting conditions. This is an extremely challenging task if you consider the likelihood that you will pull images from several different stock libraries, client-provided sources, and video frame grabs.

The key when starting out is to work on a copy of the image. This way you always have a copy to return to if something goes wrong. Open the image in question, then choose **File>Save As**, and give the corrected version a new name. In fact, this is always a good idea. Image correction is often *destructive* editing, meaning that you cannot revert to the original state at a later date. Once the modified file is closed and saved, you lose the ability for multiple undos. By preserving an original version, or employing adjustment layers, *nondestructive* editing is possible.

 The five most useful image adjustments for video:

1. Levels
2. Curves
3. Hue/Saturation
4. Color Balance
5. Desaturate

Levels

There's a very good reason this image adjustment comes first in the menu. You will need to make a Levels adjustment on *every* image. The **Levels** command allows you to correct tonal ranges and color-balance issues. That is to say, that you can fix poor exposure and adjust your white and black point. If you understand the need to white balance a video camera, the **Levels** command will soon make sense.

The key to understanding the Levels adjustment is the histogram. If you can learn to read this graph, it can serve as a visual guide for adjusting the image. To illustrate this powerful command, open up the file *Ch8ImageAdjust1.tif*. Launch the Levels dialog by choosing Image>Adjust>Levels or by pressing **Cmd+L** (Ctrl+L). Be sure the **Preview** box is checked so that you can see your changes update.

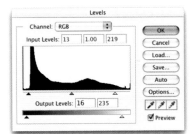

The midtones are way too dark in this image.

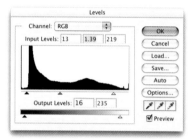

Adjust the midpoint to lighten the image.

(Photo by James Ball)

Adjust the levels for the red channel separately to improve color balance.

By adjusting the black and white input sliders, you can set the black and white points. Move the slide to the first group of pixels on each end. This will map the pixels to the values set for black and white in the Output levels area. The pixels that fall in between are adjusted proportionally in order to maintain a proper color balance. For this photo, I've adjusted the **Input** and **Output** levels to restore some of the missing contrast in the image. While a separate command exists for brightness and contrast, the levels adjustment lets you perform several improvements with one adjustment, thus cutting down on quantization (loss of quality) introduced from multiple image processing steps.

The true power lies in the middle slider. Here you can modify the gamma setting. Effectively, you can use the middle Input slider to change the intensity of the midtones, without making dramatic changes to the highlights and shadows. In a sense, you can better expose the picture, adding or subtracting "light" from the midtones. This adjustment is critical to creating a continuous flow between images. **Levels** adjustments do not offer as many precise adjustment points as **Curves** adjustments, but they are significantly easier to perform, and they generally create very good results.

So far you have been making Levels adjustments across all channels evenly. You can choose to isolate your corrections to a specific channel by clicking on the dropdown list. This can be used to remove colorcast issues, such as spill from a background or a photo shot under colored lighting. In this particular exam-

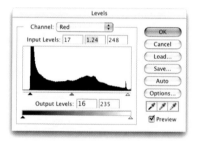

ple, I switched to the Red channel to make adjustments to the skin tones. You can automate this process a bit by using the eyedroppers. Use the black or white eyedroppers to click on an area to define its target color. For example, if you have a blue cast, clicking on a white area with the Set White Point eyedropper will remove the blue cast from the image.

What about all those other buttons? The Save and Load buttons can be used to save a color-correction setting. If you have several images from the same camera or photographer that need a common adjustment, you can save that adjustment, then load it back, and run it again. Don't waste your time with Auto; the Options button modifies the Auto button's behavior. Every image will need you to make a conscious decision; don't trust the computer to make accurate, artistic decisions about color.

Curves

Curves aren't easy, but they are powerful. The **Levels** adjustment just gives you three control points (highlights, midtones, and shadows). The **Curves** dialog gives you up to 16 control points, opening significantly more possibilities. One option is to add a single control point and pull it up to lighten the image or down to darken. The adjustment is applied evenly throughout the entire image. Multiple points can be employed for contrast adjustments based on tonal range.

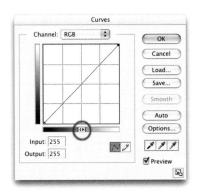

Let's take a look at **Curves** in action. I've chosen a grayscale file for the exercise because it is easier to work only on contrast issues when first using **Curves**. When you feel comfortable with grayscale images, switch to color ones, being sure to keep an eye on color shift.

Step 1   Open the file *Ch8ImageAdjust2.tif*.

Step 2   Launch the **Curves** dialog box by choosing Image>Adjust>Curves or by pressing Cmd+M (Ctrl+M).

Step 3   Right away, click on the small right-hand triangle on the bottom of the *x*-axis. This will place white at the top and right in the Curves dialog box, thus using the more familiar 0–255 scale.

(Photo by James Ball)

Currently your curve has two points on it: one representing the black point, the other, the white point. When you add additional curves and move them, you are reassigning values. For example, if you add a point at the midpoint, then move that point up (towards the lighter area on the *y*-axis); the image will lighten. Notice that the input and output values update as you drag. What differentiates **Curves** is that you have precise control over what points get mapped, whereas in **Levels**, you do not. Additionally, a **Curves** adjustment uses a curved line (rather than Levels' linear) to make adjustments that are eased through the image. It is possible to create adjustments that are easier to blend in with existing data, as opposed to Levels' frequent problem of hard clipping.

When the **Curves** Editor is open, you can automatically add control points by Cmd+clicking (Ctrl+clicking) within the image. The control points will appear in the editor. These can be moved up to lighten or down to darken.

This simple **Curves** adjustment increases the contrast of the image; doing this operation with a curve on an arbitrary map helps create a nice, organic roll-off to the adjustment.

A good image for testing the effects of the **Curves** control is a gradient such as this, where the effect on the full spectrum of values can be seen.

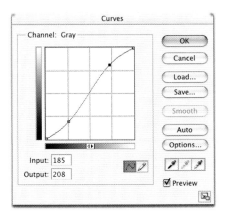

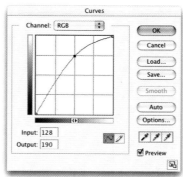

A **Curves** adjustment allows the midtones to be rolled towards the desired state. Notice how the horse and fence have regained lost details. Avoid using overly simple adjustments such as contrast; **Curves** are far superior.

To create Special FX, try using:

- Curves (with arbitrary settings)
- Channel Mixer (Load presets from Photoshop's *Goodies* folder)
- Gradient Map

So how do you know what points to pick? You click on the image itself (actually, Cmd+click on the Mac and Ctrl+click for PCs). In the **Curves** dialog box, you can then move these new points up to lighten or down to darken.

You will notice as you drag on a point that the others react as well. Be careful, because, as you add contrast in one area, it is removed from another. Radical adjustments will leave you with an undesirable posterization effect.

Because **Curves** are so complex, most people use a **Curves** adjustment layer instead of applying the adjustment directly to the source layer. An adjustment layer affects everything beneath it and has the added ability to support masks and blending modes. The results are just as effective as a traditional adjustment, but significantly more flexible. I'll look at adjustment layers in greater detail later in this chapter.

Color Balance

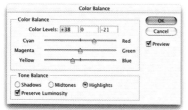

This is a simple yet useful tool. By using the **Color Balance** tool, you can change the overall mixture of colors in a particular tonal range. This is quite useful for generalized color correction. When you think an image is too blue or red, a quick adjustment allows you to tone down specific colors. The adjustment is constrained to the shadows, midtones, or highlights as specified in the dialog box.

Open up the file *Ch8ImageAdjust3.tif*. Notice how the light from the candles is a bit green? Make sure the composite channel is selected in the **Channels** palette, or the command won't work. Launch the Color Balance dialog box, or press Cmd+B (Ctrl+B). By selecting the **Highlights** radio button, you can adjust only those in the image. Leave the **Preserve Luminosity** box checked to prevent changing the luminosity. This option will allow you to maintain tonal balance throughout editing the image. Drag the sliders towards Red and Yellow; those colors will increase, while the opposite colors decrease.

The original image is too green. A **Color Balance** adjustment can help.

The new image feels warmer. *(Photo by James Ball)*

Hue/Saturation and Desaturate

This command is incredibly important for video graphics. If colors are too saturated, you will need to tone them down. Otherwise you will get "bleeding" onscreen with color data spreading from its original areas into other parts of your graphic. This can severely impact readability and is distracting to the viewer.

Oversaturation test

How do you know you're oversaturated? The best way is to import the graphics into your NLE and use features such as Final Cut Pro's **Range Check** option. Better yet, put the image onto a scope. But a quick way involves using the NTSC Colors filter.

Step 1 Open up the file *Ch8ImageAdjust4.tif.*

Step 2 If the photo is called *Background,* double-click and name it so that it's a floating layer.

Step 3 Create a copy of the photo layer by pressing Cmd+J (Ctrl+J). Make sure that you do not have a selection made.

These rich, saturated colors may cause us problems on a video monitor *(Photo by James Ball).*

Notice color shift in the red and yellow?

Step 4 Run the NTSC Colors filter on the layer. Look for any color shift. In our example, there are two areas that should show up: the juice bottles and the red tower of chalk.

Step 5 Set the filtered layer to Difference blending mode. The problem areas should be quite clear now.

Isolate for saturation

You now need to create a selection matte to isolate the saturation adjustment. Create this matte by using existing layer data.

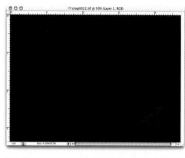

Step 1   Link the two layers together.

Step 2   Select the top layer, which is set to Difference mode.

Step 3   Hold down the Option or Alt key and choose **Merge Linked** from the layer's palette submenu. A flattened copy set to normal mode is now available.

Step 4   Desaturate this new layer by selecting Image>Adjust>Desaturate, or press Shift+Cmd+U (Shift+Ctrl+U).

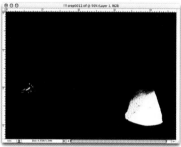

Equalize will force the matte.

Step 5   You need to expand this matte to make it more useful. To get a larger white area, choose Image>Adjust>Equalize. This will assign the lightest area to white (255) and the darkest area to black (0). The remaining pixels are dispersed evenly, thus creating a more useful high-contrast layer.

Step 6   Soften the matte by running the Gaussian Blur filter. Choose a value that generates soft edges. Depending on your image's resolution, this number will vary.

Step 7   Now the high-contrast layer will be used as a selection guide. Switch to the Channels palette (by default, it is docked with **Layers**. If it isn't, go to Windows>Show Channels).

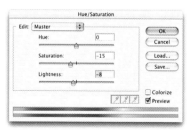

Blur the matte for softer edges in the color correction.

Step 8   Hold down the Cmd key (Ctrl) and click on the layer's thumbnail. You should now see the appropriate "marching ants."

Step 9   Further soften the selection by choosing Select>Feather.

Step 10   Switch back to the layer's palette; turn off the visibility indicator for the high-contrast matte. Select the photo layer that needs desaturating.

Step 11   Launch the Hue/Saturation dialog box by choosing Image>Adjust>Hue/Saturation or by pressing Cmd+U (Ctrl+U). Make sure the **Preview** box is checked.

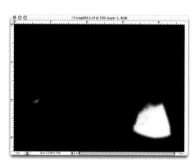

Step 12   Pull down the saturation and lightness sliders in small amounts. If you overdo it, you will get undesirable posterization.

Step 13   You may need to touch up the image using the **Sponge** tool.

With experience, you will learn to spot saturation problems visually. You can, however, always use the NTSC Colors filter as a way to spot potential issues.

The final image has the oversaturated areas corrected. You may still need to lower the output levels to 16 and 235, depending on your system.

When touching up mattes, masks, or alpha channels, you will use:

- Levels
- Invert
- Equalize
- Threshold

Useful Tools in Brief

Channel Mixer

Current channels can be combined to form a new channel. This has two distinct purposes:

Scenario 1. A digital photo had a write error and one of the channels is damaged. You can use the two good channels to create a replacement for the third.

Scenario 2. You want better grayscales. You can choose the monochromatic option and produce much better grayscales than by simply switching modes or desaturating.

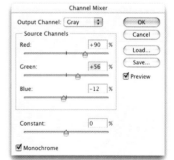

Want a better grayscale file? Use the **Channel Mixer**. *(Photo by James Ball)*

Gradient Map

The **Gradient Map** is an extremely useful effect for stylizing images. With that said, you should *always* choose to use the **Gradient Map** adjustment layer instead of the **Image Adjustment** command. What does the **Gradient Map** do? The name says it all: it takes a gradient and then maps it based on luminance values. The effect is particularly useful for colorizing backgrounds and textures. When used on photos, however, it can create some dynamic looks, especially when used with blending modes. After Effects users, you have an extremely similar effect too; in AE, it's called Colorama. To see **Gradient Map**s in action, open the file *Ch8ImageAdjust5.psd* and turn on the individual gradient maps.

When **Gradient Map**s are used as adjustment layers, they can be masked and blended. All of the effects shown used a single **Gradient Map**. There is no rendering time involved, and the original color data is preserved.

(Photo by James Ball)

Invert

This image adjustment creates an image that is a direct inverse or negative. This is very useful for reversing grayscale images—for example, reversing the masked areas of a layer mask or making a positive from a scanned black-and-white negative. When an image is inverted, the brightness of each pixel is assigned the inverse value from the 256 color-values scale. This means that a 0 value would map to 255, while a 15 value would map to 240.

Gradient Map Saves the Day.
Have an oversaturated picture and need a quick solution? Apply a black-to-white **Gradient Map** over the photo, and then set the adjustment layer's transfer mode to **Pin Light**. Fixes oversaturated colors instantly. (Thanks to Glen Stephens for this cool tip.)

Equalize command

If an image appears too dark or washed out, **Equalize** is the sledge-hammer way to pound it into a usable state. The command attempts to redistribute pixels so that they are equally balanced across the entire range of brightness values. You can tell Photoshop to look at the entire image when equalizing, or sample a smaller area that will drive the overall adjustment. The command will take the lightest area and map it to pure white (255) and the darkest area to pure black (0). Since the equalize command uses the full 0–255 range, you will need to adjust levels to keep the image broadcast safe.

Threshold command

This command is used to set the "continental divide." All pixels on one side of the new midpoint are black, the other are white. This adjustment can be used to clean up a mask made from individual channels.

(Photo by James Ball)

Not-So-Useful Tools

Brightness/Contrast. These controls are an inferior substitute for Levels and Curves, because the overall brightness or darkness is affected. Most of the time, the problem is in the midtones or gamma. A brightness and contrast adjustment will often leave your image washed out. Skip it.

Replace Color and Selective Color. These are not the most useful commands. **Replace Color** combines the select color range interface with a fill command. I personally prefer to split this step out and have fine control. The **Selective Color** command is similar to **Color Balance** (but not as easy to use) and does not produce the high-quality results that are possible with Levels or Curves. You are better off using the individual **Color Range** command (Select>Color Range) and then creating a **Levels** or **Curves** adjustment layer.

Posterize. Posterization cuts down on the number of colors used, thus producing banding. Reduced color palettes and banding are both extremely poor for video use. Skip the **Posterize** adjustment.

Skip these (unless you have no time at all):

- Auto Levels
- Auto Contrast
- Auto Color
- Variations

These may introduce *new* problems to your image:

- Brightness/Contrast
- Replace Color
- Selective Color
- Posterize

Variations. Inexperienced users try **Variations**. This wizard feels a lot like a visit to the eye doctor with its "more-and-less" approach to image adjustments. Skip it.

Broadcast-Safe Color Concerns

Whenever you adjust an image, you have to be concerned about modifying its colors to the point where they are no longer "broadcast safe." Even if you have a video frame grab that was legal, any of the previous image adjustments could push its white levels too high or blacks too low.

(Photo by James Ball)

The key is to adjust the output levels to pull things into the 16–235 broadcast safe range. In doing so, however, you don't want to overdo it, so you must monitor the adjustment. By placing targets using the **Color Sampler** tool (stored in the same well as the Eyedropper and Measure tools), you can monitor the values of white and black.

In the example, I have placed targets on the clouds (for white) and the deepest shadows (for black). In the **Info** palette, it is clear that these colors are out of the safe range. Add a Levels adjustment layer and set the output levels to 16 and 235. The colors are now in the safe range. You can leave the adjustment layer floating and modify it at any time within Photoshop.

Adjustment Layers

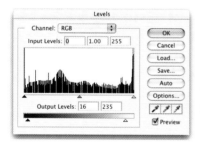

I've already mentioned adjustment layers as a helpful tool for pulling down **Levels** and for use in the Gradient Map feature. Adjustment layers are the only true way to perform nondestructive editing on an image. The adjustment layer can be blended, masked, or deleted at any time. Additionally, if you double-click on the adjustment layer's thumbnail, the **Image Adjustment** dialog box comes back. The same modifications are available in both the Adjust menu and Adjustment Layers.

If you want to apply an adjustment only to part of a layer, select as you would for any other change (see Chapter 3, "What About Transparency?"). Then, when you create the adjustment layer, it will automatically mask the adjustment to apply only to your selection. It is a good idea to feather the edges of your selection for a more believable adjustment. Otherwise you will see a hard edge that makes the adjustment very easy to spot.

Adjustment layers can also have gradient masks applied. The adjustment layer automatically comes with a mask applied. Just click on its thumbnail (the big, empty white one), and you will see the mask icon

The sign can use a little "punching up" *(Photo by James Ball).*

The new image has a different "feel." If I change my mind, editing is a double-click away.

appear next to the layer's name. You can now add a gradient or hand-painted mask to blend the adjustment in. To see these two techniques applied, open up the file *Ch8AL.psd*.

Fixing Common Problems

Photos that look useless can often be restored quickly. Color problems are one of the easiest things to fix in Photoshop.

Our next chapter, Chapter 9, "Repairing Damaged Photos," will tackle more difficult photo damage by looking at four common color problems that may affect you frequently.

Redeye

I'm not talking about what you have after a late-night editing session. The fill flash bouncing off the back of the eyeball causes *redeye*. This is a common problem for photos taken with consumer-quality cameras, because the flash and lens are very close together. Dark rooms only aggravate the problem, because the pupils are open wider . If it's your camera, look for a redeye-reduction mode. It will strobe the flash, thus cutting down on the redeye. You can also use a secondary flash with a sync cable if you are using a professional camera.

Zoom into the eyeball area. Chances are, however, you didn't take the pictures. Unless the photos are from a visit to the Inferno, you will need to clean this problem up. The discoloration won't necessarily be red. Just look for glowing eyeballs that shouldn't be there.

Step 1   Open up a photo with redeye, or use the provided file *Ch8redeye.tif*.

Step 2   Enter **Quick Mask** mode by pressing Q. Double-click on the Quick Mask mode icon; make sure it is set to show Selected Areas.

Step 3   Select a brush that is slightly smaller than the pupil. Press the [or] keys to change brush size.

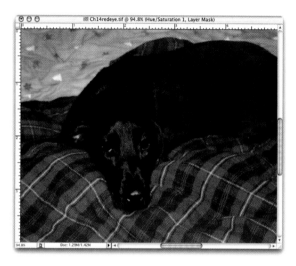

Step 4 Paint the pupil area using a soft-edge brush. For better results, click the **Airbrush** option in the Options bar.

Step 5 Press Q again to exit the Quick Mask mode. Everything but the pupils is selected.

Step 6 You may want to feather and/or expand your selection to avoid any fringe.

Step 7 Add a Hue/Saturation adjustment layer while the selection is still active. This will mask the adjustment to just the pupils.

Step 8 Pull down the Lightness and **Saturation** sliders. As an option, you may choose to colorize the pupils a darker hue to match the irises a bit more.

Step 9 If you need to touch up, just paint on the mask of the adjustment layer.

Color cast

Sometimes the light cast conditions are universally off. This could be seen as a blue cast throughout the entire shot. Maybe the wrong filter was used, or the image was not white balanced. Sometimes the problem is simply at the developing end. (When you go to a one-hour photo center at your local superstore, chances are the machine is on autopilot and is being run by someone with little or no experience.)

Step 1 Open up the file *Ch8colorcast.tif,* and you will see how easy this is to fix.

Step 2 Examine the photo. Identify a suitable white, gray, and black point. The gray point will be tricky, but you can make multiple attempts.

Step 3 Add a Levels adjustment layer.

Step 4 Select the black eyedropper and click on the darkest point in the picture.

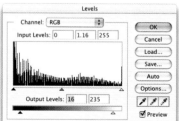

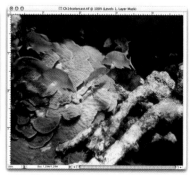

Step 5   Select the white eyedropper and click on the lightest point in the picture.

Step 6   Look for a gray point. With the gray eyedropper, click on a gray area that is representative of midtones. It may take a few attempts to find the right point in the picture.

Skin tones

It seems like old photos tend to have problems with skin tones. I look back at childhood photos from the 1970s and 80s, and I know that my skin was never that red. Improvements in film quality and processing have cut down on these color shifts, but the proliferation of digital cameras has made this problem all too prevalent. Picture fading can cause a photo to lighten or darken over time. Generally this is an even distortion, however, so a slight adjustment is all that is needed.

Step 1   To see one solution, open up the file *Ch8skintones.psd*.

Step 2   Add a Hue/Saturation adjustment layer. Roll the Hue, Saturation, and Lightness sliders until you get a more realistic skin tone. Don't worry if the image appears slightly washed out. We'll fix that next.

Step 3   Add a Levels adjustment layer and click Auto. The individual channels have been automatically adjusted. Closer, but not quite right yet.

Step 4   Now you can tweak. Switch to each channel and adjust the spread of the histogram. Bring the black and white point sliders closer to the pixel spread. Adjust the gamma or midpoint slightly until you are happy with the overall color.

Photoshop can usually restore missing color. It truly is a miracle worker.

Over time, the reds in this photo have become too dominant.

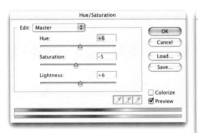
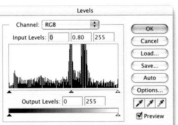
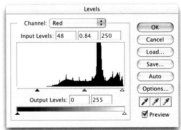
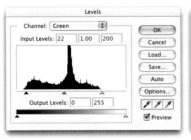
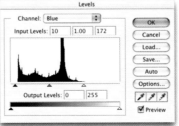

Before adjustments.

A saturation adjustment gets the "burn out."

A proper **Levels** adjustment makes everything right.

Tinting a photo

Imagine that you are working on a project showing different people, and all of your sources are full color, except one. What do you do? Dump it? Look for a tornado to carry you over the rainbow? No, you regress a bit and color it.

This technique is simple, but often overlooked.

Step 1 Create a new layer for each color you need, and place the layer in Color mode.

Step 2 Paint on the layer, and it will tint the photo below. Soften the colors with the occasional use of Dodge, Burn, Blur, and Smudge. Be sure to isolate each color on a separate layer so you have better control over the image.

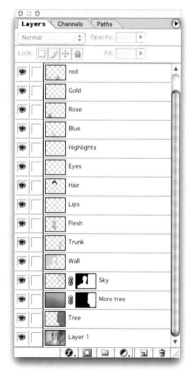

While it can be time consuming, you can hand-paint a grayscale photo to look realistic. Place each color on its own layer and set the layer to Color blending mode.

With a little time and practice, you can get great results.
Take a look at the file
Ch8ReColor.psd to   see this
techniqe in action.

Can you spot the fake? The first picture (left) is actually a hand-colored grayscale
version. The original photo is on the right. *(Photo by James Ball)*

Profile: John Mark Seck

John Mark Seck is currently the senior editor/designer at Sound Venture Productions in Ottawa, Canada. Prior to that, he worked extensively as a freelancer in Ottawa, Toronto, and Montreal. Seck works on the full range of broadcast and corporate projects. Past experiences include news, rock videos, commercials, documentaries, as well as independent films. John is an experienced and in-demand editor, but he isn't content to stop there.

"I will be called upon to create one special effect or edit and design the entire look and feel of a new series right down to the print promotional material."

This diverse range of duties is supported by Seck's design skills. Being knowledgeable in Photoshop is essential to his daily work.

"I refer to Photoshop as part of the Adobe 'holy trinity' of motion graphics production," said Seck. "Combined with Illustrator and After Effects, it is an essential and very powerful tool that should be part of any nonlinear editor's bag of tricks."

Seck was drawn to mastering Photoshop because of a need to be self-sufficient and fast. "For nonlinear editors, learning Photoshop is about as important as learning to read," said Seck. "You can get by without it, but you will always have to rely on someone else to solve problems for you."

While Photoshop serves a variety of uses for Seck, he finds it critical for documentary work. The ability to retouch, color correct, and make Levels adjustments increases production value.

"The Dust and Scratches filter is a handy, quick fix for retouching a photo. I think many people starting out think this filter will add (rather than correct) dust and scratches," said Seck. "Everyone should become good friends with the Rubber Stamp tool and the Healing Brush when it comes to retouching photos."

Seck offers additional advice on getting the most out of Photoshop:

"The layer blending modes are probably my favorite tool in Photoshop," said Seck. "When people are starting out, they tend to avoid these effects. It doesn't really matter if you understand exactly what each mode is doing. The best thing is

Copyright: Parks Canada, *Recognizing our History*, ISBN 0-662-66513-9

to dive in and try out the different looks each mode will achieve."

"Actions combined with batch processing are a tremendously powerful combination and a huge timesaver," said Seck. "If you ever do anything more than once, you should have an action for that function."

"I tend to use Photoshop layers in conjunction with After Effects a lot. I lay out multi-layered animation elements for import into After Effects. These can be either text elements or image elements."

Seck realized early on that clients and employers would expect more from editors. Because the technology and price models are changing so quickly, editors have to adapt to changing demands.

"In the past, it was possible to say, 'I'm just an editor.' That mentality is career-limiting these days.

For myself, I have chosen to develop a variety of skills. Those include editing, graphic design, motion graphics, 3D animation, and visual effects. This is a big chunk to chew on, but if you give yourself time, you find they all start to tie together and you develop a very marketable skill set."

Diversification goes way beyond what software packages you can run. To edit as an art form, it's necessary to reach beyond software "party" lines.

"I would say there is too much emphasis on what software package(s) you know these days," said Seck. "Software is just a starting point and is the easy part. Design skills and artistic aesthetics are much more elusive. Visit your local art galleries, stay in touch with current trends, and be open to new ideas."

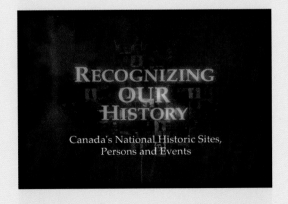

Repairing Damaged Photos

Damage, like beauty, is in the eye of the beholder. Show the same series of photos to five people and ask them to point out the mistakes; you'll get five totally different answers. Always ask your clients if there's anything they wish were different; you'll be surprised at the answers. I have had several instances where the request was as simple as cloning someone out of a group shot because they no longer worked for the company. Sometimes it will be a simple crop or color change. Always ask; don't assume that what they gave you was perfect.

Then look for the obvious things. Color correct the image first. (If you skipped it, take a look at Chapter 8, "Color Correction: How to Get It Right.") Then look for physical damage such as rips, wrinkles, pushpin holes, scratches, and ballpoint pen marks. On the second pass, look for printing or scanning errors. Is there a texture present, streaks, a misregistered scan? Finally, check for alignment and title-safe issues; you may have to rotate and clone the image to make it work. In five minutes? Yes, with practice you can fix 90% of the problems in five minutes; the other 10% you learn to live with (or ask for more time).

Scratches, creases, staple holes and dirt. This photo is beaten-up, but still usable after a little retouching work.

You'll find several of this chapter's examples on the disc. Feel free to use these for trying out the techniques.

Working with historical sources. Historical or archival photos present additional problems. There is an increased likelihood for physical damage such as tearing, water damage, or adhesive stains. The photos have also faded with time and will need touch up. It will often be easier to remove color all together from a historical source and reintroduce as the final step an overlay or sepia tone.

Working with modern sources. All of the problems with historical sources can be present in modern photographs. However, the most likely problem with modern photos, especially digital ones, is color issues. That can be followed up by physical abuse. If a photo is wrinkled, creased, punched, or scratched, look for the negative and either reprint or use a negative scanner. If the photo is dusty, smudged, or

Time is not kind to prints. Read on and learn how to fix the damage.

A USB slide scanner is an affordable option these days.

The **Clone Stamp** works very well, especially if a lower opacity brush is combined with multiple sample points.

fingerprinted, gently wipe it clean with a soft cloth, and then rescan. If rescanning or reprinting is not an option, you can fix several issues without going back to the negative.

Stamp It Out

Photoshop has several powerful options available to fix problem areas. Often the solution is to replace bad pixels with good ones. Do not think of these tools as being exclusive; it is common to employ two or more when tackling a tough problem. For all of these tools, be sure your painting tools are set to **Brush** size and your other tools to **Precise** (in your **Preferences** pane). This will allow you to better see your tools in action.

Clone Stamp

The Clone Stamp (S) is an old favorite of Photoshop users. It's been there forever, and with a little practice, produces predictable and accurate results. It works by sampling pixels from one area and applying them in another. This technique goes beyond copy and paste, however, because it uses the flexibility of Photoshop's **Brush** palette.

Step 1   Select the **Clone Stamp** Tool by pressing S.

Step 2   Select a brush from the **Options** bar or **Brush** palette.

Step 3   Experiment with blending modes. This can be useful when retouching so as to avoid visible cloning.

Step 4   Specify the alignment. If Aligned is selected, the sample point and painting point move parallel as you move. If the user clicks and starts over, the sample point picks up where it last was. If Aligned is deselected, the initial sample point is used (even after you stop and resume cloning.) The second method ensures that you are always sampling from the same area.

The **Clone Stamp** works very well, especially if a lower opacity brush is combined with multiple sample points.

You can clone from all visible layers by specifying Use All Layers. If this is deselected, only the active layer is used.

Step 5   Option+click (Alt+click) within the current document, or another open document set to the same color mode. This defines the source point for sampled pixel data.

Step 6   Click and start to paint as if you were using the **Brush** Tool (you are essentially sampling pixels from one area and painting them into another). The sampled pixels are drawn from before you click. Therefore, it may be necessary to release and start over occasionally to avoid cloning the problem area.

Step 7   Try cloning at a lower opacity from several different places to fill in a problem area. This way you can avoid too much repetition.

Step 8   Try to "follow the line" by looking for edges to follow. Straight lines such as creases in clothing are easier to follow than random spots. Look to follow the natural folds and linear paths that are present.

Healing Brush

The **Healing Brush** (J) is a new tool that is designed to correct imperfections in a photo. Similar in handling to the **Clone Stamp**, it successfully hides blemishes by taking cloned pixels and matching the texture, lighting, and shading of the sampled to the original pixels. This can often generate results in which the repaired pixels blend seamlessly together.

To get better results on an area with strong contrast, make a selection before using the **Healing Brush** Tool. The selection should be bigger than the area to be healed and should follow the boundary of high contrast pixels. For example, if healing a person's face, make a selection over the problem area that excludes the adjacent sky or clothing. This way, when painting with the **Healing Brush**, the selection will prevent color bleed-in from outside areas.

Step 1   Select the **Healing Brush** Tool by pressing J. (It's the one with a **Bandage** icon.)

Step 2   Select a brush from the **Options** bar or **Brush** palette.

Step 3   Choose a blending mode. (This can be useful when retouching as to avoid visible cloning.) The Replace option preserves noise and texture at the stroke's edges.

Step 4   Choose a source for repairing pixels in the **Options** bar. The standard source is sampled. Here pixels are taken from the area surrounding your sample point. As the brush moves, the sample

New and Improved!
The **Healing Brush** and **Patch Tool** are two of Photoshop's most exciting new features.

The **Healing Brush** was designed for challenges like this.

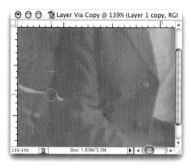

Try to "follow the line" for better results.

Use a small brush and short strokes with the **Healing Brush** for best results. The **Smudge** Tool set to Lighten or Darken mode is also useful for minor blemishes.

point also moves accordingly to ensure variety in the sampled source. The Pattern option uses a pattern from the current pattern library (accessible from a pop-up list).

Step 5 Specify the alignment. If Aligned is selected, the sample point and painting point move parallel as you move. If the user clicks and starts over, the sample point picks up where it last was. If Aligned is deselected, the initial sample point is used (even after you stop and resume cloning). The second method ensures that you are always sampling from the same area.

Step 6 You can clone from all visible layers by specifying Use All Layers. If this is deselected, only the active layer is used.

Step 7 If you are using the Sampling mode, Option+click (Alt+click) within the current document or another open document set to the same color mode.

Step 8 Click and start to paint as if you were using a brush. Because the sampled pixels are drawn from before you click, it may be necessary to release and start over occasionally to avoid cloning the problem area.

Step 9 Release the mouse to merge the sampled pixels. The stroke will look strange until then.

Step 10 Try to "follow the line" by looking for edges to follow. Straight lines such as creases in clothing are easier to follow than random spots. Look to follow the natural creases and linear paths that are present.

Patch Tool

The **Patch Tool** uses similar technology as the **Healing Brush**, but Patch is better suited to fix larger problems or empty areas. You can repair an area using pixels from another region or a pattern. To get best results, select a smaller area.

Using a Selection

Step 1 Select the **Patch Tool** by pressing J. (It's in the same well as the **Healing Brush**.)

Step 2 The **Patch Tool** can be used two different ways. You can make a selection in the area you want to repair, and then select Source in the **Options** bar. Or you can make a selection in the area from which you want to sample, and then select Destination in the **Options** bar. You can also make a selection first, and then activate the **Patch Tool**.

Step 3   Modify a selection with the standard modifier keys.

- Hold down the **Shift** key, and you can add to the selection.
- Hold down the **Option** key (**Alt** key), and you can subtract from the selection.
- To create an intersected selection, Option+Shift+drag (Alt+Shift+drag) to make a new selection.

Step 4   Place the cursor inside the selection, and then do one of the following:

- If Source is selected in the **Options** bar, drag the selection border to the area you want to sample. When you release the mouse button, the original area will be patched with the sampled pixels.
- If Destination is selected in the **Options** bar, drag the selection border to the area you want to patch. When you release the mouse button, the sampled area will be patched over the new area.

This image has several physical blemishes that can be patched.

Using a Pattern

Step 1   Select the **Patch Tool** by pressing J. (It's in the same well as the Healing Brush.)

Step 2   Make a selection in your photo.

Step 3   Select a pattern from the pop-up palette in the **Options** bar. You can also create a custom pattern in advance using the Pattern Maker filter. Once a pattern is selected, click **Use Pattern**.

The **Patch Tool** uses the same principles as the **Healing Brush** to repair an image. The option is whether or not to patch the source or the destination when you drag. By the way, you can use *any* selection tool to create your active selection, then switch to the **Patch Tool**.

Hide It:
Blur and Smudge, Dodge and Burn

The **Tools** palette offers several hands-on tools that help touch up photo damage. All of these tools are driven by brush settings: diameter, angle, roundness, and hardness will all affect the way these tools behave. If you are not familiar with the new **Brushes** palette, be sure to "brush" up first. Remember, if the **Caps Lock** key is down, brush previews are disabled.

Blur Tool   R

Sharpen Tool   R

Smudge Tool   R

Blur and Sharpen

There are two focus tools in Photoshop: the **Blur** Tool and the **Sharpen** Tool. The **Blur** Tool (R) gives you the ability to manually soften problem areas. The **Sharpen** Tool (R) helps focus soft edges.

Step 1   Select the **Blur** Tool or **Sharpen** Tool by pressing R.

Step 2   Specify the brush and brush options.

Step 3   Choose a blending mode. The Darken and Lighten modes are particularly useful for isolating the blurring effect.

Step 4   Adjust the strength for the tool. It is generally better to use a lower strength with several applications.

Step 5   Specify Use All Layers to use data from all visible layers.

Step 6   Paint over the areas that need touching up.

Be careful not to oversharpen; it will quickly introduce visible noise and distortion.

Smudge

Think of the **Smudge** Tool as the original **Liquify** command. This tool simulates dragging a finger through wet paint. The pixels are liquid, and can be easily pushed around the screen. The tool uses color from where you first click and pushes it in the direction you move the mouse. This tool is useful for cleaning up mattes and is also a quick way to clean up specks or flakes in a photo. Set the tool's blending mode to **Lighten** or **Darken** (depending on the area to be affected), and you have virtual concealer to touch up any problem.

Step 1   Select the **Smudge** Tool by pressing R.

Step 2   Specify the brush and brush options.

Step 3   Choose a blending mode. The Darken and Lighten modes are particularly useful for isolating the smudge.

Step 4   Adjust the strength for the tool. It is generally better to use a lower strength with several applications. If you are in a hurry, bump the strength up.

Step 5   Specify **Use All Layers** to use data from all visible layers.

Step 6   Paint over the areas that need touching up.

Step 7   The Finger Painting option can be accessed from the **Options** bar or activated temporarily by holding down the Option (Alt) key while painting. This technique, also known as *dipping*, smudges and simultaneously introduces color from the foreground color.

Dodge and Burn

Dodge Tool O

Burn Tool O

Sponge Tool O

Known as the toning tools, **Dodge** and **Burn** allow you finer control over lightening or darkening your image. They are similar to traditional techniques used in a darkroom, where a photographer would regulate the amount of light on a particular area on a print. These tools are helpful when touching up faded photos, especially when repairing water damage.

Step 1   Select the **Dodge** or **Burn** Tool by pressing O.

Step 2   Specify the brush and brush options.

Step 3   Choose a range of shadows, midtones, or highlights to isolate the effect.

Step 4   Adjust the exposure for the tool. It is generally better to use a lower exposure with several applications.

Step 5   Paint over the areas that need touching up.

Sponge

The **Sponge** Tool is simply elegant. It is a toning tool that can be used for subtle changes in color saturation or grayscale contrast. This tool is particularly useful for touching up spots that are too bright for television's color range. It can also be used to reduce digital grain that appears in an image.

The **Sponge** Tool can Desaturate *and* Saturate.

Step 1   Select the **Sponge** Tool by pressing O.

Step 2   Specify the brush and brush options.

Step 3   Choose **Saturate** or **Desaturate**, depending upon your needs.

Step 4   Adjust the flow for the tool. It is generally better to use a slower flow with several applications.

Step 5   Paint over the areas that need touching up.

Restoration in Action

Fixing photo damage is not a step-by-step solution or recipe. Practice is the best way to become skillful, but you can expect good results if you know which tools to use. I have seen students become proficient in just a few weeks, using Photoshop's rich suite of tools.

Use a small brush and short strokes with the **Healing Brush** for best results. The **Smudge** Tool set to Lighten or Darken mode is also useful for minor blemishes.

The challenge is knowing which tools to use, and when to use them. With that in mind, I present some common scenarios and the most likely solutions.

Wrinkles, holes, and tears

To simplify the problem, you have areas that are missing and need to be replaced. For small areas like pushpin holes, you can easily use the Clone Stamp to sample an adjacent area and fill the space in. It is possible to just "finger-paint" the problem away using the **Smudge** Tool as well. If the hole is in a dark area, set the **Smudge** Tool to Darken, and push the pixels in. This virtual spackle works extremely well.

Tears of a significant size benefit from the **Stamp** Tool. To avoid repeating patterns, try cloning at a low opacity and sample from different areas. A little bit of randomness goes a long way.

If things are really bad, consider a vignette effect and blur the outside edges. Make an elliptical selection, then reverse it by pressing Shift+Cmd+I (Shift+Ctrl+I). Then feather the edges extensively and run the Gaussian Blur filter.

 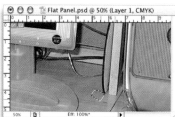 

A small blemish is visible on the desk surface. Make a selection with the **Patch** Tool, then drag to sample a clean area.

Goop, sludge, schmutz

There are several names for the problem. What I'm talking about are physical blemishes attached to the photo that could have/should have been wiped off before scanning. This problem is often caused by food or environmental debris. If the photo is still in your possession, gently clean it and rescan.

If all you have is the scan, use the new **Patch** Tool. In the sample photo *Ch9Patch Me*, you can see several areas that need touching up. Set the **Patch** Tool to Source Mode and lasso around the problem spot (feather edges for a softer transition). Drag the selection to a clear area of similar texture, using the Shift key to constrain movement to a straight line. If you want perfection, touch up with the **Blur** and **Smudge** Tools. Problem solved.

For little blemishes, use the **Smudge** Tool. If you have dark spots on a lighter background, smudge in the **Lighten** mode. For light spots on a dark background, smudge in the **Darken** mode. Because you are outputting to such a lo-res medium, these touchups are virtually unnoticeable, and they are fast. The key again is to "follow the line" (in this case, hair whorls or wood grain).

Alignment

The world is not flat, and sometimes it shows. Thin, crooked lines look very bad in video. If a photo is not straight (because it was shot or scanned at a slight angle), it is easy to fix.

Step 1 Access the **Measure** Tool (I) and find a surface you think should be horizontal (or vertical).

Step 2 Click and drag a line to measure the angle.

Step 3 Select Image>Rotate Canvas>Arbitrary. The correct value is inserted automatically from the **Measure** Tool.

Step 4 Crop the image or patch the gaps and make any additional repairs.

Shot composition

Don't forget about cropping. At print resolution, a wide shot works. On video (especially if it ends up on CD-ROM or the Internet), tighter is better. Always scan your photos at a higher resolution setting so that you can zoom in for fine corrections, and still have pixel data if you need to crop.

Step 1 Select the Crop Tool (C).

Step 2 Specify a target size (such as 720×540 for standard or 720×534 for DV) in the **Options** bar. Be sure to type *px* for pixels if your rulers are set to inches.

Step 3 Crop the photo tighter, being sure to allow a 10% gutter on each side for action-safe purposes.

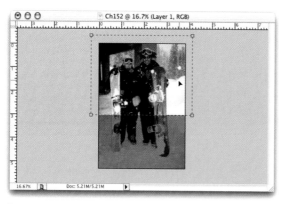

Zoom out and resize so you have room to "expand" the crop.

A little Clone Stamping and stretching of the background, and the aspect ratio is changed.

Aspect ratio

Half the time your photos will be in the portrait aspect ratio. Chances are you can't send out instructions for people to rotate their TVs 90°. The **Crop** Tool makes this an easy fix.

Step 1   Make sure the photo layer is floating. If it's called Background, double-click and rename the layer.

Step 2   Zoom Out and resize the window so that you can see some of the gray area around the photo.

Step 3   Select the Crop Tool (C).

Step 4   Specify a target size (such as 720×540 for standard or 720×534 for DV) in the **Options** bar. Be sure to type *px* for pixels if your rulers are set to inches.

Step 5   Draw the crop; initially you will be constrained to the image's area. After releasing, you can grab the individual anchor points and crop beyond the image's border.

Step 6   You can clone the missing areas in with the **Clone Stamp** or **Patch Tool**.

Step 7   Alternately, you may be able to "stretch" the edges by using the **Free Transform** feature. This works particularly well if the image is a portrait against a standard backdrop, or the background is nondescript, such as a sky. This down-and-dirty technique works very well if the sections to be filled fall outside the title-safe area.

Keystoning

If a photo is taken from a low angle, distortion is likely to appear. Open the file *Ch9Keystone.psd*. The strong horizontal and vertical lines make the distortion easy to see.

Step 1 First get the picture properly aligned horizontally using the previous technique with the **Measure** Tool. Don't worry about cropping yet.

Step 2 Zoom out and resize the window so that you can see some of the gray area around the photo.

Step 3 Make sure your rulers are visible. If not, press Cmd+R (Ctrl+R).

Original image has noticeable distortion.

Step 4 Drag two guides out to match the vertical lines. Line them up along the bottom edge if the photo was taken from a low-angle (use the top edge for a high-angle shot).

Step 5 Make sure the photo layer is floating. If it's called Background, double-click and rename the layer.

Step 6 Access the **Free Transform** Tool by pressing Cmd+T (Ctrl+T).

Step 7 Enable the Perspective transform by Ctrl+clicking or right-clicking on a two-button mouse. Drag the top handles apart to correct the keystoning of the image.

Step 8 Enable the Distort transform by Ctrl+clicking or right-clicking on a two-button mouse. Drag the corners individually to finalize the correction. Make sure snapping is off (View>Snap) or the fine-tuning will be difficult.

Step 9 Apply the transformation by pressing the Enter key or clicking the Apply button.

Once the distortion is corrected, proper perspective is regained.

Step 10 Crop the image or clone in the missing areas.

Soft focus

Under low light, cameras are more likely to generate a soft focus. The **Unsharp Mask** filter can fix blurring that is introduced during scanning, resizing, developing or even when the image was first photographed. It works by finding pixels that differ from their surrounding neighbors (specified by the threshold) and then increases their contrast by a specified amount. The effect can be limited by specifying the radius of comparison. The filter works best in the Lab color mode when run on the Lightness channel.

The glass is not quite in focus. The **Unsharp Mask** filter is the perfect solution.

Step 1   Choose Filter>Sharpen>Unsharp Mask. Select the Preview option so that you can see your changes. It is better to run the filter on the entire image instead of a specific area.

Step 2   When you click on the thumbnail in the **Filter** dialog, it reverts to the prefiltered state. You can also uncheck the **Preview** box to A/B the effect. It is a good idea to set your **Preview** window to a 100% or 50% magnification to get the most accurate preview of the filter.

Step 3   Specify a value for how much to increase the contrast of the pixels.

Step 4   Adjust the radius slider slightly.

Step 5   Modify the Threshold slider, which determines how different the sharpened pixels must be from the surrounding area before they are treated as edge pixels. A value of 2–20 is often useful for preserving flesh tones and eliminating additional noise. The default value of 0 sharpens all pixels in the image.

If you get oversaturated colors, switch to the Lab image mode. Apply the filter only to the Lightness channel.

Step 6   You may choose to defocus grainy backgrounds manually with the **Blur** Tool, or make selections, feather the edges, and filter.

Fading historical sources

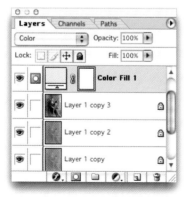

A common problem with old black-and-whites or sepia tones is that they fade. Attempting to adjust the **Levels** or **Curves** often introduces color artifacts.

Step 1   Sample the color tint if you want to retain it in the finished piece.

Step 2   Leave the image in RGB mode, but strip away the color by choosing Image>Adjust>Desaturate or by pressing Shift+Cmd+U (Shift+Ctrl+U).

Step 3   Make a Levels adjustment and restore the white and black points.

Step 4 Make any additional adjustments as needed.

Step 5 Create a color adjustment layer and use the color you previously sampled. Place the layer into Color mode, and adjust opacity and fill until you are happy with the results.

Digital blues

Many digital cameras tend to roll towards the blue tones. A simple adjustment using the **Color Balance** command can help you restore the missing reds in the shadows, midtones, and highlights. Be careful not to overdo it, because a consumer television will tend to make an image redder on its own.

Missing sky

Professional photographers spend a lot of time searching (and waiting) for the perfect sky. Unfortunately, professionals do not take many of your pictures. Skies will often be washed out and missing. By combining a few techniques, we can restore the sky in no time.

Step 1 Open the file *Ch9FixtheSky.psd*.

Step 2 Select the sky using the Color Range method (Select>Color Range).

Step 3 Subtract any stray selections in the lower half of the photo by using the Marquee Tool and holding down the Option (Alt) key.

Step 4 Copy the selection to a new layer by pressing Cmd+J (Ctrl+J).

Step 5 Adjust the Hue for the copied layer, and use the colorize option to introduce the missing blue.

Step 6 Lock the sky layer by clicking on the Lock Transparent Pixels button in the Layers palette. This will constrain the clouds to only the solid areas of the layer.

Step 7 Load a soft white and vivid blue. These colors will drive the clouds filter.

Step 8 Run the Clouds filter; then Fade Edit immediately after by pressing Shift+Cmd+F (Shift+Ctrl+F). Adjust the blending mode and opacity to screen the new clouds back.

Step 9 Run a Gaussian Blur or Motion Blur filter to spread the clouds out a bit.

Step 10 Blend the new clouds back into the original sky by adjusting the sky layer's opacity and blending mode.

Color Balance is a quick way to replace the often-missing reds from a digital picture.

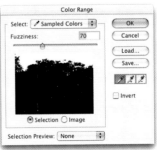

Adjust the fuzziness slider for a smoother selection.

Step 11 Unlock the sky layer and run a slight Gaussian Blur. This will be particularly helpful if you have fine details intersecting the sky because it will feather the edge.

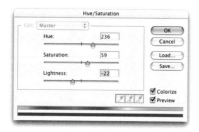

Need the perfect sky? Be sure to check the demo of Aurora (The Natural Plug-In) from Digital Element. This Photoshop plug-in harnesses true 3-D power and lets you restore missing details from photos. You can add:

- sun and star effects
- volumetric, ambient, and point lighting
- water and reflections
- haze and atmosphere

Try out the demo, and then visit www.digi-elelment.com to find out more.

Damage Control

Every time I show people how to fix a problem or take something out, someone in the audience wants to know how to add damage back in. At some point, "mistakes" like flash frames, video snow, and light leaks became "cool." So in turn, clients will ask for a distressed photo look. Here are some of my secrets.

Grain

Sometimes you may want to add some noise back into a picture. The key is to put the noise on its own layer so it's easier to control and adjust.

Step 1 Add a new layer above the photo and fill it with 50% gray.

Step 2 Create grain by choosing Filter>Artistic>Film Grain.

Step 3 Set the layer to Overlay mode.

Step 4 Duplicate the grainy layer to increase the noise.

Ripped edges

The key to pulling off this effect is to use real paper for the ripped edge. Find a piece of poster board or cardstock and rip the edge. Make sure the paper is a different color than your scanner's lid.

Step 1 Scan the ripped paper.

Step 2 Make the layer float; then delete away the white.

Step 3 Open the photo that needs a "ripped" edge. Make sure the photo layer is floating. If it's called Background, double-click and rename the layer.

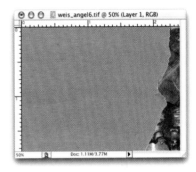

Step 4 Copy and paste the ripped layer into the photo's composition. Position the rip so the edge lines up in the desired area in the photo. Use Free Transform to modify the ripped layer. If there is an empty space, make a selection with the rectangular marquee; then Free Transform it to fill in the gap.

Step 5 Place the photo layer on top in the **Layers** palette; then group it by pressing Cmd+G (Ctrl+G).

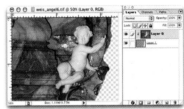

Step 6 To add a little more depth, place a copy of the ripped paper on top. Change its blending mode and add a beveled edge. Then Ctrl+click on the layer effect and tell it to create layers. Isolate the carved edge, and throw away the other highlights effect layer.

To see this effect, open *Ch9RippedPhoto.psd*.

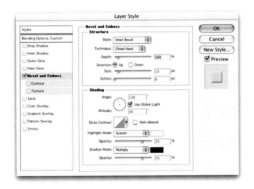

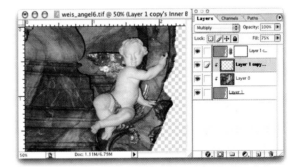

Scan lines

The digital distortion look continues to remain popular due to several web sites employing this technique. There are really several ways of doing this look. A popular, old-school plug-in called Retro-Scan by Deep Devices is available for non-OSX Mac users (http://members.aol.com/deepdevice). This can be accomplished within Photoshop as well with built-in plug-ins.

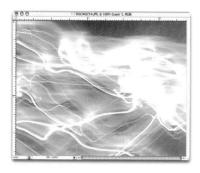

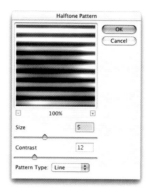

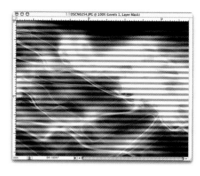

Step 1   Open an image.

Step 2   Duplicate the background layer.

Step 3   Run the Gaussian Blur filter on the duplicate layer to soften it. I used a value of 10 pixels.

Step 4   Load the default colors by pressing D.

Step 5   Run the **Halftone Pattern** filter (Filter>Sketch>Halftone Pattern…) Choose Line as the pattern and specify a width of at least three pixels. Apply the filter.

Step 6   Select the **Move** Tool by pressing **V**. We need a tool without blend modes for the next shortcut to work.

Step 7   Cycle through the blend modes by pressing Shift++ or Shift+–. Adjust the opacity of the layer to taste. I used the Luminosity mode set to 50%.

As an option, you can add a Levels adjustment layer to boost contrast.

Old photo

Want to make your own old photo? Just add noise and some tinting and you're there! The technique can even be turned into layer style or action for quicker processing.

Step 1   Open the target photo.

Step 2   Desaturate it by pressing Shift+Cmd+U (Shift+Ctrl+U).

Step 3   Duplicate the photo by pressing Cmd+J (Ctrl+J).

Step 4   Blur this copy using Gaussian Blur (Filter>Blur>Gaussian Blur). I used a six-pixel blur.

Step 5   Add some Film Grain (Filter>Artistic>Film Grain).

Step 6   Select the **Move** Tool by pressing V. We need a tool without blend modes for the next shortcut to work.

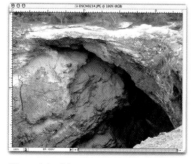

The original image.

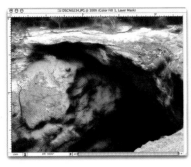 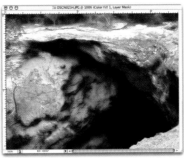 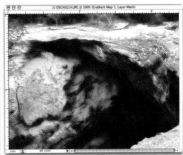

Step 7 Cycle through the blend modes by pressing Shift++ or Shift+–. Adjust the opacity of the layer to taste. I used the Multiply mode.

Step 8 Add a Solid Color adjustment layer set to the tint color you want to use. Place this layer in Color or Soft Light mode for different results. Alternately, you could use a **Gradient Map** in a similar way.

To see this effect, open *Ch9OldPhoto.psd*.

Distressed photo

In typical fashion, I stumbled across this technique while trying to get more out of my filters. I frequently will push filters into situations they weren't designed for. As a case in point, we're going to use Flaming Pear's cool cosmos/starscape generator Glitterato to distress a photo. You'll find a fully functional demo of the plug-in on the book's disc.

Step 1 Open the target photo.

Step 2 Duplicate the photo by pressing Cmd+J (Ctrl+J).

Step 3 Blur this copy using Gaussian Blur (Filter>Blur>Gaussian Blur). I used a 10-pixel blur.

  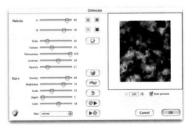

Glitterato from Flaming Pear does some really cool things!

The original image.

After blending a blurred copy.

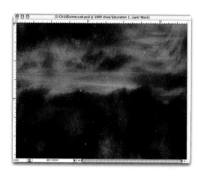

Step 4 Duplicate the blurred layer by pressing Cmd+J (Ctrl+J). Set the blurred layer to Multiply mode.

Step 5 Run the Glitterato filter and choose the Yellow Weave preset (Filter>Flaming Pear>Glitterato). Scale to taste with the Free Transform Tool.

Step 6 Soften the Glitterato layer by running the Median filter (Filter>Noise>Median). I used a two-pixel average.

Step 7 Select the **Move** Tool by pressing V. We need a tool without blend modes for the next shortcut to work.

Step 8 Cycle through the blend modes by pressing Shift++ or Shift+−. Adjust the opacity of the layer to taste. I used the Screen mode set to 50% opacity.

Step 9 Add a Gradient Map adjustment layer set to the Black-to-White gradient. Experiment with blending modes and opacity to achieve the desired look.

Step 10 Add a Saturation adjustment layer.

Strip 70–90% of the chroma out of the layer.

Step 11 Click on the adjustment layer's layer mask. Press D for default colors. Run the Clouds filter (Filter>Render>Clouds). Repeat by pressing Cmd+F (Ctrl+F) until you are happy with the random splotches.

To see this effect, open *Ch9Distressed.psd*.

Profile: Liane G. Rozzell

After freelancing as an editor for four years, Rozzell recently accepted a staff job editing for a company that specializes in producing programs for museum exhibits. While she's worked in many genres, she's most well known for her documentary work. Because documentaries rely heavily on photos, Rozzell frequently turns to Photoshop. She finds it gives her the necessary creative leverage to solve her production problems.

"How do I use Photoshop? Let me count the ways. My most basic use is in preparing a still image for import: cropping it, sizing it, adjusting the levels, and adjusting the color. Scans almost always need this sort of work. With archival photos, I'll often have to do some retouching," said Rozzell. "Sometimes I use it to prepare images that will then be animated in After Effects or using the Moving Picture plug-in inside the NLE. Every now and then, I've used Photoshop to fix a frame of an image that comes from video."

Why does she rely so much on Photoshop?

"Most of the things I do in Photoshop can't be done in the NLE itself, at least not as powerfully. For example, I can't create backgrounds as well in an NLE. I can make titles, but if I want to rotate them or create a better gradient effect, I have to do it in Photoshop," said Rozzell. "Right now, I have more control over color and levels in Photoshop, but that is changing as NLEs gain more color correction tools."

Rozzell equates mastering Photoshop to learning another language. She says a power user is one who is fluent in Photoshop: "Just as you'll never learn every word of another language (who even knows every word in their native language?), you don't

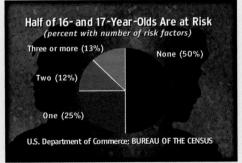

have to know everything about Photoshop."

"You start learning another language by building practical knowledge, learning how to say 'please' and 'thank you' and learning a few idioms or expressions. You can consider yourself pretty fluent when you can do the equivalent of ordering off the menu or reading a book or newspaper without having to think hard about it," said Rozzell. "Translating this to Photoshop, it means learning the basics about how the application works. How to use layers, selections, alpha channels and paths, learning what the filters do, learning how and when to use the various tools. Add "idioms" (keyboard shortcuts and plug-ins) for efficiency. And, as with a language, there is no substitute for practice, repetition, and interaction with graphic artists and other Photoshop speakers!"

To get you on your way, Rozzell offers two speed tips for Photoshop users:

- "My favorite shortcut is the simple ability to set the crop tool to the dimensions I need to create a static image. Boring, but so often necessary.

- "The tool I've gotten most excited about when it came out was the one I call "The Magic Transform Tool": Cmd+T (Ctrl+T). I just love the fact that with one tool I can resize, reposition and rotate all at the same time."

Her final advice is also important; she warns about losing track of why we use all of these great tools.

"For editors, as much as we use computers, I always get back to the fact that our work is about telling stories. Learn to use your tools to tell stories well. When you do that, your work will be good, and you'll be able to get more work!"

Creating Backgrounds for Video

While the video world often constrains itself to a 4×3 aspect ratio, the real world does not. When incorporating photos, type, and logos, there is often empty space. Some choose to leave this area empty or filled with black. I like the color black more than most people—in fact, half my wardrobe is gray, charcoal, or black. But even I'll admit that it can get pretty boring for video.

To combat this, you can wallpaper the screen. You may choose to fill the screen with blended colors, repeating patterns, or soft textures. In all cases, Photoshop proves to be an excellent tool for creating backgrounds for video. If you choose to animate these backgrounds, they can easily be imported as layered images into After Effects, Combustion, and most nonlinear packages these days. In fact, 75% of my After Effects work starts in Photoshop. With this wide-open box of possibilities, let's begin.

Backgrounds should match the 'mood' of the piece. Don't just tile the client's logo.

Gradients

Video has difficulty dealing with high-contrast ratios. Proper use of gradients exploits video's greatest weakness. A gradient is a gradual blend between two or more colors. These gradual transitions work very well on video, even after duplication to lower-quality consumer tape stock or broadcast. There are three major ways to access gradients:

- Gradient Tool
- Gradient Fill layer
- Gradient Map

However, all three use a similar interface: the **Gradient Editor**.

Be sure to go with less saturated red tones. The use of gradual blends helps hold this background together. *(Image courtesy American Diabetes Association)*

Gradient Editor

All gradients are edited using the common **Gradient Editor**. To access it, click on the thumbnail of the gradient that is loaded in the pop-up window or the **Options** bar.

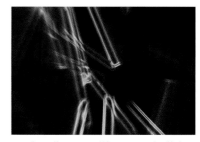

Proper use of gradients can lift your work off the screen. Gradients are essential to natural color.

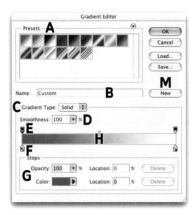

Use the , (comma) and . (period) keys to cycle through your gradient presets.

Presets (A). You have several presets to choose from. If you want to load additional preset gradients, access them from the submenu (triangle icon). You can choose to replace the existing gradients, or append (add-on) to the loaded gradients. You can also load gradients that live outside the presets folder by clicking the **Load** button. There are several gradients available online, as well as with this book's disc. You can also choose to save your own creations. The best place to store them is inside your *Presets* Folder (Application Folder>Presets>Gradients). This way they will appear in the submenu for faster loading.

Name (B). For ease of recall, gradients can be named. If you are having a particularly boring day, express yourself here.

Type (C). There are two gradients to choose from: Solid and Noise. Solid gradients involve color and opacity stops, with gradual blends in between. Noise gradients contain randomly distributed colors within a specified. Each has a different interface and will be discussed separately.

Solid Editor

Smoothness (D). Controls the rate at which colors blend into each other. It can be gradual or steep.

Opacity stops (E). Gradients can contain blends between opacity values as well. To add another stop, click in an empty area on the top of the gradient spectrum. To adjust a stop, click on it, and then modify the opacity field.

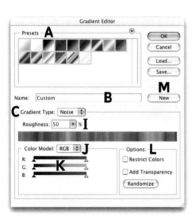

Color stops (F). The simplest gradients contain only two colors, but who said clients were simple? Often you may choose to use several colors (or even repeat colors) to achieve a desired effect. Double-click on the color stop to access the Adobe **Color Picker**.

Stop Editor (G). Selected gradient stops can be adjusted numerically. You can edit the opacity, color, and location (0–100%, read left to right.)

Midpoint (H). Between stops are midpoints. By default, the midpoint is halfway between two stops. However, it wouldn't be Photoshop if you couldn't customize it.

Noise Editor

Roughness (I). Noise gradients use a roughness setting to determine how many different colors are used to create noise.

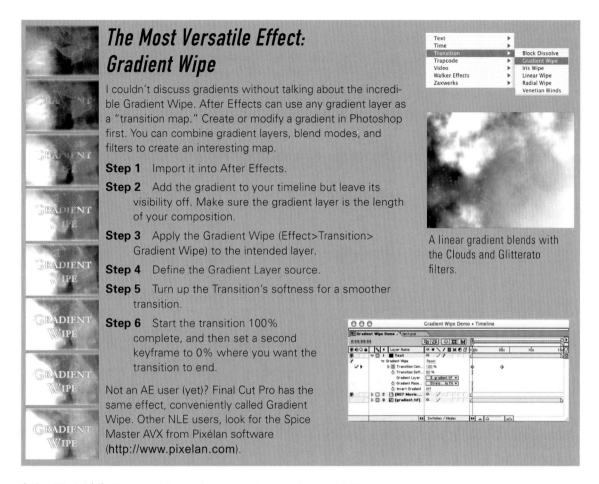

The Most Versatile Effect: Gradient Wipe

I couldn't discuss gradients without talking about the incredible Gradient Wipe. After Effects can use any gradient layer as a "transition map." Create or modify a gradient in Photoshop first. You can combine gradient layers, blend modes, and filters to create an interesting map.

Step 1 Import it into After Effects.

Step 2 Add the gradient to your timeline but leave its visibility off. Make sure the gradient layer is the length of your composition.

Step 3 Apply the Gradient Wipe (Effect>Transition> Gradient Wipe) to the intended layer.

Step 4 Define the Gradient Layer source.

Step 5 Turn up the Transition's softness for a smoother transition.

Step 6 Start the transition 100% complete, and then set a second keyframe to 0% where you want the transition to end.

A linear gradient blends with the Clouds and Glitterato filters.

Not an AE user (yet)? Final Cut Pro has the same effect, conveniently called Gradient Wipe. Other NLE users, look for the Spice Master AVX from Pixélan software (http://www.pixelan.com).

Color Model (J). You can choose between three models: Red-Green-Blue, Hue-Saturation-Brightness, or L*a*b.

Color Range Sliders (K). Adjust the range of colors available to the gradient.

Options (L). You can choose to restrict colors (which has no apparent effect for video). You can also introduce random transparency. To create a new gradient, click on the **Randomize** button. Every time you click, a new gradient will be generated.

New Button (M). To add a gradient to the **Presets** window, type a name into the name field. Click the **New** button, and an icon will be added in the **Presets** window. This new gradient is not yet permanently saved, but stored temporarily in the **Preferences** file. If this file is deleted or damaged, or if you change presets, the new gradient will be lost. You must click the **Save** button and navigate to the desired folder. Be sure to append the file name with .grd to inform Photoshop that it is a gradient file.

Use the [and] (bracket) keys to change the style of the gradient.

Gradient Tool

The **Gradient** Tool can be used to manually draw gradients on a layer. To access the **Gradient** Tool, select it from the toolbar, or press G. The Paint Bucket shares the same well as the Gradient Tool, so if you can't find the Gradient Tool, press Shift+G to cycle through your tools.

The **Gradient** Tool can use any gradient created from the gradient editor or from the **Presets** menu. To select a gradient, choose from the available ones in the **Options** bar. You can also load preset libraries or manually load gradients by accessing the palette's submenu. To access the gradient editor, double-click a **Gradient** icon.

You now must choose between five options to build your gradient:

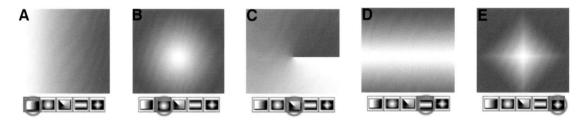

Linear gradient (image A). Shades from the starting point to the ending point in a straight line.

Radial gradient (image B). Shades from the starting point to the ending point in a circular pattern.

Angle gradient (image C). Draws the gradient in a counterclockwise sweep from the starting point.

Reflected gradient (image D). Draws a linear gradient symmetrically on both sides of the starting point.

Diamond gradient (image E). Draws the gradient in a diamond-shaped pattern outward from the starting point.

You have a few available options to further modify the gradient.

You can specify a blend mode to affect how the gradient is applied to the layer. (For more on the versatile blend modes, see Chapter 4, "Why Layers?".)

- To swap the direction of colors in the gradient, select **Reverse**.

- To create a smoother blend, choose **Dither**.

- To use a gradient's built-in transparency, check the **Transparency** box. If a preset gradient does not contain transparency, edit it and add opacity stops.

- To draw the gradient, click to set the starting point. Continue to hold the mouse button down and draw to the endpoint.

- To constrain the angle to multiples of 45°, hold down the Shift key as you drag.

Gradient Fill layer

A **Gradient Fill** layer creates a new gradient layer in your document (Layer>New Fill Layer>Gradient or from the Create New Adjustment or Fill layer menu at the bottom of the layer's palette). Instead of drawing the gradient, you access its controls from the editor and a pop-up window. The gradient can be positioned by dragging in the open document. You can also change the direction and shape of the gradient. When you are satisfied, click OK. While this gradient is not very flexible, it can be included when creating an action.

To confine the new gradient to a specific area, make a selection first. This will add a layer mask to the gradient layer. You can edit this mask at any time by highlighting the layer and using any painting tool or filter.

You can click the gradient to display the **Gradient Editor**. You can also click on the dropdown arrow to access the pop-up gradient palette. You can choose to set additional options, or edit the gradient if desired. All of the previous options and styles are available to modify the gradient. Additionally, you can move the center of the gradient by clicking and dragging inside the **Image** window.

Gradient Map

A frequently underused feature is the **Gradient Map**. The **Gradient Map** adjustment layer or image adjustment maps a new gradient to the grayscale range of an image. A two-color gradient produces a nice duotone effect. Shadows map to one of the color stops of the gradient fill; highlights map to the other. The midtones map to the gradations in between. A multicolored gradient or noise gradient can add interesting colors to an image. This is an effective technique for colorizing textures or photos for a background. I recommend using the **Gradient Map** from the **Adjustment Layers** menu, because it will provide the necessary flexibility to tweak your look.

To modify the **Gradient Map**, access the **Gradient Editor** and adjust the previously mentioned options. Remember, **Dither** adds random noise, which can smooth the appearance of the gradient fill, thus reducing banding.

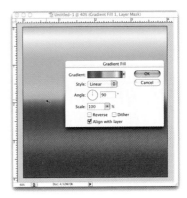

Double-clicking on the adjustment layer's icon launches the gradient controls. You can then click and drag within the window to reposition the gradient.

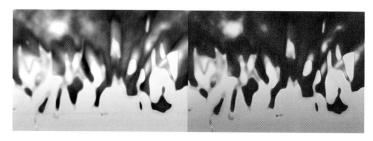

The **Gradient Map** adjustment layer is fast and flexible. You can also change the adjustment layer's blending mode to extend the effect's possibilities.

Working with Photo Sources

A background made from footage of candle flames and a map from the Hemera Photo Objects collection. The type was also done in Photoshop using layer styles. *(Image courtesy American Diabetes Association)*

One method when using a photographic source involves stripping the chroma out of your photos. I do not recommend switching to grayscale mode on the original source because you may unintentionally save the file and permanently discard your chroma. Instead, add the layer to your composition; then desaturate the layer by pressing Cmd+Shift+U (Ctrl+Shift+U). Stripping the chroma out of a photo is an excellent way to add detail to your background without competing with foreground elements. These desaturated layers can be blended over field of color or gradients to produce nice looks. You could also apply a **Gradient Map** to achieve complex color effects.

To further modify photos into backdrops, experiment with filters. While frequently overused, judicious application of the **Artistic** or **Brush Stroke** filters can simplify a photo to a pleasant image. Combine filters with fading and blending to achieve a modern look.

Sometimes the photo may serve just as a painter's palette. By applying several distortions and filters, it is possible to render a photo unrecognizable. All that is left behind are the dominant colors originally contained in the source. This is an excellent way to generate random color fields to use as backgrounds.

Using Patterned Tiles

These utterly useless patterns are built in Photoshop. Don't let them scare you away. The Artist Surfaces, Rock Patterns, and Texture Fills collection are very useful.

Tiling a pattern or texture is a nice way to fill up space. The key is to make sure the texture size is large enough that the seams are not visible. You can find several collections of patterns available, but the key is to look for seamless ones. Thanks to the folks at AutoFX, I was able to include a sampler of seamless textures on the book's disc. You can find 3,000 textures, as well as hundreds of free fonts at their web site, http://www.autofx.com.

The easiest way to make a tiled background is to use a pattern adjustment layer. The adjustment layer will create a pattern that can be easily resized and adjusted. Let's begin.

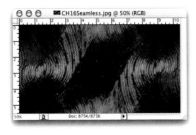

The end result, perfectly tiled and scalable. And at any time, the **Pattern** adjustment layer is editable.

Step 1 Open the file *Ch10Seamless.jpg* in this chapter's folder or any other seamless texture.

Step 1 Select the entire object by pressing Cmd+A (Ctrl+A).

Step 2 Define the pattern and name it (Edit>Define Pattern). The pattern is now temporarily stored in your **Preferences** file.

Step 3 Create or open a safe-title document sized for your edit system.

Step 4 From the **Adjustment Layer** menu on the **Layers** palette, choose **Pattern**. The last-added pattern will automatically be selected. Adjust the scaling of the pattern, but do not exceed 100%, or the pattern will soften.

Step 5 To save the pattern, click on the dropdown arrow, then the triangular submenu icon. Select **Save Patterns** and give it a unique name, adding .pat at the end to inform Photoshop that this is a pattern library. All of the visible presets in the window will be stored into this library. The best place to store them is inside your *Presets* folder (Application Folder> Presets>Patterns). This way, they will appear in the submenu for faster loading.

If you change the size of your document, the pattern will automatically expand or contract to fill the work area.

You'll also find a huge collection of seamless textures on this book's disc provided by the generous folks at AutoFX Software (http:// www.autofx.com).

Creating Patterns from Photos

If you have a photo that you'd like to turn into a seamless background, there are two key techniques: Offset (with cloning) and the **Pattern Maker** filter introduced in version 7. If you are scanning the photo, scan it at a higher resolution so you have plenty of pixels to work with. Tiled patterns look best when the tiles have fewer repetitions.

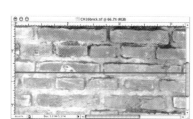

The original image.

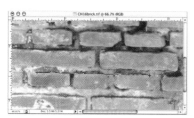

Use the **Measure Tool** to determine if the image needs to be rotated into alignment.

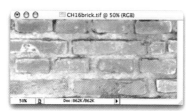

The cropped image.

Offset and Clone

The "original" method of creating seamless patterns involves the Offset filter. By shifting an image, the seams become clearly visible. You can then employ the **Clone Stamp** or **Healing Brush** to smooth out the edges.

Step 1 Open the file *CH10brick.tif* to try out this technique.

Step 2 The brick photo contains several repeating patterns. However, the photo is slightly misaligned, which will cause problems. If you have horizontal or vertical lines, check alignment using guides.

- You need to determine the specific misalignment. Select the **Measure** Tool; it is in the same well as the **Eyedropper** Tools. (To cycle, press Shift+I.)
- Measure along a straight line to determine the misalignment.
- Select Image>Rotate Canvas>Arbitrary. The appropriate measurement is automatically plugged in and will correct misalignment.

Step 3 Crop a small portion of the tile. Try to get some of the mortar along the edges as shown. This will make a more natural tile.

Step 4 Choose Filter>Other>Offset to push the image over. Be certain to select the **Wrap Around** option. This step will show the seams that must be removed to create a tile.

Step 5 Erase the seams using a combination of the **Clone Stamp**, **Healing Brush**, **Smudge**, and **Blur** Tools. Remember to clone from several parts of the image to avoid "twins" syndrome.

Step 6 Select All and choose Edit>Define Pattern. You can now use the pattern as a seamless tile.

Step 7 To use a seamless tile, add a pattern adjustment layer.

Be sure to save your custom patterns to your *Presets* folder. The **Save** menu can be accessed from the Pattern palette's submenu.

You can move the pattern at any time to tweak the fill. Highlight the adjustment layer, and then click in the composition's window and drag. Open the file *Ch10Wall.psd* to see the results.

After cloning the seams, the tile is ready.

Pattern Maker

The **Pattern Maker** can be found under the filter menu. It can be used to generate tiling patterns. These patterns do not often match their initial source; the pixels are "scrambled" to generate a seamless tile. Because the pattern is based on the pixels in a sample, it shares visual characteristics with the original image. This filter works well for small patterns, but not on large objects. The **Pattern Maker** command is available only for 8-bit images. Let's explore this useful filter.

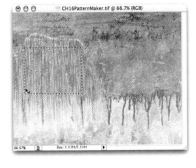

Step 1   Open the file *CH10PatternMaker.tif*.

Step 2   Size the image for your video editing system by cropping or using the **Image Size** command.

Step 3   The layer you make the selection from will be replaced by the generated pattern. It is a good idea to copy the layer by pressing Cmd+J (Ctrl+J).

Step 4   Make a selection with the rectangular **Marquee** Tool around the area you want to use as the basis for the tile.

Step 5   Choose Filter>Pattern Maker.

Depending on your source, you may need to increase the Smoothness and Sample Detail to a higher value. If the pixels in the sample lack contrast, increase the Smoothness value to decrease edges. If the sample contains details that are being chopped up, increase the Sample Detail value. Increasing the Smoothness and Sample Detail increases render time.

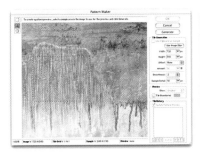
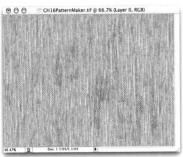

 Increasing the Sample Detail and Smoothness improves the appearance, but significantly increases render time.

Step 6   Tell the **Pattern Maker** that you want to generate a full-size tile by clicking on the Use Image Size button. This produces the best results as the pattern is sized to fill the whole layer.

Step 7   Click **Generate Again** to create additional patterns. You can use the same options, or make adjustments and click **Generate Again**. You can flip back through all generated tiles using the Tile History panel.

Step 8   When you're happy with the preview, click **OK**.

Softening the Background

Be sure to hold down the Option (Alt) key when choosing Merged Link. This will preserve your layers.

Getting the right balance between focus and detail will require some experimentation. To produce a natural defocused effect, you can harness the powerful **Gaussian Blur** filter. Unfortunately, there is no Gaussian Blur of Focus adjustment layer. Normally this would require you to flatten the layered background, or make a copy and flatten it. This is inefficient, because it requires backing up and managing multiple files.

A better option to soften the background is targeted flattening, first introduced in Chapter 4 (page 80) as an alpha channel solution. The technique is relatively simple, but it opens up several new design options.

Step 1   For this technique to work, all layers must be floating. The bottom layer is likely named *Background* and is technically not a layer yet. Option (Alt)+double-click to float the layer.

Step 2   Select the top-most layer by pressing Option+Shift+] (Alt+Shift+]).

Step 3   Create a new layer by pressing Shift+Cmd+N (Shift+Ctrl+N).

Step 4   Link all of the visible layers in your composition to the top layer. Leave the top layer highlighted as the active layer.

Step 5   Hold down the Option key (Alt) and select **Merge Linked** from the layer palette's submenu. All layers will be flattened to the target layer.

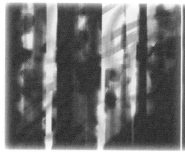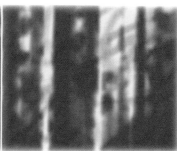

The softened background will make a better backdrop for foreground elements. Use blurred copies and blending modes for new looks.

Step 6   You can now defocus this layer by using one of the natural blurs such as **Gaussian Blur** or **Motion Blur**.

This technique has many other implications, especially when blending multiple copies of layers together. Try targeted flattening periodically while building a composition. Apply assorted filters, such as **Radial Blur** (Zoom) to these intermediary copies, and then adjust blending modes. Several new techniques can be developed.

Some Recipes

To get you started, 23 backgrounds created entirely within Photoshop are included. The first 11 were created using built-in filters. The second group was created using various third-party filter packages (demo versions of most can be found on the book's disc). Instead of eating up page space printing long lists, I've captured these backgrounds as actions.

You'll find an *Actions* file on the DVD for all of these backgrounds. Feel free to modify these backgrounds and use them in your projects.

Step 1 To load a set of actions, call up the **Actions** palette.

Step 2 Go to the palette's submenu and choose Load Actions.

Step 3 Navigate to the *CH10.atn* file in this chapter's folder. You can view all of the steps used by flipping down all of the triangles in the palette. You can also use these actions to quickly create the featured backgrounds (the first 11 will always work; the second 12 will require you to install/purchase specialized filters.)

Keep it Legal! Be sure to check the **Levels** on your image. Several of these backgrounds use filters set to generate random results (and colors). Additionally, your modifications to the Adjustment Layers may push them past broadcast safe. Always check your **Levels** as a last step, setting your output levels to 16 for the black point and 235 for the white point.

Step 4 To view the individual steps in an action, change the action's playback speed. From the **Actions** palette submenu, choose Playback Options>Pause for (X) seconds. You can now see the action playback one step at a time.

Remember, there is no exact science to these backgrounds, just some controlled experimentation and a little bit of luck. By employing the **Actions** palette, you can capture these experiments for later use. For more on Actions, see Chapter 11, "Automation."

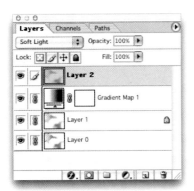

Intermediate layers are preserved so that you can further modify the new background. Change the blending modes, add adjustment layers… automatic is good, but flexible is better.

You can see the recipe by flipping down the action. Feel free to modify these to create more automatic backgrounds.

Water

Bubble Wrap

Nebula

Microbes

Swirls

Curtain

Interference

InSphere

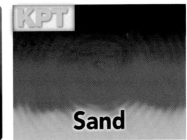

Sand

Stained Glass

Velvet

Whorl

Profile: Kevin Oleksy

Kevin Oleksy is an experienced video pro working for the U.S. Government. He produces re-enactments, documentaries, training pieces, and live satellite talk shows.

"I've been in video production for about 15 years. I've spent time in news as a cameraman, reporter, anchor, producer, technical director, and director. The majority of my career I've spent time in postproduction, doing military, corporate, and commercial editing and finishing," said Oleksy. "I was first introduced to the Avid back in the 5.0 days when you had the edit monitor doubling as the client monitor on an AMP (Avid Media Processor) system."

Oleksy soon discovered the power of Photoshop to enhance his video projects. He started with Photoshop version 4 and has been a huge fan since. Photoshop also helped him expand into After Effects as well.

"When I worked for the military, I mainly used Photoshop for Over-The-Shoulder graphics within the nightly newscast and the week in review. I would take still shots that highlighted the story and create a layered and keyable graphic that I could either fly in layer-by-layer live or import into the Avid for post work," said Oleksy. "I continue to use Photoshop to make mattes and backgrounds as well as titling. I do all of my titling in Photoshop. The flexibility and power for titles are awesome."

Oleksy thinks that Photoshop is the perfect companion application for any NLE package. He says it has become a required skill for editors to know.

"Learning Photoshop is crucial in the video world. The flexibility and versatility it provides allow you to create more visually appealing productions. NLEs are great for editing, but their titling, masking, and background abilities are often limited and weak."

To learn and keep his skills sharp, Oleksy takes every opportunity to attend training sessions and conferences. He's a firm believer in pushing himself to learn more.

"No matter how far you get, there's always somewhere further to get to. You can never say, 'I have enough knowledge to be the best that I can.' Take every opportunity to attend training and trade shows. Also, watch what others are doing and try to build on that. Nobody is the be-all, know-all editing or graphics god. Some of the best ideas spawn from something done before that triggered an idea. So, yeah, steal an idea, but build on it to make it better."

Automation

Automation is fast, easy, and surprisingly fun. Selecting the right automation tool depends on your situation:

- Actions offer the ability to generate extremely complex results.
- Batch processing allows you to run an action on an entire folder of images.
- Droplets place the convenience of Photoshop actions into a drag-and-drop utility on your desktop.
- The final category, **Automate** commands, performs complex tasks with minimal efforts.

Customize your keyboard! Photoshop actions can be mapped to the keyboard, giving you up to 60 customizable keys by using the F keys and modifiers.

Actions

Virtually every command (and better yet, series of commands) can be captured and played back later. Basic actions will play back one command, such as a resize command or image mode change. In fact, these simple actions often can take advantage of your empty function keys on the keyboard. By combining the **Shift** and **Option** (Alt) key modifiers, a standard keyboard has 48–60 customizable keys.

Call up the Actions palette (Window>Actions). Go to the palette's submenu and make sure that the Button mode is not checked. One of the first things you'll notice is a familiar interface. This is one tool that is clearly video influenced: the **Stop**, **Record**, and **Play** buttons function like their video counterparts. The other three buttons appear similar to those found in other palettes. The **Folder** icon creates sets; a set holds individual actions just as bins hold clips. The **Page** icon creates a new (empty) action. The **Trash** icon performs the obvious role of deleting items.

The key to speed in Photoshop: Actions. These macros are easy to program and generate incredible results. Take the time to learn Actions; it will pay off.

To get started, let's work with one of Photoshop's built-in collections. Go to the Actions palette submenu and choose *Textures.atn*. (This file should have been loaded when you installed Photoshop.) Any actions stored inside of the *Presets* folder will appear in the submenu's list (Application Folder>Presets>Photoshop Actions). These texture actions are not specifically designed for video, although you may find them useful for creating texture layers.

Actions are very literal. If you click on a layer, the action records the name of the layer selected. Use keyboard shortcuts wherever possible so that your action will work on other documents.

Open or create a video-sized frame. Then click on the Obsidian action and press **Play**. Photoshop quickly creates a realistic texture by combining several built-in filters and adjustment techniques.

Next, try the Rusted Metal option. Highlight the name and press **Play**.

Depending on your processor speed, Photoshop should have finished rendering about...now. I hope you are impressed. Flip down the triangles in the Actions palette and look at how elaborate some actions are. You may be thinking that these are somewhat interesting, but surely they will get old quickly.

The built-in Rusted Metal action can be useful for text effects or backgrounds.

Enable Dialog Boxes for future variations.

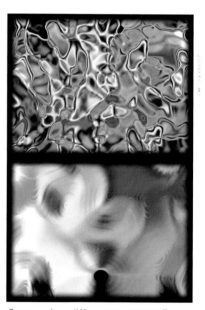

Same action, different outcomes. Turn on the Dialog Boxes for new results.

Turning on **Dialog Boxes** allows you to interact more with an action. In fact, it can open up hundreds of new possibilities.

This is not the case. Modifying actions is simple. The easiest way is to turn **Dialog Boxes** on. Normally, an action will play all the way through, using the original values assigned to the filters or image adjustments. By clicking in the column next to the name (the empty space next to the checkmark), you can enable dialog boxes for a filter or adjustment. These dialog boxes let you enter variables and influence an action's outcomes.

To try this out, turn on **Dialog Boxes** for the Rippled Oil action. You can click through the first few options about naming layers. Try different inputs for the **Clouds**, **Chrome**, **Gaussian Blur**, and **Unsharp Mask** filters. By modifying these actions, several different outcomes are possible. Flip down the triangle next to the action's name, and you will see the list of steps. It is possible to turn on only some of the dialog boxes by clicking next to the specific step.

The Best Things Are Free

A sample of Photoshop's built-in Image Effects Actions

If you are excited by the little you've seen so far, keep reading. We have only scratched the surface. Actions open up all sorts of options, both for creative and technical outcomes.

Where to Find Actions That Help the Video Editor

Entire Web sites and commercial products have been developed that significantly extend Photoshop's ability as a video tool. The accompanying DVD includes samples of some of these products.

The *Tools for Television* package (http://www.toolsfortelevision.com) builds safe title documents for every format, resizes square pixel documents, and helps build alpha channels.

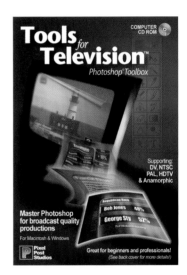

The first package of actions ever released commercially was originally called Neal's Efex!. These have since been refined into two packages called nik Efex! And nik Type Efex! The first package offers a set of image effects that can completely change the look of a photo, add interesting edge effects, and produce stylized type. The second package is all about type.

One source that has both free and for-sale actions is the diverse Web site, ActionFX (http://www.actionfx.com) Members have access to thousands of Photoshop actions, as well as other add-ons. You'll find free items to try out before joining.

If you're not in a position to purchase add-ons to your system, there's one incredible free resource worth mentioning. With the release of Photoshop 5.5, Adobe launched a Web site originally called Action Xchange where users could share their actions; see http://www.adobexchange.com.

Need to flatten your layer styles with a push of a button? Create the following action and map it to your keyboard. Highlight the styled layer; then record the following action.

Step 1   Create a new layer named Flattened. (It will be created by default right above selected layer.)

Step 2   Press Option+[(Alt+[) to select the layer below to be flattened.

Step 3   Link to the layer named Flattened.

Step 4   Choose merge linked from the palette's submenu.

Press STOP. (You can choose Option (Alt)+Merge Linked instead for targeted flattening).

Thanks to Todd Siechen at www.realeyz.com for the co-development.

If you download actions from a Web site, they are probably compressed. The files should have the extension .atn after them, so Photoshop knows that they are actions.

When you successfully download actions (or create your own), you will want to store them in two places. If you install them into your *Presets* folder (Photoshop Application>Presets>Photoshop Actions), they will be available from the Actions palette submenu. Storing them in your *Presets* folder is convenient, but if you have to reinstall Photoshop, it will erase the Photoshop Actions and replace them with the defaults. Therefore, back up a copy of your actions to another location so that you can quickly load them in after future upgrades.

Creating and saving actions

Actions can be assigned to F-keys for easy access.

Throughout this book, I've offered several keyboard shortcuts (and there is more in Appendix A). Many of them will be useful, but I have no doubt that you've wished for more. Wouldn't it be nice to have a convert to RGB mode button, or a de-interlace button, or, better yet, a create safe-title area button? But Photoshop doesn't have a mappable keyboard, right? Wrong. You've got 15 function keys and three modifier keys, for a total of 60 keys that you can customize.

StuffIt Expander™ gives you free access to virtually any file on the Internet.

Mapping your keyboard involves a few steps. First, you must create a set to hold your actions. Sets hold actions, and there's no limit to how many actions in a set, or how many sets you can load. For example, you could create a set with 60 actions mapped to the F Keys. You could have another set mapped to the same keys and simply swap it out. The possibilities are endless. Let's try it out.

Step 1   Open an image.

Step 2   Call up the **Actions** palette and click on the **Folder** icon.

Step 3 Name the set, making sure to add the extension .atn at the end.

Step 4 Click on the new Action icon.

Step 5 Name the action and assign it to F2. If you want, you can also assign a color to the action. Colors help identify actions when you are in the simplified **Button** mode.

Step 6 Under the **Filter** menu, choose the De-Interlace filter (Filter>Video>De-Interlace).

Step 7 Click Stop. Congratulations! You've just made Photoshop faster and more video-friendly.

Step 8 Now save your work. Click on the action set (not the individual action, the entire set). Go to the **Actions** palette submenu and choose Save Actions. By default, the Photoshop *Actions* folder will be chosen. If it isn't, search for it.

Repeat these steps as needed. Virtually every menu command or button can be recorded (although manual items from the **Tools** palette do not record properly). Actions can be duplicated, modified, and deleted. Explore all of the options in the **Actions** palette submenu, look at other people's actions, and experiment by creating your own actions. With a little practice and imagination, you'll be amazed at what you can accomplish.

 Want to add a safe-title overlay to your open document? Record the following action:

Step 1 Create a New Layer.

Step 2 Select All.

Step 3 Choose Select>Transform Selection; specify 90% in the **Options** bar.

Step 4 Press return.

Step 5 Load a Red swatch.

Step 6 Choose Edit>Stroke and specify 5 pixels centered. This is the action safe area.

Step 7 Select All.

Step 8 Choose Select>Transform Selection; specify 80% in the **Options** bar.

Step 9 Press return.

Step 10 Choose Edit>Stroke and specify 5 pixels centered. This is the title safe area.

Press STOP.

General tips for better actions

The **Actions** palette provides a video-friendly graphic user interface (GUI) for computer programming. Here's some general advice to get results quickly.

Choose layer above	Option+] (Shift+Alt+])
Choose layer below	Option+[(Alt+[)
Choose top layer	Shift+Option+] (Shift+Alt+])
Choose bottom layer	Shift+Option+[(Shift+Alt+[)

You can also arrange layers with shortcuts. These will move the current layer:

Up the layer stack	Cmd+] (Ctrl +])
Down the layer stack	Cmd+[(Ctrl +[)
To the top	Shift+Cmd+] (Shift+Ctrl+])
To the bottom	Shift+Cmd+[(Shift+Ctrl+[)

- Brush strokes, cloning, and most manual tools from the toolbox do not work. There are several alternatives, such as using a **Gradient Fill** layer instead of the **Gradient** tool.
- To play a single step of an action, double-click on it.
- Button mode lets you launch actions quickly; it's in the palette's submenu. You'll need to disable it to get recording and editing features.
- Set the Playback Options from the **Actions** palette submenu to play back an action accelerated. Photoshop can process faster than it can redraw the screen.
- You can batch multiple folders at once. Create aliases or shortcuts within one folder that point to the desired folders. Be sure to click the Include All Subfolders option.
- Back up your custom actions to two folders, the default location and a secondary backup. This way, a reinstall or upgrade won't blow your custom actions away.
- To create an action that will work on all files, you must record some commands with the rulers set to percentage.
- Use File>Automate>Fit Image to resize images for a specific height *or* width.
- Photoshop will record the names of layers as you select them. This may cause playback issues, because the action will look for specific names. Use keyboard shortcuts to select layers and such so that the action won't look for a specific name for that step.

Batch Processing

Photoshop allows you to run actions on an entire folder of images. This can significantly cut down your production time. Use batch processing to convert an entire folder from CMYK to RGB mode. Resize a folder of images, de-interlace a bunch of screen captures, and remove the blue tint from a group of improperly exposed photos. Anything you may need to do to one image, you can do to several.

Step 1 To apply an action to a group of images, place those images into one folder.

Step 2 Make sure the action you want to run is loaded in the **Actions** palette.

Step 3 Choose File>Automate>Batch.

Step 4 Select the desired set and the action.

Step 5 Select the folder to process in the Source area. When you first start out, it's a good idea to work with a duplicate copy so that you don't accidentally erase your images.

- As an alternative, you can choose Import to import images, Opened Files to process all open documents, or the **File Browser** (see the "The Versatile File Browser" on page 206).
- Select **Override Action 'Open' Commands** in order to ignore open commands recorded in the original action.
- Select **Include All Subfolders** to process even nested files in the original folder.
- Select **Suppress Color Profile Warnings** to ignore any profile warnings.

 Batch processing is a great thing for lunch breaks or overnight.

Step 6 Choose a destination folder for the new images from the **Destination** menu. Choose **None** to leave the files open or **Save and Close** to overwrite the original images.

Step 7 Be sure to choose an error processing method: **Stop for Errors** or **Log Errors to File**.

 If you don't want an action to abort when it hits an error, be sure to specify Log Errors to File.

Step 8 Click OK.

Droplets

If you live in a drag-and-drop world, then droplets are for you. A droplet is a Photoshop action conveniently stored as an icon on your desktop. Files or folders can be dragged on top and batch processed. For example, I have created an action and then a droplet that converts an image to RGB mode while preserving layers. I could use this to ensure that all my graphics were in the proper mode for my edit. The important thing to remember is that you can't have a droplet without first having the action you want to put in it.

Save your droplets in a convenient location for drag-and-drop.

Step 1 Choose File>Automate>Create Droplet.

Step 2 Click Choose in the Save Droplet In section of the dialog box. Specify a location to save the droplet where you can get to it easily. Many users set the target as the desktop.

Step 3   Choose the specific set and action from the Set and Action menus. The action you want to use must be currently loaded.

Step 4   Specify Play options for the droplet:

- Override Action "Open" Commands ignores any file names specified in the action.
- Deselect Override Action "Open" Commands if the action is designed to work only on open files or if the action contains Open commands for specific files needed by the action.

Step 5   Decide if you want to include all subfolders to process files in subdirectories of drag-and-drop.

Step 6   Select **Suppress Color Profile Warnings** to ignore color policy messages. These can cause a batch to hang waiting for your input.

Step 7   Specify a destination for the batch-processed files in the Destination menu:

- None leaves the files open without saving changes (unless the action contains a Save command).
- Save and Close rewrites the files to their current location.
- Folder to specify a new location.

Step 8   If Folder is the chosen destination, specify a file-naming convention for the batch-processed files.

Step 9   Specify an error-processing option from the Errors pop-up menu. **Log Errors to File** is generally best for batching. I use a similar approach in my batch digitizing, because this is when I stand up to stretch my legs a bit.

Web Gallery

Use the Web Gallery for dynamic storyboards.

Here's a real-world scenario: Imagine that you're working on a video that needs some stock photos of the healthcare industry. Your clients provided you with a shot list, but they are across town and can't approve things until they come in tomorrow. After searching for the right stock photos, you've narrowed it down to 25 choices, about three per each shot needed. You could: (a) sit on your hands, (b) e-mail the client a bunch of attachments that are likely too big and will get stuck in their corporate firewall, or (c) just go ahead with your gut and redo things later.

Photoshop provides you a fourth option: one of the hugest time savers of all, the **Web Photo Gallery** feature. After a couple of clicks, Photoshop can take an entire folder of images, instantly resize them for the Web, author a preview page complete with thumbnails, and set up the whole site while you take a break. Don't worry; it's perfectly safe and leaves your original files and layers intact. Just think of the time savings. You can e-mail the whole folder to your client or post it to your company's site with a blind link. (The folder is there, but there is no visual link on your Web site's home page; customers access it through a text link you send them.)

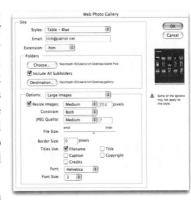

Photoshop gives you several templates to choose from for use in the **Web Photo Gallery** command. If you know HTML, or if you have a web developer on staff, you can use a customized style for pages that feature your company logo and colors.

This automation feature makes it easy to get your images in front of an off-site client. A convenient thumbnail (or lightbox) page links to a much larger preview pane.

Step 1   Choose File>Automate>Web Photo Gallery.

Step 2   Specify the site's appearance:

- Choose a style from the pop-up menu.
- Enter an e-mail or other contact info to be displayed on the page.
- Choose an extension (.htm or .html) for your pages. To determine which one, look at your corporate page. The .htm is more likely these days.

Step 3   Under Folders, specify the image source:

- Choose or Browse to identify the folder that contains the images you need. Don't worry about making copies first, the originals will not be permanently modified.
- Include All Subdirectories if there are folders inside your targeted folder.
- Specify the destination. You cannot save the images into the same folder where they came from because this would cause an endless loop. Specify a final destination.

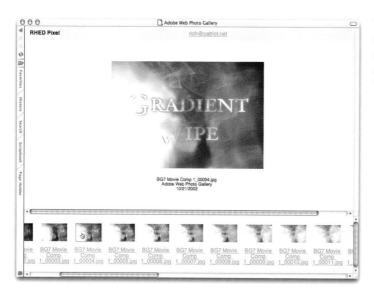

The web browser is an easy way to show your client's animations or storyboards, especially if your client has a slower-speed Internet connection or is traveling.

Step 4   Modify the banner options with the rest of the site information that you want displayed.

- For Site Name, enter the project's name.
- For Photographer, enter your client's name.
- For Contact Info, tell the client whom to call with questions.
- For Date, enter the date that the page was built or modified.
- Specify fonts and font size. Remember, the default web sizes on Mac and PCs differ. Text that looks just right on a Mac will be significantly bigger on a PC.

Step 5   Choose Large Images from the Options pop-up menu and specify how big the display images should be. A higher-quality JPEG will take up more space and take longer to load. A setting of 6–8 is usually sufficient for preview purposes. Be sure to tell Photoshop to display the file name as a caption so that you and your clients are speaking the same language when they call.

Step 6   Next, modify the thumbnails from the **Options** pop-up menu. Choose a size for the thumbnails, and then specify how many columns and rows that you want on each index page (if the style you choose uses index pages).

Step 7   If you want, modify the colors for the page.

Step 8   You can add a watermark over each image (such as Confidential or For Approval Purposes) by choosing Security from the **Options** pop-up menu.

When you run the automation, Photoshop will go into autopilot and begin building the site. In the destination folder, you will find an images subfolder, a thumbnail subfolder, an htm subfolder, and an index page. The index page should be opened in a standard browser to view the preview site (or light box).

Posting animations

Step 1   In After Effects you can change a composition's setting to be 2 frames per second. This technique can also be used as a way to get an animation's storyboard approval. You can render out a PICT or TARGA sequence, then post two or three frames from each second to a thumbnail page.

Step 2   Add the Composition to the render queue.

Step 3   Specify a target folder and output an image sequence.

Step 4   Return to Photoshop and use the **Web Photo Gallery** feature.

Have an animation you want to show, but don't want to deal with codecs and unknown media players? Export the movie as a 2-fps PICT sequence, and then process it as a Web Gallery.

Importing PDF Files

Photoshop has given you the ability to use Portable Document Format (PDF) files two ways. If you choose Place or Open, a dialog box allows you to specify which page, and Photoshop places it like an EPS file or opens it to a new window. If you choose Import PDF Image, a preview box of thumbnails allows you to pick one or all of the images contained in the PDF.

To finalize our control over this flexible format, Photoshop now gives you a third way to access your PDF sources. The final automate command we'll examine is the Multi-Page PDF to PSD command. This action is simple, but very fast.

Step 1   Choose File>Automate>Multi-Page PDF to PSD.

Step 2   Under Source, choose the file you want to import.

Step 3   Under Page Range, specify which pages to import.

Step 4 Under Output Options, specify a resolution and color mode. Be sure to select the Anti-alias option for smoother on-screen appearance.

Step 5 Specify a Destination and a base name for the generated files.

Step 6 Click OK.

New and Improved!
The File Browser (originally developed for Photoshop Elements) is a convenient way to browse and batch process images.

The Versatile File Browser

The **File Browser** can also be thought of as an automation tool. It allows you to browse, organize, and batch process images. You can create new folders; rename items; move, copy, and delete files. One of the most useful features is the ability to rotate a group of images.

Displaying the File Browser. By default, the **File Browser** is docked in the palette well. If it's not visible, choose File>Browse (Shift+Cmd+O/Shift+Ctrl+O) or Window>File Browser. If you want to display the **File Browser** in a separate floating window, choose **Show in Separate Window** from the **File Browser**'s submenu. The submenu contains many other options. You can change the thumbnail sizes, rotate images, and reverse matchframe to the original image location.

Navigating the File Browser. To open a folder, double-click. Large thumbnails of images make it easy to find what you're looking for. You can navigate through a hierarchical view of a folder to view its contents. You can also sort by clicking on the pop-up menu at the bottom of the **File Browser**, offering several different sorting options.

To select a file, click on it. To choose multiple files, hold down the **Shift** key. When you have the desired images selected, press Return/Enter on the keyboard, or double-click. To further prove Photoshop's ability to offer too many ways to do the same thing, you can also choose Open from the palette's submenu or drag the images out of the palette.

You can rotate, delete, and move images from within the **File Browser**.

Viewing file information. There are several pieces of metadata attached to your Photoshop files. Quick access to creation dates, modification dates, resolution, file size, width, height, image menu, and bit depth. Selecting the right image is a lot easier with all of a file's details. This information is available in the lower left corner when you click on an individual thumbnail. The details view option will display this information next to each thumbnail.

Batching items. There are several items you can batch process in the **File Browser**. You can choose **Batch Rename** from the palette's submenu and rename a group of images. You can Shift+click to select a group of images, and then press the Delete key to erase the images. You can also move a group of images from within the file browser. Experienced Photoshop users may tend to overlook this new feature, but it's worth the effort to learn it because it saves a lot of time.

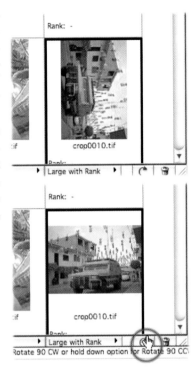

Profile: Glen Stephens

Glen Stephens is an experienced broadcast designer who makes time to actively contribute to the Photoshop community. Stephens is the developer of Tools for Television, a Photoshop add-on that brings many features and actions that are needed for broadcast design. You can also find him co-moderating the Adobe Photoshop and Illustrator forum at Creative Cow (http://www.creativecow.net). He also contributes a monthly column on video graphics to *Photoshop User Magazine* (http://www.photoshopuser.com).

"I've spent many years studying and researching to find resources and techniques that help me as a designer for video," said Stephens. "Because Photoshop users in the video industry are hard to come by, those sharing resources and tips are equally elusive. This is why I do everything I can to make the learning process easier for those eager to expand their skills."

Stephens would not be in a position to offer all of this advice if he were not actively involved in the production community. To get his designs done, Stephens relies heavily on Photoshop.

"Photoshop is my scratch pad and design platform. In most situations, the images for projects, lower thirds, opens, bumpers, and closes are all created or conceptualized in Photoshop. If the client doesn't want or require any animation, then Photoshop is my final output. If motion is needed, then to After Effects I go," said Stephens. "All photographs, scans, digital images, frame grabs, or any clip art that is used in my composites will always get color corrected and stylized in Photoshop before it is used anywhere."

Stephens also uses Photoshop's superior text handling to complement his Final Cut Pro editing system. "Photoshop is my character generator. All of my lower thirds, full-screen images, over-the-shoulder graphics are all created in Photoshop. I am currently working on an application that makes Photoshop a standalone character generator."

Stephens sees a definite need for any video pro to focus on Photoshop. In fact, he sees it as the single most important complement to any video application.

"In my opinion, it is critical to anyone's career. Doesn't matter what industry you are in, Photoshop will be there. Even if it is only a supplemental application for you, learn it," said Stephens. "Many times Photoshop is all you have, and the more you know, the less you will turn to other applications for other tasks. It is the single most powerful image creation/manipulation tool, and failing to learn it is career suicide."

While Photoshop may appear daunting, with hundreds of features and menu items, an organized approach can get you through it. To get you started, Stephens offers some favorite tips.

"Apply a black-to-white gradient map adjustment layer above an oversaturated photo; then set the adjustment layer's transfer mode to pin light. Pulls oversaturated colors down to an acceptable range without affecting other portions of the image."

Stephens also encourages you to try the Tools for Television package. "I may have written and created it, but I use the tools on it every day!" Stephens has included a sampler on the book's DVD-ROM.

While the process of learning may be challenging due to time constraints and workload, Stephens encourages editors and graphic artists to push themselves further. "Take seminars, classes, read, interface with others, and just get in and use Photoshop. Then learn After Effects, Illustrator, Commotion, Final Cut Pro, and any other desktop video/graphic tool you can," said Stephens. "The more you know, the more marketable you will be, and the quicker you can get your work done and surprise your client with fresh ideas and the correct execution of them."

Stephens' Web sites are **www.pixelpoststudios.com** and **www.toolsfortelevision.com**. He is always open to ideas, input and suggestions for products and tools that make graphic design easier and more intuitive. He is also available for training, consulting, and graphic design contracting for a wide variety of broadcast and video projects. You can write Glen at **glen@pixelpoststudios.com** with any questions or suggestions.

The Road to the NLE

If you bought this book, then you must intend for your graphics to end up on video. If you're on a deadline (okay, you're always on a deadline), you may have jumped to this chapter right away. Please go back. In one chapter, it would be impossible to discuss the several issues that make designing video graphics a challenge.

If you've made it through most of the book, then you are likely anxious to see your work on screen, on air, or on tape. I realize that Photoshop can be painful at times. Unlike your NLE, Photoshop is not designed to be a video application exclusively. There are very few safety nets to keep you from choosing a filter/style/image adjustment that will send your graphic reeling into the land of nonbroadcast safe.

What you will find here are several methods to check your work, suggestions on getting your client to buy in and sign off, and some general tips on resizing and deciding upon the right file format. I'll discuss the importance of file extensions and reinforce methods to prepare for future changes (because "approved" only means "for now").

(courtesy of Hemera Photo Objects)

The tips in this chapter come from years of experience. Special thanks to Glen Stephens, creator of Tools for Television, for his insights as well. What you'll find here are strategies for success. Techniques for tiny budgets, as well as those for deeper pockets, are offered. Please go with the best solution you can afford.

Final Testing on an NTSC/PAL Monitor

There's no way around it: you have to test your graphics. If you're building them in the edit suite, this should be easy. But what happens if you're building them for someone else, or you're on the road, or you don't own a vectorscope?

VHS

There is absolutely no replacement for the least common denominator. If they look good on VHS, they will certainly look good on beta or broadcast. Just batch import into an NLE and go straight to VHS. With the right video card, you may be able to go right out of your

Mac or PC. Most video makers hate VHS for its low quality, but it is the final test for all videos.

Video CD

I call this the "less-than-VHS" approach. A Video CD (VCD) uses the MPEG-1 format to store video. The two advantages of VCDs are that they are cheap and that they will play back on most set-top DVD players. There are several different solutions out there for making VCDs, including Roxio's Toast Titanium or Easy CD Creator Platinum.

Step 1   Create a QuickTime movie or MPEG-1 of your graphics.

a) This can be done with free video apps such as iMovie or Windows Movie Maker. Roxio lets you skip these other steps and export directly to VCD from these apps with a plug-in. Be sure to visit their Web site for details and compatibility (http://www.roxio.com).

b) You can also open all the graphics in ImageReady, and export as a QuickTime movie (see the following sidebar, "Video Export from Photoshop?").

Step 2   Launch Toast or Easy CD Creator and choose Video CD from the **Other** menu.

Step 3   Drag the movie in or choose it.

Step 4   Click the Record button.

Step 5   Let the disc verify, and then view it on a DVD player. Some users report better performance using CD-RWs instead of CD-Rs.

DVD-RW/DVD-R

Have a DVD recorder? Chances are it shipped with all the software you need. Most DVD authoring applications will allow you to import full-screen graphics (the proper size is 720×480 nonsquare pixels). Look for a slideshow feature to bring in a folder full of graphics. If not, author a QuickTime movie or MPEG-2 file that contains your graphics.

Most DVD-R drives can also use rewriteable discs. These are an excellent way to check your graphics in a DVD player.

The DVD-RW format is not as widely promoted. Discs cost about three times more than a burn-once disc. These have the benefit of being able to be reused hundreds of times. The DVD-RW discs generally take twice as long to burn, but you are likely only testing a small amount of data. Every DVD-R drive that's shipped with a Mac or a computer with a Pioneer drive inside also writes DVD-RW. I recommend avoiding the DVD+R and DVD+RW formats because the committee that sets standards for DVD does not approve them.

Video Export from Photoshop?

Photoshop has built-in QuickTime creation? Well, sort of. ImageReady is the bundled "web app" that comes with Photoshop. One of the formats it supports is QuickTime. By using it, you can convert your files into a QT movie and transcode to an MPEG-1 file with Toast or Easy CD Creator. These applications will also burn a Video CD that can be played in most set-top DVD players.

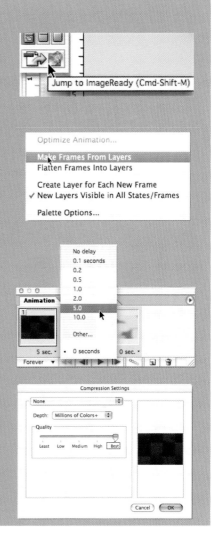

Step 1   Create a single document sized 720×480 and paste each graphic on its own layer. Don't worry about pixel aspect ratio; this is just for a quick test.

Step 2   Send the Document into ImageReady by clicking on the Jump to ImageReady button or by pressing Cmd+Shift+M (Ctrl+Shift+M).

Step 3   Call up the Animation window.

Step 4   From the Animation palette's submenu, choose Make Frames From Layers.

Step 5   Click on the first frame, and then Shift+click on the last frame to select all frames in the Animation palette.

Step 6   Specify duration of 5 seconds per frame by clicking below a frame. The duration should change on each frame if you had them selected.

Step 7   Choose File>Export Original.

Step 8   Name the file and choose **QuickTime Movie** as the output format. Click OK.

Step 9   You now must specify a compressor. None or Animation works well.

Step 10   Launch Toast or Easy CD Creator and follow the steps for creating a Video CD.

High-end video cards

There is no better way to preview your graphics than using a high-end video card and a broadcast monitor. This solution is pricey, but opens up several possibilities. A video card with Serial Digital Interface or component output will allow you to check your graphics. Hands down, this is the best solution, but prepare to dig deep into your pockets. Cards will range between $1,500 and $14,000, depending on the types of inputs and outputs you want. If you already have a non-linear edit system hooked up at your facility, you may just choose to harness its ability to output to video or a scope for testing purposes.

Digital Voodoo manufactures several popular video cards designed for video editors and broadcast designers.

Low-end video cards

Several consumer-oriented video cards have the ability to export Composite and S-Video signals. These cards will often require you to specify which port should be used, meaning you can output to the computer monitor or the video device, but not both simultaneously. Hook these cards up to a consumer television, or better yet a TV/VCR combo set. Set **Photoshop to Full Screen Mode** (press F twice) and remove your palettes (press Tab). You can now output and test your graphics on consumer equipment, which is where your audience will probably see them. These cards do not necessarily scale the video properly and may have interlace issues. There is also a chance that the luminance/chrominance will be off. But if you have to get a second monitor card for dual display, pick one up with an S-Video port for quick previews.

Laptop

Several laptops come with AV or S-Video ports. These are primarily designed so that businesspeople can send presentations out to a TV. Plug in the S-Video cable and check your control panel to enable the port. You may have to restart your machine. If you have enough VRAM, you may be able to drive the main screen and video monitor simultaneously.

FireWire output

If you have a FireWire-based DV camera or a DV converter (bridge), it is very easy to send your graphics out. You can use bundled DV editors such as iMovie or Windows Movie Maker to send a stream out. Adobe After Effects also supports (limited) video output. Go to your Video Preview preferences pane and specify FireWire as the output path. Nearly all DV cameras ship with a converter cable to go from an AV miniplug to RCA plugs. Some cameras even have S-Video ports. For a standalone solution, buy a DV converter from companies such as Canopus or Dazzle.

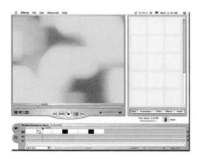

iMovie is an affordable way to send your graphics out over DV.

For more on FireWire output, take a look at the following companies.

Canopus:	http://www.canopus.com
Dazzle:	http://www.dazzle.com
Synthetic Aperture	http://www.synthetic-ap.com

Echo Fire

This affordable product from Synthetic Aperture offers several excellent features for desktop video users. Photoshop and After Effects users have the ability to send their work to a video monitor for immediate previews. With After Effects, this includes full-motion previews with audio. The plug-in works with Mac and PC FireWire devices or several cards from Digital Voodoo, Pinnacle Systems, Aurora, and Media 100.

Echo Fire offers a very flexible solution for video previews, for both Photoshop and After Effects.

Features that come in handy for Photoshop include:
- Video previews in Photoshop by pressing a key or from the Export menu
- Ability to handle 4×3 and 16×9 aspect ratios
- Direct overlays of a waveform monitor, vector scope, and test-pattern displays within Photoshop
- A video-safe color picker
- Proper handling of video interlace and color for accurate previews

You'll find a full-featured demo on this book's disc that will let you try it out for three days. If you like it, be sure to visit Synthetic Aperture's site for a special discount on purchase.

VideoScope

This shareware utility is available only for Macintosh computers (both OS9 and OSX). It is designed to monitor video input; however, it works quite well to check graphics. You can drag and drop a graphic into the viewer monitor and then have access to a software-based waveform and vectorscope. It appears to be as accurate as several NLEs' built-in scopes, but cannot fully replace a hardware-based scope. This application gives you the ability to use a software scope on systems that are not running a full NLE package. For more information, visit http://www.evological.com.

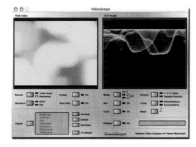

Tools that make life easier (and they're on the book's DVD-ROM)

Test-Pattern Maker. This free Mac utility produces standard video and audio test patterns, including SMPTE, EIA and EBU bars, luma step and ramp patterns, and convergence and overscan tests. It supports NTSC and PAL frame sizes, pixel aspect ratios, black and white levels, and saves in numerous image file formats.

HiQual. This free Macintosh utility sets the high-quality flag in DV-compressed QuickTime movies. This flag only affects playback on the computer, not DV output.

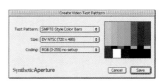

Quickly create test patterns for checking your monitor with TPM from Synthetic Aperture.

Getting Client Approval

Unfortunately, the VHS rule applies here as well. If it looks good on VHS, it'll look good anywhere. Chances are your client has access to a VCR. Always send along a printout of the graphics as well so that the client can mark them up with comments. Adjust the graphics image size to print at 150 dpi (without resampling), and you will get an acceptable image. The Genuine Fractals product from Lizard Tech (http://www.lizardtech.com) can also be used to bump up lo-res graphics to acceptable print qualities.

Photoshop's **Save for Web** feature is the easiest way to prepare web graphics. Be sure to reduce the image size for quicker downloads.

The Internet, however, is proving popular for client approvals. By harnessing Photoshop's **Save for Web** command (File>Save for Web), you can reduce the image to half-screen size and get the file size down to a comfortably portable 10 KB. Be sure to stick with JPEG compression. (A quality setting of 60 is sufficient.) Also resize the image to 50% of its original size and click Apply. The **Save for Web** feature will not alter your original file; all size and layer data is preserved. It also saves the file in the smallest format possible, automatically leaving off features such as image previews and custom icons, which just beef up file size and serve no purpose on the Internet.

Another great web approval method is the Web Photo Gallery (File>Automate>Web Photo Gallery). This automated wizard allows you to instantly build an entire Web site with thumbnail preview pages and larger images to view online. Additional features like contact information and watermarking allow you to quickly get client feedback, while protecting your content online. For more on this great feature, see Chapter 11, "Automation."

For both web options, be sure to explain the concept of title safe to your clients. They may be bothered by "all that extra space." The PowerPoint user in them will rise up and command you to fill every pixel with small, unreadable text. Fight the power!

How to get NLE-specific Information:	
Adobe	http://www.adobe.com/support/main.html
Apple	http://www.info.apple.com/
Avid	http://www.avid.com/support/index.html
Canopus	http://www.canopus.com/US/support/
discreet	http://www.discreet.com/support/
Media 100	http://media100.com/PlatinumSupport.asp
Pinnacle Systems	http://www.pinnaclesys.com/support
Sonic Foundry	http://www.sonicfoundry.com/support/

When to Resize

Every edit system is different, as is every version. You simply must keep up on what your manufacturer recommends for graphics. It would be impossible to keep this chapter 100% current because every NLE has a different upgrade cycle.

Glen Stephens offers the following advice:

"If you work in a DV-only environment, you can get away with working at 720×534, but I always recommend working at 720×540 so that you have the option to go to DV or D1 at any time in the process.

"Resizing the production file is the last step before you go to the NLE. A 720×534 file resizes to 720×480; a 720×540 file resizes for D1 at 720×486. If you designed at 720×540 but need to go to DV, first resize to 720×486, and then crop to 720×480."

If you are working with interlaced material, be sure to crop two lines from the top and four from the bottom using the **Canvas Size** command (Image>Canvas Size). First anchor the bottom edge, and then crop two lines. Repeat the step, but anchor the top edge, and crop four lines. If the material is entirely created in Photoshop (with no interlace issues), just change the canvas size to 480.

How do you find out what size your NLE needs? The best piece of advice I ever received was RTFM (Read The @#$! Manual). Every edit system expects that you will want to import graphics. Photoshop is the #1 choice for that need. Inside of every NLE's manual or the online help section, you will find a section on Photoshop and still graphics. A quick visit to a manufacturer's Web site will often have a PDF available for download as well.

Stephens offers another technique for quickly determining what size is needed:

"If you aren't sure about the NLE requirements, take a still frame from your edit system into Photoshop and check its size. Otherwise, if you are going in DV, it is 720×480; if it is D1 it is 720×486."

But to show I didn't try to dodge this bullet, check out Appendix D, "Working with Other Applications." You'll find guides for several popular NLEs and compositing applications.

Of course, by the time you read this, things may have changed again. I suspect we will see Photoshop's support for nonsquare pixels (just like After Effects) in a future version. This is a moving target that's easy to hit. Always check with your NLE's manufacturer to see what's recommended.

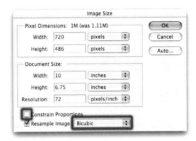

If your NLE requires it, you will "stretch" your images in Photoshop. Be sure the **Constrain Proportions** box is unchecked. Use Bicubic resampling for best results.

Choosing the right file format

You used to have two choices for file formats that NLEs recognized. Macs took PICT files; PCs took TARGA files. That list has gotten significantly longer over the years to include virtually every file format that Photoshop can export. For more on what each format is good for, see the "Glossary" beginning on page 279. Here are five general tips:

1. There's a reason that PICT and TARGA were the first video-friendly formats. Stick with them. Be sure to not add any compression, and use with the maximum bit size.

2. Just because you can import a .psd file doesn't mean you want to. Most NLEs cannot handle blending modes and layer styles. Even After Effects chokes on some items. Be sure to selectively flatten items that don't travel well.

3. Always save your design files. These are essential for future changes. Save a separate version using the **Save A Copy** option (now merged with Save As), which can be accessed by pressing Cmd+Option+S (Ctrl+Alt+S).

4. Be sure to include an alpha channel if you have transparency.

5. Avoid web formats at all costs; these are delivery formats, not authoring formats. The compression artifacts will taint your project.

File Extensions

Repeat after me: "I will always use file extensions." That two- or three-letter code is critical to preserving your file. The extension tells the computer (which is the least intelligent creation ever made) which application created the graphic and what can open it.

Mac users have been historically lazy with extensions, because the Mac OS had written the file type into the header information. This does you no good if the fie is copied to a PC-formatted disc, moves across a PC or UNIX network, travels the Internet, etc. Always use file extensions.

Not seeing your file extensions at all? Windows machines may have these turned off by default. Go to the Folder Options control panel and access the **View** pane. Disable the setting called **Hide Extensions For Known File Types**.

Under OSX, you must access the Finder preferences. Choose Finder>Preferences. To show the extension for all files, choose Preferences from the Finder menu. Check the box for **Always Show File Extensions**.

In our cross-platform world, file extension types are critical (especially for Mac users). Be sure to change your preferences to always append file extensions so that you don't have to memorize a bunch of two- and three-letter codes.

Mac OSX user? You've got to start using file extensions. Your new OS is dependent upon them.

But what are all the file extensions? Don't worry about it; simply tell Photoshop to always use them. In the Preferences menu (location varies depending on OS), access the File Handling options. Tell Photoshop to **Append File Extension Always**, and check the **Use Lower Case** checkbox. Problem solved; you can now work cross-platform.

Preserving Flexibility

While *done* is a four-letter word you like, it frequently leads to several others you may not want your mother to hear. Thanks to nonlinear editing and the Internet, nothing is ever done. It is always subject to tweaks, revisions, and repurposing. If you cut corners in the design and archiving stages, you will regret it later.

Never flatten your Photoshop Design files. Create a second copy for Production purposes, or use the **Save A Copy** feature mentioned earlier. Chances are you archive your source tapes, project files, and EDLs for your video programs, not just the finished master. For the same reasons, you must save your Photoshop layered files.

Thanks to adjustment layers, several of the image adjustments and filters previously used can now be applied to the layered file. Additionally, you can apply effects applied to a layer filled with 50% gray; this can then be blended with layers below it, providing an AE-style adjustment layer. Lastly, use the **Copy Merged** command to **Flatten Visible Layers** to an intermediate copy. This will allow several filter and blend mode combinations. Change the way you work, and it won't be as much work to make changes.

Annotation tools

Annotating a file is a helpful way to insert "sticky notes" for later use. Photoshop offers two annotation options, one for notes and one for audio. The Audio option is a waste of file space, so stick with the **Notes Tool** (N).

What should you put into notes? Information such as fonts or colors used. It may also be helpful to specify which filters were used. Better yet, save an action for the look and include a note identifying it. Video treatments often drive the appearance of web and print collateral materials. Follow the Golden Rule; make it easy for someone else to do their job, and the karma will return to you eventually.

What about clients? If they have Photoshop, they can easily add notes, but most clients don't have (or understand) Photoshop. Save your file in the Portable Document Format (PDF) and ask reviewers to use the full version of Acrobat to add annotations. To bring these into Photoshop, choose File>Import>Annotations and identify the PDF file.

Archiving your work

Storage-media prices have fallen to incredible levels. A DVD-R disc can hold 4.5 GB and is priced less than $5 per disc. Don't need that much room? CD-R discs have fallen in price to the point where you can find spindles on sale that end up being free after rebate. You have no economic reason not to save your work.

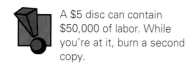 A $5 disc can contain $50,000 of labor. While you're at it, burn a second copy.

I keep a binder with project files burned to CD-R and DVD-R. This proves invaluable for future projects for clients and for revisions. (Don't ever believe that "It's done" actually means something.) To make sure I wasn't compulsive, however, I asked Glen Stephens about his backup strategy.

"You should back up not only all the Photoshop files, production and design, but also all fonts, original artwork, Illustrator logos, animations, and After Effects files. *Everything!*" said Stephens. "Make two copies at least of the project files, because the client almost always comes back and asks for one."

Several designers and companies I have worked with are nervous about giving clients all of the assets for a project. If you have a good relationship with the customer, you should at least be comfortable handing over your production files. If you are concerned about getting paid, hold onto things until the checks come in. Clients come back because of your creativity and level of service, not the fact that you hold their project's assets hostage.

Profile: Michael H. Amundson

Michael Amundson studied film at The University of Iowa and soon found himself a freelancer in film production. He worked as First Assistant Camera on 16mm and 35mm shoots, camera operator on 16mm and video shoots, and other jobs ranging from dolly grip to sound recordist. He then went to work for a production company, where he became an Avid editor, making commercials, videos, and interactive media. Amundson then pulled up roots and moved across the country to Boston, MA.

"I am an editor for the PBS TV show *Frontline*, the only regularly scheduled long-form public-affairs documentary series on American television. My duties include online and offline editing of the films and promos," said Amundson. "I do design work for the open titles and credits, promo end pages, and graphics. I occasionally design and update packaging elements."

To create these numerous graphics, Amundson frequently relies on Adobe Photoshop. He always uses Photoshop to prepare photographs and other scanned elements for use in the documentaries. Amundson says that Photoshop is "indispensable" to the broadcast TV business. "Photoshop is great for retouching problem photos to eliminate scratches or distracting elements in the image," said Amundson. "I also create graphic elements such as main titles and credits in Photoshop, then animate or effect them in After Effects. Photoshop support is integrated perfectly in After Effects, making the work very easy and more creative. I then render a QuickTime movie with After Effects to be imported into our finishing system, an Avid Symphony." Amundson says Photoshop's accessible and affordable toolset is a perfect complement to an NLE suite. "Our online system has excellent color correction and scratch-removal tools, so I don't use Photoshop as much as I used to for that," said Amundson. "However, not everyone has access to expensive broadcast tools, and Photoshop can accomplish many of these tasks at a great price." Amundson offers two pieces of advice for nonlinear editors.

- Rely on the **History** palette. "I use the **History** palette to undo my screw-ups, which are many."

- Remember the need for collaboration. "Being in tune with the people in your edit suite is half of the editing process."

Keyboard Commands and Shortcuts

 Keyboard shortcuts are the secret to unlocking Photoshop's speed. More than any NLE, Photoshop relies on key combos to get complex tasks done quickly.

Overlooked Commands

Command:	Shortcut:
File Menu	
Close All	Cmd+Option+W (Ctrl+Alt+W)
Save As	Choose from 18 formats (more through special plug-ins). Photoshop is the ultimate graphic converter. Shift+Cmd+S (Shift+Ctrl+S)
Save for Web	It doesn't get any more intuitive. Choose the two-up window, resize and compress your image for the web or e-mail. Now you can safely send the client an approval copy without having to worry about messing up your original. Shift+Option+Cmd+S (Shift+Alt+Ctrl+S)
Place	Can't open it? Try placing it. This is how you can bring in EPS, AI, or PDF files. It allows you to position and scale an image (via a bounding box). When you click OK, Photoshop will rasterize it at the proper size, position, and resolution.
Automate Submenu	These are some of the most useful tools for preparing client comps. Whether for print, web, or e-mail, the **Automate** options take boring tasks and make them quick and easy. Think of this menu as Photoshop's batch rendering option. (Think of batch rendering as the only chance you may get for caffeine, nicotine, or vending machine—the vices for an editor.) To learn more, see Chapter 11, "Automation."

Overlooked Commands (continued)

Command:	Shortcut:
Edit Menu	
Step Forward and Step Backward	Multiple undos. See Chapter 6, "A Sense of History." The keyboard shortcut varies based on your user-specified preferences in the General Preferences tab.
Fade	Not happy with the results of a filter or an adjustment? Choose this immediately after running the filter. By the way, did I mention this adds blending modes to _all_ filters? Your filter collection just grew 2100%. Try it now! Give your filters new life! Remember: you must choose this immediately after running a filter. This is quite possibly Photoshop's most underused feature. (Shift+Cmd+F/Shift+Ctrl+F)
Copy Merged	Copy multiple layers into one layer on your clipboard. Why flatten unnecessarily? (Shift+Cmd+C/Shift+Ctrl+C)
Check Spelling, Find and Replace Text	We asked; Adobe listened. In my opinion, worth the upgrade price alone. (Literally, because spelling errors are generally nonbillable).
Free Transform	This tool does it all. Access every layer transformation by **Ctrl**+clicking (right-clicking) while in free transform mode. Cut downs on image degradation by applying all your sizing, warping, and perspective changes at once. Cmd+T (Ctrl+T)
Purge	Free up space by deleting undos, clipboards, history! This will enable you to save and close when you get the dreaded "Scratch Disks Are Full" message.
Layer Menu	
Group and Ungroup	Similar to using a track matte. Apply a layer to its downstairs neighbor, but only in areas where there is opacity. This is often used to constrain a fill layer to a lower text layer for a Paste Into effect. It is also used internally by many layer styles to create proper clipping for bevel effects. Group: Cmd+G (Ctrl+G) Ungroup: Cmd+Shift+G (Ctrl+Shift+G)
Arrange Layers	You can move layers around from the keyboard.
Bring to Front	Cmd+Shift+[(Ctrl+Shift+[)
Bring Forward	Cmd+[(Ctrl+[)
Send Backward	Cmd+] (Ctrl+])
Send to Back	Cmd+Shift+] (Ctrl+Shift+])
Align Linked and Distribute Linked	Because your eyes aren't that good. Link the layers together and access these controls from the menu (or use the Move tool and Options bar for a graphical interface). Want something centered on the screen? Link to the background layer and highlight it. The highlighted layer is the basis for all centering and distribution.

Overlooked Commands (continued)

Command:	Shortcut:

Select Menu

Reselect	Brings back the last selection made, even if it was a long time ago. (Shift+Cmd+D/Shift+Ctl+D)
Feather	Proper feathering is the difference between good glows and shadows and bad ones. It is also a critical step when creating masks and alpha channels. Use this method to feather *after* you have made a selection. Several tools have their own feathering which can be applied from the Options bar. Cmd+Option+D (Ctrl+Alt+D)
Select Color Range	This tool uses an interface similar to After Effects Linear Color Key effect. Use the **Eyedropper** to click on the color you want to select, then add or subtract with the **Plus** and **Minus Eyedroppers**. You can smooth your selection out using the **Fuzziness** slider. This powerful selection tool does not get enough use.

View Menu

Zoom In	Cmd++ (Ctrl++)
Zoom Out	Cmd+– (Ctrl+–)
Fit On Screen	Cmd+0 (Ctrl+0)
Show Actual Pixels	Cmd+Option+0 (Ctrl+Alt+0)
Show	Hide selections and guides. Very useful to see your work and nothing else. By the way, slices are for the web. If you see annoying white numbers in the corner of your document, you've turned slices on accidentally (by selecting the Slice tool, for example). Get rid of them by accessing View>Show>Slices and unchecking it. To hide all, press Cmd+H (Ctrl+H)
Snap	Use those guides for something useful. Objects will snap to position as you drag them near a guide. (Shift+Cmd+;/Shift+Ctrl+;)
New Guide	A more precise way to add guides to your project. Choose View>New Guide and specify an exact location.

Window Menu

Cycle through open windows	Ctrl+Tab
Hide Tools	Tab
Steal Attributes for New Image Size or Canvas Size	This one is tricky. By default, Photoshop offers to make a new document from the size of the image on your clipboard. You can choose from more options, however. First, make a new window. Before clicking OK for the size, access the Window menu. You can now select from any open document in the list.

Overlooked Commands (continued)

Command: **Shortcut:**

Help Menu

There is no shame in using the Help menu. It's all there (at least the dryly written official answer). The Help menu allows you to keep the users manual in a quick access format (it uses a standard web browser).

System Info	You'll need this when calling tech support. It's also a great way to call up a list of all your filters so that you can check on manufacturer's web sites for updates.
Adobe Online	Get updates and news on your favorite products. You can access software updates directly.

Full Screen Modes

One picture at a time, please! Cutting down on clutter can be tough with all of Photoshop's floating palettes and open windows. Fortunately, there are two full-screen modes that help you isolate your active window. You can cycle through these by pressing the F key. If you'd like to apply a full-screen mode to all open documents, Shift+click on the corresponding icon.

Full Screen Mode With Menu Bar	This mode puts you into a windows-like environment where the active window blocks the others out. The area outside your image is filled with gray, and scroll bars disappear. You can cycle to other windows by pressing Ctrl+Tab or selecting the item from the Window menu.
Full Screen Mode	This mode blacks out the background and loses the menu bars. To complement this environment, press the Tab key to hide all of your palettes, and press Cmd+0 (Ctrl+0) to zoom your image to full screen. This mode works well for reviewing and approving images. The Ctrl+Tab shortcut will work here as well to cycle through open windows.

Shortcuts

There are many valuable shortcuts when it comes to layers. Think of the **Layers** palette as your timeline, and you will grasp the importance of mastering these. And remember, you can activate multiple visibility and link switches by clicking on one then dragging through the other layers in the palette.

Layer Shortcuts

Command:	Shortcut:
Load a Layer	Cmd+click (Ctrl+click) on layer icon
Add to Loaded Layer selection	Shift+Cmd+click (Shift+Ctrl+click) on other layer icons
Subtract to Loaded Layer selection	Cmd+Option+click on other layer icons Ctrl+Alt+click on other layer icons
Activate Layers palette	F7
New Layer	Cmd+Shift+N (Ctrl+Shift+N) or Click on New Layer button
New Layer via Copy	Cmd+J (Ctrl+J)(must have item selected)
New Layer via Cut	Cmd+Shift+J (Ctrl+Shift+J) (must have item selected)
Duplicate Layer	Cmd+J (Ctrl+J) or Drag Layer to the New Layer Button
Delete a Layer	Click Delete Layer Button or Drag Layer to the Delete Layer Button
Delete Multiple Layers	**Step 1** Link them together. **Step 2** Cmd+click (Ctrl+click) on the Trash icon in the Layers palette.
Solo a Layer	Option+click (Alt+click)on Eye icon
Activate Next Visible Layer	Option+] (Alt +])
Activate Previous Visible Layer	Option+[Alt+[)
Activate Top Layer	Option+Shift +] (Alt+Shift +])
Activate Bottom Layer	Option+Shift+[(Alt+Shift+[)
Move a Layer Up One Position	Cmd+] (Ctrl +])
Move a Layer Down One Position	Cmd+[(Ctrl +[)
Move a Layer to Top	Cmd+Shift +] (Ctrl+Shift +])
Move a Layer to Bottom	Cmd+Shift+[(Ctrl+Shift +[)

Layer Shortcuts (continued)

Command:	Shortcut:
Change Opacity by 10% increments	Type a single number (i.e., 3 = 30%)
Change Opacity by 1% increments	Type two numbers quickly (i.e., 67 = 67%)
Cycle through Blend Modes	(must have tool selected *without* blending modes)
Cycle to Next Blend Mode	Shift++ (plus)
Cycle to Previous Blend Mode	Shift+– (minus)
Convert a Background Layer	Double-click on icon and rename
Group Layer	Option+G (Alt+G) Option+click (Alt+click) between layers
Ungroup Layer	Cmd+Shift+G (Ctrl+Shift+G) Option+click (Alt+click) between layers
Merge Active layer Down	Cmd+E (Ctrl+E)
Merge to Target Layer	Link desired layers to target, choose **Merge Linked** from submenu of **Layers** palette
Merge to Target and Preserve Layers	**Step 1** Create new target layer. **Step 2** Link desired layers to new target. **Step 3** Hold down Option (Alt) key and choose Merge Linked from submenu of Layers palette.
Toggle Layer Mask Off/On	Shift+click on Layer Mask thumbnail
Toggle Layer Mask and composite	Option+click (Alt+click) on Layer Mask thumbnail
Turn on alpha channel	\ (toggles rubylith mask off/on)
Make Layer Active	Cmd+~ (Ctrl+~) Click on layer thumbnail
Modify Layer Mask View	Double-click on Layer Mask icon

NOTE: Holding down the **Shift** key while changing a type layer's attributes in the **Character** or **Paragraph** palette will change the same attribute on all linked layers.

Type Shortcuts

Command:	Shortcut:
Enter Edit Mode	Double-click on T icon in layer palette
Reposition Type without exiting	Hold down Cmd (Ctrl) and move with mouse
Toggle Eyedropper	Option (Alt)
Select a Word	Double-click on word
Select a Line	Triple-click on word
Select a Paragraph	Quadruple-click on word
Select All	Cmd+A (Ctrl+A)
Cycle through fonts	Click in **Type** field in **Options** bar and use up and down arrows to select font
Adjust point size	Click in **Point Size** field in **Options** bar and use up and down arrows to adjust size
Adjust point size of selection	Cmd+Shift+< or > Ctrl+Shift+< or >
Hide "reversed out" selection	Cmd+H (Ctrl+H)
Create new type layer	Shift+click with **Type** tool to create a new type layer (if you're close to another type block)
Toggle Hyphenation	Cmd+Option+Shift+H (Ctrl+Alt+Shift+H)

Kerning Shortcuts (place cursor between characters)

Increase by 2/100 Em Space	Option+right arrow (Alt+right arrow)
Decrease by 2/100 Em Space	Option+left arrow (Alt+left arrow)
Increase by 10/100 Em Space	Cmd+Option+right arrow (Ctrl+Alt+right arrow)
Decrease by 10/100 Em Space	Cmd+Option+left arrow (Ctrl+Alt+left arrow)

Leading Adjustment Shortcuts (must highlight text)

Increase by 2 points	Option+down arrow (Alt+down arrow)
Decrease by 2 points	Option+up arrow (Alt+up arrow)
Increase by 10 points	Cmd+Option+down arrow (Ctrl+Alt+down arrow)
Decrease by 10 points	Cmd+Option+up arrow (Ctrl+Alt+up arrow)
Select Auto Leading	Cmd+Option+Shift+A (Ctrl+Alt+Shift+A)

History Palette Shortcuts

Command:	Shortcut:
Redo Key Option 1	**(Cmd+Z)/(Ctrl+Z)**
Toggles Undo/Redo	Cmd+Z (Ctrl+Z)
History State Backward	Cmd+Option+Z (Ctrl+Alt+Z)
History State Forward	Cmd+Shift+Z (Ctrl+Shift+Z)
Redo Key Option 2	**(Cmd+Shift+Z)/(Ctrl+Shift+Z)**
Toggles Undo/Redo	Cmd+Option+Z (Ctrl+Alt+Z)
History State Backward	Cmd+Z (Ctrl+Z)
History State Forward	Cmd+Shift+Z (Ctrl+Shift+Z)
Redo Key Option 3	**(Cmd+Y)/(Ctrl+Y)**
Toggles Undo/Redo	Cmd+Option+Z (Ctrl+Alt+Z)
History State Backward	Cmd+Z (Ctrl+Z)
History State Forward	Cmd+Y (Ctrl+Y)

Filter Shortcuts

Command:	Shortcut:
Extract	Filter>Extract Cmd+Option+X (Ctrl+Alt+X)
Repeat last filter	Cmd+F (Ctrl+F)
Reopen last filter with same settings	Cmd+Option+F (Ctrl+Alt+F)
Fade last filter	Cmd+Shift+F (Ctrl+Shift+F)
Cycle Through Gradients	Previous, (comma)/Next. (period)
Default Colors	D
Toggle Foreground/Background	X

Lighting Effects Filter

Duplicate light	Option+drag light (Alt+drag light)
Delete Light	Delete
Adjust light footprint w/o changing angle	Shift+drag handle
Adjust light Angle w/o changing footprint	Cmd+drag handle (Ctrl+drag handle)

Filter Shortcuts (continued)

Command:	Shortcut:
Retouching Tools	
Toggle Blur and Sharpen	Hold down Option (Alt) while using one of these tools
Toggle Fingerpainting Smudge	Hold down Option (Alt) while using the Smudge tool
Toggle Dodge and Burn	Hold down Option (Alt) while using one of these tools
Switch Modes while Toning	Shadows: Option (Alt)+Shift+S Midtones: Option (Alt)+Shift+M Highlights: Option (Alt)+Shift+H Cycle: Shift++ or Shift+–
Set the Sponge tool	Desaturate: Option (Alt)+Shift+D Saturate: Option (Alt)+Shift+S Cycle: Shift++ or Shift+–

Selection Shortcuts

Command:	Shortcut:
Add to a selection	Shift+Selection tool
Subtract from a selection	Option+Selection tool (Alt+Selection tool)
Create intersection selection	Shift+Option+tool (Shift+Alt+tool)
Select All	Cmd+A (Ctrl+A)
Deselect	Cmd+D (Ctrl+D)
Reselect last selection	Cmdl+Shift+D (Ctrl+Shift+D)
Inverse selection	Cmd+Shift+I (Ctrl+Shift+I)
Hide Marching Ants	Cmd+H (Ctrl+H)
Use Move tool temporarily	Hold down the Cmd (Ctrl) key to temporarily switch (Except with vector tools)
Use Hand tool temporarily	Hold down the spacebar
Feather	Cmd+Option+D (Ctrl+Alt+D)
Load a Layer	Cmd+click (Ctrl+click) on a layer
Add to Loaded Layer	Cmd+Shift+click (Ctrl+Shift+click) on a layer
Subtract From Loaded Layer	Cmd+Option+click (Ctrl+Alt+click) on a layer
Intersect From Loaded Layer	Cmd+Option+Shift+click (Ctrl+Alt+click) on a layer

Selection Shortcuts (continued)

Command:	Shortcut:
Load a Channel	Cmd+Option (Ctrl+Alt) and the channel number Cmd+click (Ctrl+click) on the Channel icon
Constrain Marquee	Shift+drag with initial selection
Draw from Center with Marquee	Option+drag (Alt+drag) with Elliptical Marquee
Reposition Selection as it's drawn	Hold down spacebar
Move Selection 1 pixel	Arrow keys when Marquee/Lasso/Wand selected
Move Selection 10 pixels	Shift +arrow keys when Marquee/Lasso/Wand selected
Move Selected Pixels 1 pixel	Switch to Move tool; then use arrow keys
Move Selected Pixels 10 pixels	Switch to Move tool; then use Shift+arrow keys
Center selection in new document	Shift+drag selection to new document
Lasso Tool	
Activate Lasso tool	L
Toggle Lasso tools midselection	Hold down the Option (Alt) key and drag
Close Selection	Double-click or press **Enter**
Cancel	Escape

Levels, Curves, and Color Shortcuts

Command:	Shortcut:
Levels	
Levels	Cmd+L (Ctrl+L)
Use Last Levels Settings	Cmd+Option+L (Ctrl+ Alt+L)
Auto Levels	Cmd+Shift+L (Ctrl+Shift+L)
Auto Contrast	Cmd+Option+Shift+L (Ctrl+Alt+Shift+L)
Curves	
Curves	Cmd+M (Ctrl+M)
Use Last Curves Settings	Cmd+Option+M (Ctrl+Alt+M)
Pinpoint Color on Curve	Cmd+click (Ctrl+click) in image
Pinpoint Color on Each Curve	Cmd+Shift+click (Ctrl+Shift+click) in image

Levels, Curves, and Color Shortcuts (continued)

Command:	Shortcut:
Color	
Color Balance	Cmd+B (Ctrl+B)
Use Last Color Balance Settings	Cmd+Option+B (Ctrl+ Alt+B)
Auto Color	Cmd+Shift+B (Ctrl+Shift+B)
Hue/Saturation	Cmd+U (Ctrl+U)
Use Last Hue/Saturation Settings	Cmd+Option+U (Ctrl+ Alt+U)
Desaturate Image	Cmd+Shift+U (Ctrl+Shift+U)
Invert	Cmd+I (Ctrl+I)

Advanced Learning Opportunities, Recommended Reading, and Resources

I love books. I own hundreds of them. I hope you keep this book next to your nonlinear editing system so that it can be truly useful. Books aren't people, however, and no matter how conversationally I try to write, this book will never replace the personal connection you may experience with a trainer, instructor, or professor.

You need to look for a personal training opportunity that matches your needs. I am not a fan of those big, rolling caravans that advertise three-day "Master Workshops" where you sit in an auditorium and learn everything. Education needs to be a personal experience.

I tell folks to consider is enrolling in a college class. This will most likely place you with twenty or so others for a few months. Chances are the class will focus on print and web and not video. There are exceptions, however, with several schools offering Digital Media Production or Broadcast Journalism programs. A college class has the benefit of homework and the subsequent feedback loop. I spent about a third of my professional life teaching college students the ins and outs of video and motion graphics. I am sure that these students frequently fail to realize just how new and exciting this field is.

Adobe Certified Training Providers

There's a high likelihood that you don't have the time to take a college course. For working pros, there's a better solution: Adobe Certified Training Providers. There are several classes and resources to choose from. The best place to start is Adobe's web site (http://www.adobe.com/misc/training.html).

Adobe carefully selects and screens its training centers and trainers. By ensuring that all of the trainers have passed a standardized exam, an objective level of quality control is maintained. Carrie B. Cooper, Training Partner Relations Manager within the Adobe Solutions Network, said that Adobe tries to offer variety. "Adobe Certified Training Providers (ACTP) offer beginning, intermediate, advanced to

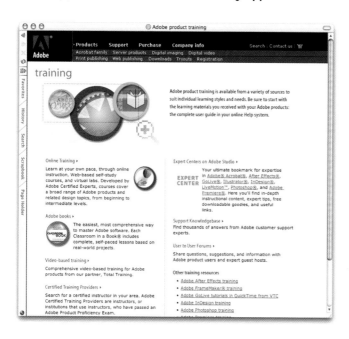

 Adobe's training page offers several alternatives to advance your skills. Be sure to visit http://www.adobe.com/misc/training.html and look for authorized learning opportunities near you.

more specific courses like Photoshop for Photographers," said Cooper. "The best thing to do is to check out the training centers' web sites and catalogs."

One of those centers is Future Media Concepts. With offices in six East Coast cities, FMC offers a full range of Photoshop and video-oriented courses (http://www.FMCtraining.com). Ben Kozuch, President and co-founder of FMC, explained his company's approach to training:

"We offer hands-on training in an intimate environment of no more than six people. Instructors are certified by Adobe, so participants are assured the highest-level quality training. Instructors are not professors, but industry professionals. We offer training on all Adobe software, varying in level from beginner through advanced."

When searching for a center, be sure to check their references. Ask for customer testimonials, and be sure to check Adobe's site to make sure they are listed as an ACTP (http://partners.adobe.com/asn/partnerfinder/search_training.jsp). You should also expect flexible and accessible scheduling (including weekend classes). Ask if instructors are working professionals. Some centers also offer a satisfaction-guarantee policy and financing plans.

(Photo courtesy Future Media Concepts)

"Training is a major investment of time and money. You want to make sure that it is done right the first time so you don't have to spend time again after a bad experience," said Kozuch. "Bad habits are tough to un-learn. At an authorized training center, you learn the software the way the manufacturer intended it to work."

Industry Certifications

So you want proof that you're as good as you think? Certifications offer Photoshop pros a chance test their mettle. The most recognized certification is the Adobe Certified Expert or ACE. To become certified, one must pass the Adobe Product Proficiency Exams for Photoshop (While you're at it, you can pick one up for After Effects, Premiere, and most other Adobe products.)

Adobe Certified Expert

Exams are computer-delivered, closed-book tests. The exam consists of 60–90 multiple-choice questions. The tests are administered locally at Prometric computing exam centers located around the world. You'll know whether you passed immediately after the exam. Diagnostic information is also included in your exam's report to help identify areas of strength and weakness. The ACE program was created by Adobe to fill a specific need for users and instructors.

"It started as a vehicle to objectively measure instructors' ability on the products," said Carrie B. Cooper, Training Partner Relations Manager within the Adobe Solutions Network. "We expanded that audience to include all types of experts on the products, be they consultants, students, designers, etc."

To become certified, Adobe recommends the following five steps:

Step 1   Study for the Exam. You need to be familiar with the topic areas and objectives in the Exam Bulletin for the Photoshop exam (http://partners.adobe.com/asn/training/PDFS/031_bulletinPS.pdf).

Step 2   Review the Adobe Certified Expert Program Agreement. The ACE agreement is available as a PDF for your review (http://partners.adobe.com/asn/training/PDFS/ace_agmt.pdf).

Step 3   Register for the Adobe Product Proficiency Exam. In the United States and Canada, you can call 1-800-356-3926. Outside the U.S./Canada (or if you don't like being on hold), visit the Prometric web site (http://www.2test.com). When contacting Prometric, you must know the name and number of the exam you want to take. (http://partners.adobe.com/asn/training/aceexamlist.html).

Step 4   Pass the Adobe Product Proficiency Exam. There is no limit on how many times you can retest, but you must pay for each exam. If you don't pass on the first attempt, when you register to retake, use the discount code RETEST, which will give you a 25% discount.

Step 5 Receive your welcome kit in four to six weeks and begin using your benefits. You'll get a certificate stating your achievement. You'll also have access to the ACE logo for your business cards and résumé.

NAPP Certification

Another certification route is now available for those who want to supplement their ACE certifications. The National Association of Photoshop Professionals (NAPP) is developing specialized exams for specific skill areas. David Moser, COO of the NAPP says that the different certifications will be a distinct accomplishment. "We will make sure that is a quality certification," said Moser. "You can be proud when you say that you pass the test."

The NAPP (http://www.photoshopuser.com) has announced its first two certifications. The initial program will include NAPP Certified Web Expert (CWE) and NAPP Certified Print Expert (CPE). David Moser says that a Video or Multimedia certification is being considered, along with one for Photoshop educators.

To find out more about the test or to register, be sure to visit http://www.photoshopcertification.com. Members of the NAPP will receive a discount on the exam.

Recommended Reading

Becoming a good designer is a continuous journey. Below you will find the favorite items from my bookshelf. All of these books and CD-ROMs I have personally read and used. I recommend them strongly.

Books on Photoshop

Photoshop Power Shortcuts	by Michael Ninness	*The* shortcut guide written by a man inside Adobe. This book has *every* keyboard shortcut.
Photoshop Restoration and Retouching	by Katrin Eismann, Steve Simmons	This book digs deep into fixing problem photos.
Creating Graphics for Avid Xpress DV 3.5 with Adobe Photoshop	by Avid Technology Inc.	This book looks at the essential skills needed for the beginning Avid Editor.
Photoshop Channel Chops	by David Biendy, Bert Monroy, Nathan Moody	This book takes a very close look at channels and transparency. It is the only other book out there that covers video-specific information.
Photoshop Down and Dirty Tricks	by Scott Kelby	These two books are filled with cool tips and tricks.
Photoshop Killer Tips	by Scott Kelby, Felix Nelson	

Books on Photoshop (continued)

The Photoshop Wow! Book	by Jack Davis, Linnea Dayton	These books are very web- and print-centric, but they offer timesaving techniques.
Adobe Photoshop One-Click Wow!		
Photoshop Bible	by Deke McClelland	The name says it all. This book is thick and detailed. It offers great general knowledge, but no video-specific information.
Adobe Photoshop and Illustrator Advanced Classroom in a Book	by Adobe Creative Team	If you own Illustrator, this book will help you get more out of it.
Avoiding the Scanning Blues	by Taz Tally, Ph.D.	The most in-depth book on scanning available.

Need to know more about type?

I dug deeper into typographic theory in Chapter 5, "Some Words on Words, Logos, and Symbols." There are many more aesthetic decisions to be made, as well as some guidelines on legibility, alignment, and white space that need to be reviewed.

Books and CD-ROMs on type

www.type	by Roger Pring	A look at web type and how to use it at low resolutions.
Stop Stealing Sheep and Find Out How Type Works	by Erik Spiekermann, E. M. Ginger	The title says it all (albeit obscurely).
Typographic Principles with Don Barnett	by Lynda.com	A great primer on how type works.

Books on motion graphics

Creating Motion Graphics	by Trish and Chris Meyer
After Effects in Production	by Trish and Chris Meyer
Creative After Effects	by Angie Taylor
Adobe After Effects Essentials	by Jayse Hansen
Motion Graphics	by Steve Curran
Moving Type	by Matt Woolman, Jeff Bellatoni

Books on color

Global Graphics: Color	by L.K. Peterson, Cheryl Dangel Cullen	Color examined globally.
Global Color Combinations	by Leslie Cabarga	Color examined globally.
Color Correction for Digital Video	by Steve Hullfish and Jaime Fowler	Also part of CMP Books' "DV Expert Series."
Color Index	by Jim Krause	A small color guide that will find its way to your desk.
Color Harmony Workbook	by Lisa Sawahata	A helpful book for finding harmonious color combinations.

Books on design

Brain Darts	by Turkel Schwartz and Partners	An inside look at the ideas that go into advertising campaigns.
The Best of Business Card Design 2	by Rockport Publishers	
Creative Edge: Letterhead+Business Card Design	by Lynn Haller	Business cards only have a small imageable area and several design constraints... sound familiar?
Robin Williams Design Workshop	by Robin Williams and John Tollett	
Idea Index	by Jim Krause	A useful jump-start to a good idea.

Photoshop Web Sites

A quick online search will leave you over-whelmed. If you judge by quantity, Photoshop is a well-loved product. Since your time is limited, I offer a scaled-down list of some of the best sites out there. Be sure to look for valuable resources and alternative points of view. Also, keep in mind that the majority of these sites are written from web and print perspectives. In general, web-oriented sites are the next best thing because they discuss designing for the screen as well.

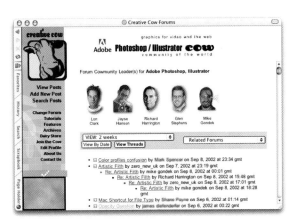

Creative Cow offers several video and motion graphics oriented forums. Their Photoshop forum is a very popular spot.

Tutorials and support

Adobe Evangelists	www.adobeevangelists.com
BPSource	www.bobsphotoshopsource.co.uk
Creative Cow	www.creativecow.net
Lynda.com	www.lynda.com
Photoshop Café	www.photoshopcafe.com
Photoshop Roadmap	www.photoshoproadmap.com
Pixel Foundry	www.pixelfoundry.com
Planet Photoshop	www.planetphotoshop.com
PS Workshop	www.psworkshop.net
Team Photoshop	www.teamphotoshop.com

Filters

Alien Skin Software	www.alienskin.com
Auto FX Software	www.autofx.com
Camera Bits	www.camerabits.com
Digital Film Tools	www.digitalfilmtools.com
Flaming Pear Software	www.flamingpear.com
Lizard Tech	www.lizardtech.com
The Plugin Site	www.thepluginsite.com
Nik Multimedia	www.nikmultimedia.com
Procreate	www.procreate.com

Actions, styles, and add-ons

Action FX	www.actionfx.com
Adobe Xchange	www.adobexchange.com
DeepSpaceWeb	www.deepspaceweb.com
Elated.com	www.elated.com/actionkits
Tools for Television	www.toolsfortelevision.com
Web Teknique	www.webteknique.com

Publications with Frequent Stories about Photoshop

There are several great computer magazines that routinely discuss Photoshop and related topics such as third-party plug-ins, motion graphics, and video. A magazine has a certain timeliness to it and can provide excellent tips on Photoshop updates and add-ons.

Publications

Photoshop User	www.photoshopuser.com	The official publication of the National Association of Photoshop Professionals. All Photoshop, every page. They've even added a section on Photoshop for Video.
Mac Design	www.macdesignmagazine.com	A sister publication to *Photoshop User*. This magazine covers Photoshop, After Effects, Final Cut Pro and several other design applications.
Computer Arts	www.computerarts.co.uk	This English magazine has consistently good articles and fun tutorials. It always comes packaged with a great disc as well.
Graphic Exchange	www.gxo.com/index.html	This concise publication from Canada is published six times per year.
Mac Addict	www.macaddict.com	This unconventional publication frequently publishes articles and tutorials on digital imaging and video.
Macworld	www.macworld.com	This magazine offers several great articles for the graphics-oriented editor.
DV	www.dv.com	This book wouldn't be possible without *DV*. The magazine has been a tremendous resource to video pros.
Cinefex	www.cinefex.com	This magazine goes in deep. Each issue looks at visual effects–driven movies and tells you how they were done.

Professional Organizations and Users' Groups

Be sure also to look locally as well for users' groups. For example, the Los Angeles and Boston Final Cut Pro user groups provide several resources to help their members integrate graphics into their video projects.

User groups

National Association of Photoshop Professionals	www.photoshopuser.com
American Institute of Graphic Arts	www.aiga.org
Media Communications Association-International	www.mca-i.org

Free and Affordable Software Online

If you're looking for more, just go to the Internet. The following sites offer several free or affordable items.

Free or Cheap Software

Version Tracker	www.versiontracker.com
Download.com	www.download.com
Mac OSX Software Guide	www.apple.com/downloads/macosx
The Plugin Site	www.thepluginsite.com
Flaming Pear	www.flamingpear.com
Free Photoshop	www.freephotoshop.com

Tech Support

Like anything related to computers, Photoshop will occasionally fail. I can safely say that it is rock solid, but not perfect. When pushing Photoshop's limits (yes, there are a few), it is possible to "break it." There are several technical support options available from Adobe directly. Often times, a solution is available already; the documentation, however, just might not be available to you. Adobe also needs to hear about user problems so they can release bug fixes and create new features that meet users' needs.

If you are a registered owner, you get 90 days tech support for new copies and 30 days for upgrade copies.

1. Limited Complimentary Phone Support is available from 6 a.m. to 5 p.m. Pacific Time. You get 90 days support on a new copy of Photoshop and 30 days for a purchased upgrade. The counter ticking starts when you first activate the phone support.

    • MAC   206-675-6203
    • WINDOWS   206-675-6303

2. "Pay as you go" service is also available for $2 per minute (ouch!), but it's only available in the U.S. and Canada.

    • MAC   900-555-3300
    • WINDOWS   900-555-2200

3. Annual support agreements are available in a variety of packages. Prices start at $149 per year for a single user running Photoshop to $399 per year for annual support for all registered Adobe applications. Companies can purchase a package for $1,999 per year for ten users using multiple applications. (Only available in the U.S. and Canada.)

4. Online information is plentiful. Start at www.adobe.com for different technical documents. You can also send an email to techdocs@adobe.com to get a listing of more than 1,000 reference documents, FAQs, and technical articles. The Adobe Web site has a very good search feature. Software is dynamic and with new versions, there will be incompatibility issues. Frequent visits to the Adobe site will keep Photoshop (and you) up to date.

You were supposed to keep this book... chances are you didn't. All the essential tech support information is summarized here. The Adobe help staff is highly trained and ready to answer your call.

More Tech Support

While straight from the horse's mouth is probably the best method, the horse isn't always available (and it ain't cheap to talk to.) Because you will be working crazy hours, I am providing my "Ten Tips for Tech Support." These steps will solve 95% of your problems. I've been using (fighting with) personal computers for twenty years, so these are born from tough experience.

1. **Save (if you can). Quit. Shutdown. Count to 20 and Restart.** Believe it or not, this fixes 60% of computer errors. Sometimes a clean boot will do it.

2. **Try another file.** If you keep getting errors on your current document, open another file and see if the same problems occur. Sometimes individual Photoshop files get corrupted. If you isolate the problem to a single file, you can try running a disk repair utility to see if the individual file can be saved. Chances are pretty slim for corrupted files however.

3. **Try another machine.** Open up the "questionable" document on another computer. If it works correctly, then your machine may be the culprit.

4. **Trash your preferences file.** Sometimes your preferences file goes bad and causes Photoshop to misbehave. Quit the application, locate the preferences file, throw it away, and re-launch.

Mac OSX	Macintosh HD\Users\<username>\Library\Preferences\ Adobe Photoshop 7.0 Settings
Mac OS9	Macintosh HD\System Folder\Preferences\ Adobe Photoshop 7.0 Settings
Windows 98	Windows\Application Data\Adobe\Photoshop\7.0\Adobe Photoshop 7.0 Settings
Windows NT	WinNT\profiles\<username>\Application Data\ Photoshop\7.0\Adobe Photoshop 7.0 Settings
Windows 2000 and XP	C:\Documents and Settings\<username>\Application Data\ Photoshop\7.0\ Adobe Photoshop 7.0 Settings

5. **Check for updates.** Launch the Adobe Online utility and check for updates. Run your Operating System updater. Visit third-party plug-in sites or go to VersionTracker.com. If you really think about it, it's amazing that our computers run at all considering how much random code we stuff into them.

The Application Data folder is a hidden folder. Go into: Windows Explorer>Tools>Folder Options> View and check the option **View Hidden Files and Folders**.

6. **Evaluate hardware.** Has anything changed? Any cables loose or unplugged? If you've added a new scanner, mouse, tablet, etc., it may be interfering with your OS or with Photoshop. Remove the device and see what happens. Check the manufacturers' Web site and see if there are updates. Just because products are sold in stores doesn't mean the manufacturer supports it. Before adding hardware, visit the company's site and see when they last updated their tech support page. "Mac Compatible" doesn't mean it will work on OSX natively. Windows users frequently experience problems as well, especially with native support for XP.

7. **Reinstall Photoshop.** Sometimes a fresh copy will solve your problems.

8. **Reinstall plug-ins and drivers.** Uninstall all third-party items and then reload them one at a time. Check to see when the error occurs. Remove all offending software.

9. **Repair or reinstall your Operating System.** Some errors are tied directly to the Operating System. For example, if Photoshop misbehaves when opening files, the Directory Services portion of the OS may be damaged. Remember, the OS and Photoshop work together. Some problems have nothing to do with Photoshop (even if that's where you first notice them.) Try disk utilties first, then if needed, you may have to freshen up the OS. A full system reinstall is the last resort.

10. **Take it to the Web.** There exists a wonderful assortment of online resources to help Photoshop users. One of the best forums for Photoshop and Video exists at www.CreativeCow.net. Make sure to search the archives first to see if your problem has been discussed recently (chances are it has). When you do post questions looking for troubleshooting help (or just new ideas), make sure you specify which version of Photoshop you are using, the type of machine, and which Operating System.

Technical Support on the Web

The Internet provides a wealth of knowledge—not all of it is good however. Several users turn to community-based forums as an alternative. These moderated forums offer a chance to post your questions and get answers (often in a very timely fashion). To improve your results, follow this advice.

1. Always specify what version software you are using.

2. Give details about the hardware and OS you are using.

3. Avoid excessive abbreviations as many are *not* standards.

4. Be sure to consult the built-in help features for the application. If an answer is obvious, you might not get a response.

5. Run a search through recent posts. Your problem might have already been answered recently. Moderators will assume you've skimmed the post index first.

6. Post your question in the appropriate forums. If your question is about Photoshop and Final Cut Pro, post it to both forums.

7. If your problem is solved, confirm it so others don't keep posting answers.

8. Say thanks. I moderate a forum for free because I believe in giving back. I have drawn upon the advice and wisdom of many kind people in the past and now I can return the favor. A "thank you" goes a long way.

Tech support Web sites

2-Pop.com	www.2-pop.com	This site specializes in Final Cut Pro, but has recently expanded its vision. Avid, Apple, Media 100, and Adobe editing products all have active forums. There is no specific graphics forum, but users can post questions in their respective NLE's section.
Creative Cow	www.creativecow.net	This site offers a dedicated and active Adobe Photoshop and Illustrator forum hosted by a team of experts. You will also find a huge area of After Effects resources and forums devoted to nearly every video editing, motion graphics, and DVD authoring application.
Worldwide Users Groups (WWUG)	www.wwug.com	Users can come here for discussions on Adobe Photoshop as well. Several threaded topics are available.

Working with Other Applications

Integrating Adobe Photoshop with Adobe After Effects

by Jayse Hansen

This miniguide is written to assist some of you more ambitious editors who want to create dynamic motion for your videos using After Effects. It's not a guide to using After Effects; that is a book in itself. Rather, this is a guide to preparing Photoshop files to transfer properly *into* After Effects.

 You'll find source files for this appendix on the DVD-ROM in the *Chapter Files* folder.

Now that you've got a fairly good handle on Photoshop, it may please you to know that, in the process, you've also learned a lot about After Effects. Many people think of After Effects as "Photoshop with a Timeline," and I certainly agree.

One of the most exciting features of After Effects is that you can take a layered Photoshop file directly into After Effects and begin animating each layer's opacity, position, blur and so on. Many people create their source work within Photoshop and then animate the elements and layers within After Effects.

I'm going to show you how to import a layered Photoshop file into After Effects so that you can begin animating it. The basic steps are:

1. Create your Photoshop File.

2. Evaluate how you've set it up.

3. Import into AE as a composition.

4. Evaluate the imported file within AE.

5. Animate layers.

Step 1   Create your Photoshop file

Not all Photoshop features will transfer perfectly into After Effects. Some alterations are needed. You will also create your Photoshop document at a different pixel dimension than you will be working in within AE.

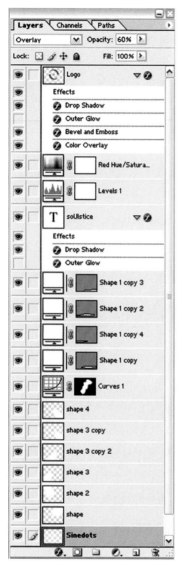

Normally you'd think I'd tell you to work within these limitations and set your file up accordingly. However, other than setting my pixel dimensions correctly, I will usually create my Photoshop files using whatever techniques are easiest and quickest without really worrying about how it will all translate into After Effects. This frees my design up immensely. I know that later on, when I want to import it, there will be tricks I can use to get exactly what I want.

Sometimes I will also create my files at double or triple video resolution. I do this because there's a good chance the client will want to use the graphics I create in print materials—and I dislike doing things twice.

However you decide to create your artwork, the first step is to create your Photoshop file using layers.

This is a simple mockup design I'll use to demonstrate how different advanced layers translate into After Effects. We'll want to be able to animate various aspects of this once we are inside AE. Let's examine the makeup of this image.

Step 2   Examine your layers

Here are the layers that make up this image. As you can see, I have several layers with layer styles added to them—drop shadows, glows, Bevel and Emboss, etc.

From top to bottom, I have:
- Logo with layer styles applied
- Hue/Saturation Adjustment layer in which I've changed the hue, making all the layers below that were once blue appear red. Turn off this layer to see its effect on the layers below.
- Levels Adjustment layer. This was added to boost the contrast.
- Normal text layer with a drop shadow and outer glow (turned off)
- Vector shapes along the bottom that I drew with the pen tool and changed their transfer mode to Overlay. I essentially drew one shape, copied the layer a few times, flipped and repositioned them.

A few things to notice are:

• Some layer styles will transfer. However, most times, I recommend doing what the book suggests: Flatten your layer styles before exporting.

• My layers are not in folders (layer sets). This is because layer sets are translated as compositions in AE. I want all my layers to be able to be animated, so I'm keeping them out of folders, especially since I'm using transfer modes and they don't import correctly into AE when using layer sets.

- Curves adjustment layer to get some of the highlights in the background. Turn it on and off to see its effect.
- Amorphous shapes I created with the lasso tool. I simply filled roughly drawn shapes with white and blurred them to a great degree. I then changed their transfer mode and opacity to suit my taste.
- Sinedots layer. This is a free plug-in from Dragonfly (http://www.philipp-spoeth.de/). It produces high-resolution sine patterns that are gorgeous. I set its transfer mode to **Overlay**.
- Background Layer. Just a layer filled with a dark blue pattern. (It's the Hue/Saturation Adjustment layer that is making the final piece red.)

Now, admittedly, this is a lot to throw into a single Photoshop file, but not uncommon for most of my files. I also want to illustrate how various layer styles, text, and transfer modes translate into After Effects. Save the file and let's jump into After Effects.

Step 3   Import into AE as a composition

Now that we have a good idea of the makeup of our Photoshop document, we'll take it into AE and see how it gets interpreted.

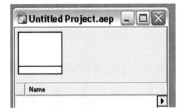

Open up After Effects. Double-click in the blank area of the Project Window (or type Cmd+I (Ctrl+I), or you can do the more tedious File>Import>Import File.). This will bring up the Import **File** dialog box.

Select the Photoshop file you'd like to import. For this exercise, I've selected *Soulstice.psd*.

The most important step here is to change the Import As dropdown menu from **Footage** to **Composition**. Here are the differences:

- Footage will import the document either as a flattened image or import a single layer only.
- Composition imports the Photoshop document and keeps its layers separated.

Step 4   Evaluate the imported file within AE

The following figure shows how our Photoshop file comes into After Effects after we've imported as a composition.

We get a composition and a folder. The folder contains every layer that was in the Photoshop file. Double-click on the composition to see what you have to work with.

Even though there were quite a few different Photoshop effects, transfer modes, layer styles, text, opacity levels, adjustment layers, etc., the image looks just about exactly the same as it did in Photoshop. All of

A few things to notice are:

• Layer Styles have been split into separate layers and grouped into Layer Effects Comp. If you Option+double-click this, you'll see that it is composed of the logo's original, bevel highlight/shadow and color overlay.

This can come in handy because you can now animate the layer's effect properties individually.

• Text is now an image. If you want to update it:

a. Update the text in Photoshop and save it.

b. In After Effects, find the layer within the folder in the Project window.

c. Ctrl+click or right-click on the layer and choose **Reload Footage**.

Alternately, you can try Edit Original by pressing Cmd+E (Ctrl+E) to open the text layer in Photoshop. Make your updates, then close and save. Your changes should appear in the timeline.

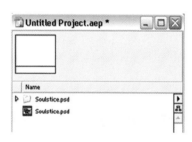

these settings transfer over quite well. And the layers are now on the timeline, ready to animate each individually to your heart's content.

Step 5   Animate layers

Congratulations! You are now ready to animate each layer individually using the After Effects timeline. This guide is meant only to deliver you safely to the door; you will need to explore After Effects on your own. If you need help animating with After Effects, see Jayse's training series at http://training.jayse.us. Trish and Chris Meyers' book *Creating Motion Graphics* is also useful.

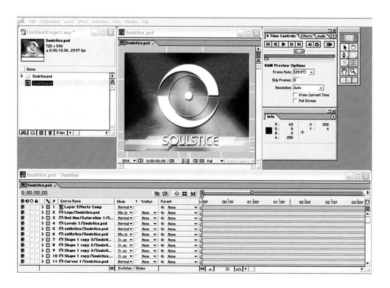

Integrating Adobe Photoshop with Adobe Premiere

by Tim Kolb[1]

Why Photoshop integration is important for this system. Adobe's Photoshop is an application that changed the way we all think about image editing. Adobe's Premiere was one of the first software-based video editing applications on the scene. It's only natural that they would be designed to work hand-in-hand. Converting and processing still images and graphics and creating graphic elements and masks for compositing will always be a critical part of creating video programs. Whether you're creating a video for deployment on tape, CD-ROM, or DVD, Photoshop is a critical accessory for high-quality video production with Adobe Premiere.

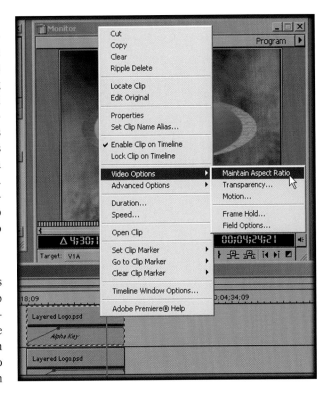

Proper frame size to create graphics for Adobe Premiere in square pixels. 720×534 is the best frame size to compose Photoshop graphics with square pixels to transfer to Premiere. Premiere will automatically scale the image to the proper frame dimension on import. Maintaining the original aspect ratio of the graphic is optional and can be chosen for each clip individually.

Supported file types. Premiere will import:

- PSD and PSD sequence
- Filmstrip
- PICT and PICT sequence
- PCX
- PICS animations (Mac only)

- GIF and animated GIF
- JPEG
- TARGA and TGA sequence
- BMP and BMP sequence

Supported Image Modes. RGB, 8-bit images can be used in Premiere projects.

---

1. Tim Kolb is an Emmy Award-winning director with a 16-year history of video and television production. He has been a principal in Kolb Syverson Communications since its inception in 1990 and serves as a program producer and first unit director for video programs, television commercials, CD-Roms and DVDs. His work has been seen on the CBS Evening News, ESPN, ESPN 2, and CNN, and he has been known to freelance for the likes of Court TV and ABC Sports. Besides Emmys, his shelf holds American Advertising Awards, Tellys, International Television Association Honors, and Communicator Awards. He judges Emmys and Tellys and is an advisor to Adobe Systems and Canopus Corporation. He tends to hang out at several industry-related forums at creativecow.net, where he is a host. Tim can be reached at kolb@kolbsyverson.com.

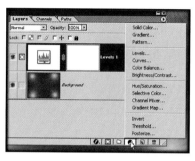

Designing graphics to use in Adobe Premiere. There are several color-handling options for designing for Adobe Premiere in Photoshop. Working within the generally accepted RGB level limitations for NTSC video of 17–235 may sound like a sensible way to design. Unfortunately, it can be very easy to introduce an illegal color during design, not to mention that your constant focus on staying in gamut isn't going to streamline the process. Daniel Brown from Adobe Systems had several other options to consider that may be more effective for individual users:

Option 1: Design in full gamut RGB and, just before final save, duplicate the final document into a merged, single-layer document and run the NTSC-safe filter on that layer. The only possible drawback is that the colors that are out of gamut may go completely flat because this filter has a relatively harsh curve. (Such detail may or may not have been lost in the transition to video in any case.)

Option 2: Design in full-gamut RGB and apply the NTSC-safe filter on the file in Premiere. This method ensures that all graphics are processed, but will cause the now-filtered graphic to be rendered when a properly prepared Photoshop document would not.

Option 3: Add an adjustment layer over the entire document that forces the white and black points to be within the desired ranges. This method would actually bring the image into compliance by shifting the overall value of all colors rather than just rounding a few of them, which is how the NTSC-safe filter works. The adjustment layer can be active while editing, which will display the safe colors while you work, even though the colors you are actually using are beyond NTSC safe range. This adjustment layer can be saved with the original document, which will load into Premiere when you load the document as merged layers.

Personal preference will always reign in choosing any method of working for design in Photoshop, but my choice would be option #3 in most cases.

Major Photoshop features that import. Premiere can import:

• Photoshop files as merged layers. Most features of Photoshop will load properly when loading a document as merged layers. Layer blending and opacity are preserved when the document is loaded as merged layers with only a specific individual or group of layer(s) saved as visible.

• Each independent layer of a document to use each layer as a separate element. Layer sets can't import as a group. However, the individual layers are visible and can be loaded from within a layer set. Blending modes and opacity settings for layers as well as layer masks aren't read by Premiere when layers are imported individually.

Importing graphics into the system. Photoshop outputs image files in a variety of file types. Of those, Premiere imports:

- Tagged Image Files or TIFF and TIFF sequence
- Truevision TARGA or TGA and TGA sequence
- Compuserve GIF or animated GIF
- JPEG
- PSD and PSD sequence
- Windows Bitmap or BMP and BMP sequence (Windows only)
- PICT and PICT sequence.

Still graphics are represented in source-clip bins just like video clips. Premiere can be set to automatically interpret alpha channels when the clip is placed on video track 2 or above and offers three ways to interpret alpha channel transparency (white alpha, black alpha, or straight alpha channel). Default duration for still images can be set in the preferences, but length can be easily adjusted on the timeline after the clip is placed as well.

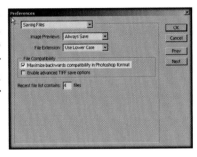

Exporting video frames. Stills can be exported from Premiere as:

- Tagged Image Files or TIFF
- Compuserve GIFs
- Truevision TARGA or TGA
- Windows Bitmap or BMP (Windows only)
- PICT (Macintosh only)

Tips. Be sure **Maximize backwards compatibility in Photoshop format** is checked in the Photoshop preferences for the broadest import capabilities. This will assure that Photoshop saves a rasterized version of vector layers within the Photoshop file for proper interpretation upon import into Premiere.

For composing graphics in Photoshop that I know will be used in a DV format Premiere project, occasionally I have used a 640×480 frame size. Once the document is final, I use the image size dialog to stretch the image to 720×480, which will appear stretched in Photoshop but will compress back to their correct aspect once inside Premiere. While this may go against most conventional recommendations, I've found there are times (usually involving large circular elements or large, sweeping curves) when I prefer Photoshop's horizontal pixel upsampling in this case (stretching 640 to 720) to Premiere's vertical downsampling when you import a 720×534 image into a 720×480 DV video project. You would need to uncheck the Maintain Aspect Ratio option for this method to work properly.

Tim Kolb thanks Daniel Brown and Richard Townhill of Adobe Systems for their critical assistance in assembling this supplement.

Integrating Adobe Photoshop with Boris

by Tim Wilson[1]

Why Photoshop integration is important for this system. Boris is the leading developer of integrated effects technology for nonlinear editing systems. Three major products–Boris FX, Boris GRAFFITI, and Boris RED–provide a full range of solutions to enhance the power of nearly two dozen editing applications on both Macintosh and Windows platforms. Our goal is to provide editors all the animation and effects capabilities they need without leaving their NLEs. Of course, that includes the ability to incorporate Photoshop graphics into their work.

Proper frame size to create graphics for this system with square pixels. FX, GRAFFITI, and RED all automatically convert square pixels to rectangular pixels, with a variety of options. For example, projects may be set up to use square pixels throughout, or imported graphics automatically resized to fit the project.

Users who choose to bypass these internal algorithms and prepare their images more precisely should follow the guidelines presented elsewhere in this book.

Note that, like other video applications, Boris assumes a resolution of 72 pixels per inch, which displays at the same size in both Photoshop and Boris. With a 300-pixel resolution in Photoshop, the image will be roughly four times larger in Boris. This may be useful when animating larger images, but, to be honest, it gives me a headache. I'd rather start with the image at the right size and resolution, and end the day doing a little less math.

Supported file type. FX, GRAFFITI, and RED use QuickTime to read still images. As long as QuickTime is installed, any format supported by QuickTime is supported by Boris. These include:

- PICT
- GIF
- PNG
- Silicon Graphics
- TARGA
- JPEG
- PDF
- Photoshop (.psd), which users will generally find the most flexible format

---

1. Tim Wilson is the Product Manager for Boris RED and Boris FX, as well as the Director of Marketing for Boris FX, Inc. Before joining the company in 2000, he ran his own video production business, where he used Boris products daily in projects for a wide range of corporate and government clients. A video editor for more than 20 years, he started in computer graphics long before Photoshop, but was hooked for life by version 2.

Although Photoshop EPS files are not supported directly–they should be resaved in Photoshop as .psd–Boris RED imports Illustrator EPS files while retaining full control over every aspect of their vector information. This includes the ability to edit, animate, add and delete individual control points, stroke, and fill, as well as the ability to extrude any or all layers in the Illustrator file.

Supported image modes. 8-bit RGB files are the only mode supported reliably. Indexed color files may be imported, but the indexing is limited by the colorspace of the Boris project, which in turn is set by the host editing application.

Design with RGB or 601 levels. There's no question that artists will have the most control over their levels if they do indeed exercise control over their levels. That said, FX, GRAFFITI, and RED all include options for limiting output to NTSC safe levels, as indeed do all of our host applications. Users who'd rather not pay attention to levels need not. They're not, however, likely to have read this far.

Major Photoshop features that import perfectly. The default for importing Photoshop files is to treat them as flattened files.

In this state, all features import perfectly, with two limitations:

- Boris products released prior to April 2003 support only a single alpha channel or mask.
- Files are limited to 4091 pixels in either dimension.

Both of these limitations are addressed in Boris products scheduled to be released after April 2003.

Once imported into Boris RED, the Convert to Container command separates the file into layers, retaining the layer names used in Photoshop.

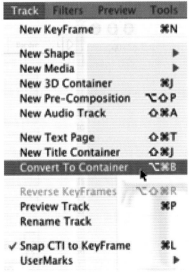

The container track allows the layers to be animated and filtered as a group. Both of these are much more flexible than most other applications, which, if they support Photoshop layers at all, allow users to decide how to handle files only at import, and, if layers are chosen, do not allow an easy way to continue to treat the layers as a group.

After separating into layers, users may opt to add additional layers to the containers, including filters acting as adjustment layers, vector masks, or video layers.

Photoshop features that do not import perfectly. As long as images remain flattened, all visible Photoshop features import perfectly. (Others, such as watermarks, aren't immediately relevant to the world of video, and are ignored.)

Once separated into layers, however, there are some limitations. Most obviously, Photoshop's layer styles are handled internally by the Photoshop format and disappear when the image is broken into its component layers in Boris RED. This needn't be a serious limitation, because RED offers even more options for effects than Photoshop does. Better still, the effects in RED, including **Apply** modes, are fully animatable. If you have no interest in animating layer styles, then there's likely no reason to unflatten an image, and all will be well.

Alternatively, text with layer styles can be saved as a single document, and additional elements may be saved separately. Once in RED, one click will assemble all of these into a single element (a container) which will allow them to be animated and filtered as a group, without sacrificing the ability to animate and filter elements individually.

One element that can cause difficulties when .psd files are converted to a container is adjustment layers. To work around this, simply turn them off by clicking on the **Eye** icon for that track.

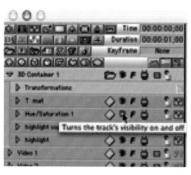

Boris RED 3.0 and later simply ignores the adjustment layers, although they are imported with the proper name. The effect can then be replaced in RED, where *all* filters act as adjustment layers with no limitations whatsoever. This is another area where RED offers a significant enhancement to Photoshop files.

How to import graphics. Every track in Boris FX, GRAFFITI, and RED has a pop-up menu that allows media to be imported. When Still Image is selected, a standard OS dialog box opens. There's also a **Shortcut** button on the timeline for adding a new track with still image media.

The Boris Preferences have a tab devoted to behavior when importing media. Although the default is to use straight alpha, I suspect that anyone bringing in many Photoshop files with transparency will want to select the **Premultiplied White** option.

Regardless of the default setting, Boris attempts to guess correctly. If for some reason it doesn't or if users want to override those settings (most typically to turn alpha off altogether), the Media tab provides a speedy way to do this without digging into the Prefs. (The same panel in the Controls window offers speedy options for flipping the image.)

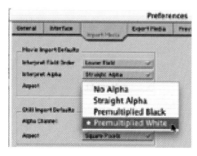

If an image's transparency has been premultiplied with something other than black or white, it's better to leave the alpha as Straight and apply the Premultiply filter, which can use any color.

How to export video frames. The default is PICT on Macintosh, TARGA on Windows. Since all layers in Boris have alpha already, you just need to be sure to have some of the checkerboard exposed, perhaps as easily as turning off background video tracks. The images are automatically exported as Millions of Colors+, which includes the alpha channel.

An even wider range of options is provided in the Export Movie dialog, which also allows animations to be output as sequential numbered stills. Exporting a single frame to, for instance, a JPEG "movie" allows for basic compression, as well as options for interlacing or not, in a simple dialog box.

General tips on usage. Boris FX, GRAFFITI, and RED may all act as plug-in filters to media on NLE timelines. This offers profound workflow advantages, since complex, multilayer composites may be created in the NLE without having to import or export footage. That said, Boris applications offer profound advantages for importing Photoshop files themselves, rather than being applied as filters to still images placed on the NLE timeline.

Chief among these is that most NLEs limit still frames to the project size, while Boris allows images much larger to be used. Along with Boris's elegant approach to Bézier keyframing, FX, GRAFFITI, and RED all easily create pan-and-zoom documentary-style animations.

Additionally, most NLEs fail to pass alpha channel information to plug-ins, including Boris. Better to import Photoshop files into Boris, which also offers more control over alpha blending than most NLEs.

Still images are useful not only for their most obvious nature as visible elements in the foreground of a composition. All Boris applications offer a number of ways to let imported graphics drive animation effects. Here are a handful of examples:

- The Burnt Film filter creates gradient wipes. The default simulates a layer dissolving in the manner of a piece of film melting in a projector, but the pattern may also be generated by an imported graphic with alpha.
- Displacement Map uses the luminance information in one file to push the pixels in another layer, so that a Photoshop file, with or without alpha, can distort another layer.
- Natural effects filters such as Fire, Rain and Snow may be mapped to the edges of imported graphics. These filters also contain interaction channels, so that users can make snow accumulate on a Photoshop file's alpha channel, or have rain bounce off it.
- Particle effects such as 2D Particles Advanced, 3D Image Shatter, and Particle System all allow imported images with or without alpha to create custom particle shapes, so that a layer can explode into logo-shaped shards.

These same filters can use gradients to drive particle wipes. Instead of a standard gradient, much more dramatic effects can be achieved when using the alpha channel of an imported graphic to drive a wipe. Imagine a layer exploding into particles *except* for the area defined by an alpha channel.

There are many, many others, but this should offer some idea of the range of effects that can be driven by Photoshop files.

A few more tips. A one-pixel vertical motion blur in Photoshop can frequently smooth out single-pixel elements that can flicker when crossing scan lines.

Some graphic elements, especially those with alpha, look better when rendered with fields. Choose Preferences>Local Project>Enable Better Field Rendering. (Earlier versions of Boris call this **Render Fields as Frames**. Because it results in longer render times, try to render without this option first.)

As mentioned earlier, many users will find it easier to go to the Preferences and set the default for still image import to Premultiplied White. If there's no premultiplication, the image comes through untouched, but it can otherwise save a click or two per image, which can add up quickly over the course of a project.

Rather than build complex layer styles in Photoshop, build them in FX or RED. They have more filters (all of which may be used as adjustment layers), more flexibility, animated apply modes, and a robust style palette to quickly apply favorite parameters. GRAFFITI and RED also feature native vector text with animation features not found elsewhere. Let Photoshop do best what it does best. Let Boris do the rest.

Integrating Adobe Photoshop with discreet combustion

by Lee Roderick[1]

Why Photoshop integration is important for this system. It is to be expected that a client or designer will hand you resources created in Photoshop. The Photoshop file can be directly imported into combustion retaining layers, transfer modes, and opacity. While the discreet combustion Paint Module itself uses image editing procedures similar to Adobe Photoshop, tools such as Custom Brushes, the Healing Brush,Liquify, and Layer Styles are available only in Photoshop.

Proper frame size to create graphics for this system with square pixels. Because combustion is resolution independent, it will not automatically resize images from square-pixel applications such as Photoshop.

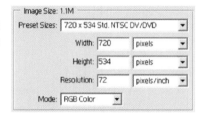

Step 1   When preparing full-frame graphics for a combustion DV NTSC composite, create a 720×534, Photoshop document. Photoshop 7 has a dropdown menu for Preset Sizes in the menu File>New.

Step 2   Create the graphic and save the file. This will be the original file to return to for modification.

Step 3   From the menu Image>Image Size, uncheck the Constrain Proportions box

Step 4   Set Resample Image to Bicubic

Step 5   Change the Height from 534 to 480. Click **OK**.

The image should look squashed down or fatter. Save this file for combustion. When combustion imports the graphic, the squashing is compensated by the nonsquare (.90) pixels in the combustion DV NTSC composite.

When preparing full-frame graphics for a Standard NTSC 601 (D1) composite, follow the same steps but create a 720×540 Photoshop document and change the Height from 540 to 486 before saving for combustion.

1. Lee Roderick was handed a life sentence in video production in 1984 with no possibility of parole. He teaches and works out of North Gate Studios, his facility in San Rafael, California, and is one of the world's six Certified discreet Training Specialists for combustion as well as a co-author of Discreet's Combustion 2 Courseware. Lee's work is not limited to graphics; he is an editor, director, producer, CD-ROM/DVD author and photographer for a wide array of clients throughout California and beyond. "Rod" (he says he likes that) can be contacted at rod@northgatestudios.com. Thanks to Josee Belhumeur, Gary M. Davis, and Ken LaRue for contributing to this supplement.

By default, the combustion viewports display a pixel ratio of 1:1 (square pixels), so an imported full frame Photoshop file may still appear to be squashed. In the combustion menu, enable Window>Use Aspect Ratio to scale the viewport and display the output accordingly.

Supported file types. File formats supported by combustion are:

- PSD (with layers, opacity and blend modes)
- GIF (32-bit, transparency support)
- PNG (32-bit, full alpha support)
- TIFF (32-bit, full alpha support)

- BMP (24-bit only, no alpha support)
- JPEG (24-bit, no alpha support)
- TARGA (32-bit, full alpha support)

Supported image modes. Combustion supports files created in:
- grayscale
- index
- RGB

combustion does not support files created in CMYK, Lab, or multi-channel modes.

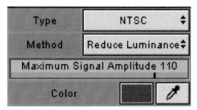

Design with RGB or 601 levels. Design in Photoshop RGB. If the composition is being used for broadcast, it may be necessary to bring the graphic within color safe. After importing the graphic into combustion, apply a broadcast safe color operator (Operators>Video>Broadcast Safe Colors) to reduce the luminance or saturation or to identify NTSC illegal colors for manual correction, such as with the discreet Color Corrector. If the composite contains numerous layers imported from Photoshop, the Broadcast Safe Color Operator can be applied on the final output and optionally nested; this makes all layers safe. Of course, if you are doing genuine broadcast work, always use a vectorscope.

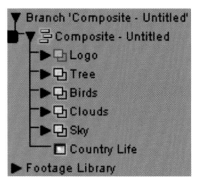

Major Photoshop features that import. Photoshop layers are independently recognized by combustion. Layers can be manipulated and modified individually or as a group. Photoshop layers with visibility turned off will import into combustion **Off** and can be turned **On** by clicking the **Layer** icon (see figure, right) in the workspace. Photoshop layer names are preserved on import.

Photoshop layer blend modes are compatible with combustion layer transfer modes and can be changed easily in combustion. However, new (Photoshop 7) Layer blend modes will import as Normal; these include Linear Burn, Linear Dodge, Vivid Light, Pin Light, and Linear Light.

Photoshop layer opacity imports perfectly and the full range of opacity can be modified and animated in combustion. The advanced blending fill opacity is not acknowledged.

Photoshop clipping groups are imported seamlessly using combustion's Stencil Layer option found in the Surface Controls. The Stencil Layer option is automatically set to Alpha.

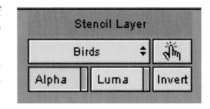

Photoshop features that do not import. combustion does not recognize the following features:

- layer sets. All layers are imported in order from top to bottom, disregarding layer sets and layer set names.
- layer styles when the file is saved as a Photoshop file. Merge a layer containing a layer style down into an empty layer to rasterize it. However, if a Photoshop file is saved as a still image (BMP, GIF, JPEG, PNG, TARGA, or TIFF), layer styles are saved in the image, and there is no need to rasterize.
- Adjustment layers
- Vector type, which is rasterized on import into combustion. If text needs to be scaled or edited, modify the original Photoshop file or use the combustion text tools.
- Vector shape layers, which are ignored on import and must be rasterized before being saved in Photoshop.

How do you import graphics into the system? When importing Photoshop files into combustion, a dialog gives details on how many layers are in the file and offers one of three import options:

- **Merged Image.** The entire Photoshop file becomes a flattened single layer in combustion. Even after merging the file into a single layer, individual layers can be displayed one at a time through the Footage Controls>Source>Source Layer. Uncheck Merge Layers and choose a layer from the dropdown.
- **Grouped.** The Photoshop file is imported as individual layers parented to a null object. Each layer can be controlled and modified separately or manipulated together using the Transform controls for the null object.
- **Nested.** The Photoshop file is imported as individual layers parented to a null object within a nested composite. Each layer can be controlled and modified separately or manipulated together using the Transform controls for the null object. the additional benefit of a nested import is that filters and operators can be applied to the nested composite, affecting the entire group of layers uniformly.

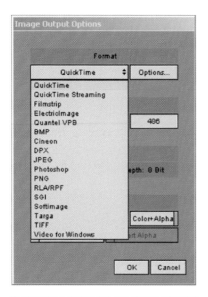

How to export video frames from your system. A single image can be exported from combustion in more than a dozen formats using File>Save Image, with options for compression, frame size, bit depth, and alpha channel. Be aware that the image is saved at Viewport Quality, so change the Viewport Display Quality to Best before saving an image.

An image sequence in any of the standard formats can be exported through combustion from the menu File>Render.

General tips on usage. If the Photoshop file is less than full frame (titles, icons) or larger than full frame (an image you want to pan and zoom around in), the square-to-nonsquare-pixel ratio may not be as obvious. In this event, in the combustion Footage controls, choose From File in the Pixel Aspect Ratio dropdown.

If a file looks squashed or too wide in an NTSC combustion composite and its origin can't be determined, try scaling the layer down 90% on the *y*-axis. If that fixes it, it was created with square pixels, most likely in Photoshop. Remember to enable Window>Use Aspect Ratio to display the proper aspect ratio in the viewport.

Integrating Adobe Photoshop with Sonic Foundry Vegas

by David Hill[1]

Why Photoshop integration is important for this system. At some point, the Vegas user may need the services of an image editing application, and Adobe Photoshop is the natural choice. With Photoshop, you can create a title graphic, tweak an alpha mask, retouch a still image, or convert a vector graphic to a raster graphic for a Vegas project.

Proper frame size to create graphics for this system with square pixels. Vegas can stretch images internally, so it is not mandatory to compensate for pixel aspect ratio at the still image creation stage. If you load the image into Vegas, choose **Event Pan/Crop>Match Output Aspect** (see graphic). Vegas will stretch the image using high-quality internal scaling algorithms. You will usually notice little, if any, distortion from stretching. Also, with this method, you will not have to resize your still images if you are rendering to multiple formats with different pixel aspect ratios.

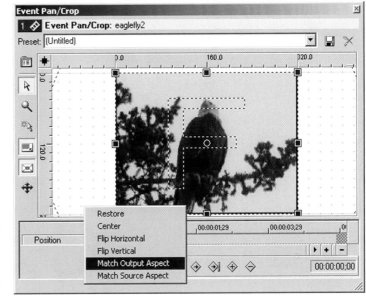

Of course, there may be times when using a pixel-aspect-correct source file is desirable–for instance, when creating masks to be used along with video footage or when ultra-high quality is desired. To create pixel-aspect-correct static graphics in Photoshop to use in Vegas, multiply the destination format's frame width times the destination format's pixel aspect ratio. For example, for DV, which is 720×480 with a pixel aspect ratio of 0.9091, use a still image size of 655×480.

---

1. David Hill has been the engineering manager for Vegas Video since 1999 and continues to work on Vegas with an exceptionally talented team of developers at Sonic Foundry's Madison, Wisconsin, headquarters. Dave has been involved in the television industry for more than 20 years, dating back to the Quad epoch. He has done time as an online editor, offline editor, post house creative director, tape and film cameraman, live sports technical director, documentary producer, and software publisher. Though he has won numerous industry awards for his work, none of them ever had any positive impact on his day rate. Dave can be reached by e-mail at drdropout@sonicfoundry.com

The math is simple.

720	×	0.9091	= ~655 pixels
destination frame width, in pixels		(Pixel aspect ratio of NTSC DV)	This is the width you should use when creating NTSC DV graphics in Photoshop. Height remains unchanged at 480 pixels.

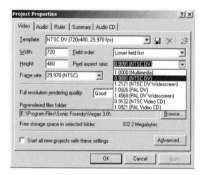

You can find a large list of pixel aspect ratios in Vegas>Project properties, as shown in the figure.

What file types are supported. Sonic Foundry supports the following file formats:

- PSD (including alpha channel)
- PNG (including alpha channel)
- TARGA (including alpha channel)
- BMP
- TIFF (requires QuickTime authoring components to be installed)
- JPEG
- GIF

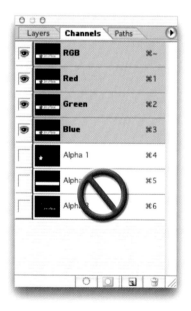

The PNG format, while less commonly used than PSD or TARGA, is an excellent choice for graphics destined for Vegas. In addition to producing high quality, Vegas can autointerpret the presence of alpha channel in PNG files.

Image modes supported. Vegas provides support for both 8- and 16-bits per pixel. The following color modes are supported:
- RGB
- indexed
- grayscale
- CMYK

The following color modes are not supported: Lab and multichannel.

Design with RGB or 601 levels. Choose RGB or 601, depending on the destination format you are working with. If needed, color correction filters can be applied in Vegas to deal with illegal color values in RGB files.

Major Photoshop features that import. The first alpha channel is properly understood on import. Do not save more than one alpha channel with your native .psd file.

If you are planning to zoom in on the graphic using motion effects within Vegas, it is a good idea to make the graphic larger than the video frame. If you double the frame size (for NTSC DV, this would be 1310×960), you'll be able to zoom in on the image with no distortion and get the "Ken Burns" look.

Photoshop features that do not import. Feel free to use all of Photoshop's features. If your file contains layers, layer sets, layer styles, blending modes, vector type, or vector shapes, Vegas will properly interpret them on import. The .psd files will be opened with all visible layers flattened. Alpha channel will be retained and can be enabled (with several interpretation options) in the Vegas Media Properties dialog.

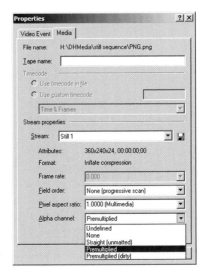

Importing graphics. Vegas opens supported still image files like any other file type. You can adjust the alpha channel interpretation in the Media Properties dialog. You can also save the alpha channel settings so that any file you subsequently open that has the same parameters will use the same alpha interpretation.

Exporting video frames from your system. Vegas can save a timeline snapshot PNG (with alpha). Set the Vegas Preview window to project size, best quality; cue to the frame you want to capture; apply any needed processing (filters, de-interlace, etc.). Vegas will save a pixel-aspect-corrected still (either a PNG with alpha or a low-quality JPEG). Timeline snapshots are WYSIWYG—what you see in the Vegas Preview window is what you will see when you open the file in Photoshop for editing.

General tips on usage. Rendering using the **Best** video rendering quality setting will produce the cleanest results because the highest quality scaling algorithms are used. Render time will likely increase using **Best**, so it is a good idea to do a test render using the Good setting. In many cases, this will look excellent and require less render time.

If you are zooming in on still images in a Vegas project and notice flickering or combing artifacts in the moving image, you may want enable the Reduce Interlace Flicker (event switch). There is no one setting that produces perfect results under any circumstance, so some experimentation is often needed to obtain the perfect look.

Integrating Adobe Photoshop with Avid Editing Systems

by Richard Harrington

Alias
BMP
Chyron
Cineon
ERIMovie
Framestore
IFF
JPEG
OMF
PCX
Photoshop
PICS
√ PICT
Pixar
PNG
QRT
Rendition
SGI
Softimage
SunRaster
TARGA
TIFF
Wavefront
XWindows
YUV

Why Photoshop integration is important for this system. Avid editing systems are the most widely used option for video postproduction. They are indeed an *edit* system and not a *paint* package, however. The proper use of Adobe Photoshop gives Avid users access to advanced titling opportunities as well as a chance to prepare logos and photos for import. Avid recognizes this important connection and even offers an advanced course through Avid Education Centers called *Creating Graphics and Mattes with Avid Media Composer and Adobe Photoshop.*

Proper frame size to create graphics for this system with square pixels. Depending upon which Avid system you are using and which video standard (NTSC or PAL) used in your particular country, your graphic size may vary. All graphics should be properly sized before you import them. Improperly sized graphics are prone to distortion and loss of quality.

For those working with standard definition video, such as Avid Media Composer, Avid Symphony, and Avid Xpress, use the following sizes:

Format	4×3 Aspect Ratio Square Pixel	16×9 Aspect Ratio Square Pixel	Native Size [1] Nonsquare Pixel
NTSC	648×486	864×486	720×486
PAL	768×576	1024×576	720×576

1. Native size is the actual frame size stored by the Avid system.

There are two square-pixel sizes listed for the 4×3 aspect ratio for flexibility. Designing at the 720×540 standard allows you to carry graphics to both NTSC and PAL. A small crop to 720×534 will also allow them to be used with DV footage or DVD titles.

For those working with the digital video formats on Avid Xpress DV, use the following sizes:

Format	4×3 Aspect Ratio Square Pixel	16×9 Aspect Ratio Square Pixel	Native Size [1] Nonsquare Pixel
NTSC	648×480	853×480	720×480
PAL	768×576	1024×576	720×576

1. Native size is the actual frame size stored by the Avid system.

Supported file types. Avid systems support 24 still-graphic file formats. The two most common formats that Avid recommends are TIFF and PICT. The following table lists the most common formats you will likely encounter. For a complete list, see the Avid online help file or the user's manual.

Format	Extension	Alpha?	Comments
Alias	.als	No	Alpha must be a separate file.
BMP	.bmp	No	
Chyron	.chr	Yes	Images must be saved as a frame store file.
JPEG	.jpg	No	CMYK images are not supported.
Photoshop	.psd	Yes	CMYK images and files with more than four channels are not supported.
PICT	.pct	Yes	
PNG	.png	Yes	
Softimage	.pic	Yes	
TARGA	.tga	Yes	
TIFF	.tif	Yes	RGB and grayscale images import correctly, as do layered TIFF files created with Adobe Photoshop 6 or newer. CMYK and files with more than four channels do not import correctly.
Wavefront	.rla	Yes	

Supported image modes. Both 8-bit and 16-bit RGB are supported reliably. Note that at this time, Photoshop images that contain layers do not support the 16-bit format.

Design with RGB or 601 levels. You have three choices for color levels when importing with an Avid system: RGB, RGB Dithered, and 601. The method you choose to use will affect how you work in Photoshop.

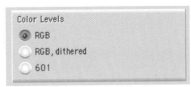

RGB. This is the most common color model used. Most computer-generated graphics use RGB graphics levels (0–255). If you choose RGB when you import to the Avid system, your graphics will be remapped to appropriate ITU-R 601 (formerly CCIR 601) video color. The blackest black in the document will be assigned video black levels, and the whitest white will be mapped to video white.

RGB Dithered. If your file contains complex color effects–such as a gradient or complex glow–and you are importing at a high resolution (2:1), choose this option. The 8-bit limit of 4:2:2 video encoding is prone to banding with fine gradients.

601. Use this option if the imported graphics file has video levels based on the ITU-R 601 (formerly CCIR 601) standard. This would include frames of digitized video that were exported and processed in Photoshop. This also includes Avid color bars or images that include superblack for luma-keying.

If you are exporting a frame from your Avid system for touch up in Photoshop, export it with 601 levels. Once you take it into Photoshop, be sure to avoid any adjustments to levels or saturation, or a visible color-shift will likely occur.

All other graphics that originate in Photoshop can be designed using the full color range of the RGB format. However, be certain to specify RGB or RGB, dithered levels when you import.

Major Photoshop features that import. The following properties transfer correctly into Photoshop:

Opacity. The imported layer's opacity becomes the Foreground Level control in the Effect Editor.

Layer Group. Layer grouping is ignored. However all layers, including grouped layers, are imported as individual layers.

Layer Set. All layers within a layer set are imported to individual layers.

Type Layers. Type is rasterized.

Solid Layer. Solid layers are brought in as a graphic with a full-screen, opaque alpha channel.

Gradient Layer. Gradient transparency is preserved upon import.

Pattern Layer. Pattern adjustment layers make the trip.

Photoshop features that do not import. B

lending Modes. Merge the blended layers together. Only normal mode is supported.

Layer/Set Mask. Layer and set masks are ignored. To keep the mask's transparency, you must merge the set or layer with an empty layer. Highlight the empty layer as a target.

Layer Effects. Layer effects must also be merged in order to travel.

Adjustment Layers. Merge the adjusted layers together.

How to import graphics. Importing graphics into your system is pretty straightforward. However, you need to understand a few options.

Step 1   Select the bin where you want the imported file(s) to be stored.

Step 2   Choose File>Import.

Step 3   Navigate to where the files are located.

Step 4   Select the files to import. Hold down the Cmd or Shift key (Ctrl or Shift key) to select multiple files. The **Shift** key selects contiguous files; the Cmd (Ctrl) key selects noncontiguous files.

Step 5   Choose a Media Drive and specify the resolution settings that best match your project. Remember, compressed and uncompressed footage cannot be mixed.

Step 6   Click the Options button and specify the options that best match your project and source materials.

601, nonsquare	This is the default setting. It assumes that your video has been properly sized for import to your Avid system. Use this option to import images with the native dimensions used by the Avid system: 720×480 (NTSC DV), 720×486 (NTSC), or 72×576 (PAL). Also use this option for 720×540 images or other images that match the 4×3 aspect ratio.
Maintain, nonsquare	This option never scales or resizes. In a D1 environment, use this with images sized for DVD or DV (720×480). The image is centered and padded with black at top and bottom to fill out the 486 scan lines for those systems that need it. In Xpress DV, up to 480 (NTSC) or 576 (PAL) lines are preserved. The extras are removed or missing lines are padded with video black. Use this option for DV-sized material being used in a D1 project, or vice-versa.
Maintain, square	This is for images that use square pixels and are smaller than the video frame. This will prevent enlarging the image and thus softening it. Square pixels are resized for nonsquare usage, and the empty areas are filled with video black.
Maintain and Resize, square	This option assumes that the image aspect ratio is incorrect. It will letterbox the image and scale to fit the 720 pixel width or the 480 (NTSC DV), 486 (NTSC), or 576 (PAL) size. It will also compensate for square pixels. For best full-screen resolution of files created with square pixels, use 648×480 (NTSC) or 768×576 (PAL). To create a single resolution for both NTSC and PAL, use 720×540. Do not use this option to bring in a full-screen, square-pixel image that has already been stretched to nonsquare-pixel dimensions.
File Field Order	Leave set to **Noninterlaced** for still graphics.
Color Levels	Choose from RGB, RGB Dithered, or 601, based on the criteria outlined in "Design with RGB or 601 levels" on page 269.

Alpha

Use Existing	Applies only to images that have an attached alpha channel. If you create your alpha channels with the **Save Selection As Channel** button, this method will not work properly.
Invert Existing	This method inverts the Alpha Channel. This one is generally more useful to Photoshop users.
Ignore	Alpha channel is disregarded.
Single Frame Import	Specify a length for the clip.

Step 7   When satisfied with your options, click OK to close the dialog box.

Step 8   Click OK to begin import.

Step 9   Specify how you want the files imported. Your Avid system can import a Photoshop graphic in three different ways: as a flattened image or as a multilayered graphic with some or all of the layers.

If you intend to key the graphic without any complex reveal or animation, such as a lower third, choose **Flattened**.

If you are going to use the layers to build an animation or complex reveal, choose to import as a sequence of layers or select layers. Each layer imports as a separate object (a matte key or master clip). These can then be manipulated individually like any other matte key or master clip.

Upon import, the Avid system presents you with a sequence with each layer on a separate track. This will allow you to edit all of the layers into a final sequence. The names and order of the layers are preserved from the original Photoshop file.

How to export video frames

Step 1   Load the clip or sequence that contains the desired clip into your source or record monitor.

Step 2   Park on the desired position with the position indicator (blue bar).

Step 3 Choose File>Export.

Step 4 The pop-up list at the bottom of the dialog box contains saved Export settings. You can use these or create specialized exports.

Step 5 Click the **Options** button to access the Export Settings dialog box.

Step 6 Choose Graphic from the Export As menu.

Step 7 Specify the following options:

    a. Use Marks—If selected, the in point is used. If deselected, the position indicator is used.

    b. Use Enabled Tracks—If selected, the highest active track is used. If deselected, the highest monitored track is used.

    c. Graphic Format—Specify the output type. Avoid JPEG and GIF; they introduce undesirable compression.

    d. Format Options—Access specific options for each format.

    e. Width, Height—Use the presets to specify an output size. Use square pixels for print and web. Use native size when touching up and reimporting or going to After Effects.

    f. Scale to Fit or Crop/Pad—How the image is forced to fit the export size.

    g. Color Levels—RGB is used most of the time. Specify 601 levels if you plan to reimport after touchup.

    h. File Field Order—The Single Field option is best when exporting.

Step 8 Deselect Sequential Files option.

Step 9 Click Save As to save the setting for future use.

Step 10 Navigate to storage destination.

Step 11 Enter name for graphic with version number. Avoid alpha-numeric characters and spaces.

Step 12 Click OK to save.

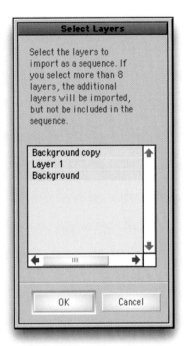

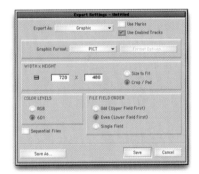

General tips on usage. It is important to note that:

- Opacity levels from Photoshop are converted to Foreground level in the Matte Key effect.
- Layer order and layer names are preserved during import to the system.
- A hidden layer will be imported as a matte key.
- Vector text and shape layers are rasterized during import to the Avid.
- Graphics must be RGB (8 or 16 bits) or grayscale.

Integrating Adobe Photoshop with Apple Final Cut Pro

by Richard Harrington

Why Photoshop integration is important for this system. Early versions of Final Cut Pro lacked a strong titler. This fact combined with Photoshop's strong reputation helped it make inroads with the FCP-user community. Final Cut Pro's excellent support for importing layered documents and the flexibility to make changes with the External Editor's tab has proven a viable option for creating more graphically intense videos.

Proper frame size to create graphics for this system with square pixels. If you are right out of the box or using Firewire to capture or converter box, you are probably using the DV format. Whether you are using DV, DVCPRO, or DVCAM, your end result is a frame size of 720×480.

Format	4×3 Aspect Ratio Square Pixel	16×9 Aspect Ratio Square Pixel	Native Size [1] Nonsquare Pixel
NTSC	720×534	960×540	720×480
PAL	768×576	1024×576	720×576

1. Native size is the actual frame size stored by the FCP system.

If you are working on a hardware-accelerated system, you are most likely working at a 601 frame size. Here I offer general guidelines, but always confer with the documentation that shipped with your hardware capture board, or check the manufacturer's Web site.

Format	4×3 Aspect Ratio Square Pixel	16×9 Aspect Ratio Square Pixel	Native Size [1] Nonsquare Pixel
NTSC	720×540	864×540	720×486
PAL	768×576	1024×576	720×576

1. Native size is the actual frame size stored by the FCP system.

The final step is to resize the square pixel graphic to the desired non-square pixel size. To do this, choose Image>Image Size. Uncheck the **Constrain Proportions** box in type in the native size from the previous chart. The graphic will now display correctly when played back from the timeline.

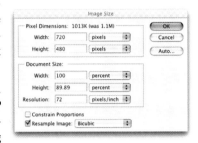

It is also possible to bring in a graphic that is larger than the screen. Make sure that the graphic is a single-layer document. This way, FCP will recognize the square-pixel nature of the graphic and automatically compensate. Using a high-resolution image is useful for creating backgrounds or simulating motion control photography. Keyframed motion parameters such as Center, Anchor Point, and Scale parameters in a clip's Motion tab allow panning and zooming. Be certain not to scale over 100%, or image softening will occur.

Supported file types. Final Cut Pro Systems are capable of supporting several graphic formats. Because FCP is QuickTime based, it can draw upon a wide variety of formats. Some of the most popular formats include:

Format	Extension	Alpha?	Comments
BMP	.bmp	No	BMP: Windows bitmap format. This format supports color depths from dithered black-and-white to Millions of Colors.
JPEG	.jpg	No	CMYK Images are not supported. A popular file format because it can create highly compressed yet good-looking graphics files. This format is not well suited for additional compression by editing into a video sequence.
Photoshop	.psd	Yes	CMYK images and files with more than four channels aren't supported. Supports color and grayscale 8-bit graphics, Millions of Colors, and alpha channels.
PICT	.pct	Yes	A common image format used on Mac computers.
PNG	.png	Yes	Allows color depths from black-and-white to Millions of Colors+.
TARGA	.tga	Yes	An uncompressed file format that is supported by nearly every media application.
TIFF	.tif	Yes	RGB and grayscale images import correctly. Advanced TIFF files created with Adobe Photoshop 6 or newer import correctly. CMYK and files with more than four channels do not import correctly.

Supported image modes. Both 8-bit and 16-bit RGB are supported reliably. Note that at this time, Photoshop images that contain layers do not support the 16-bit format.

Design with RGB or 601 levels. When a graphics clip is edited into a sequence, its levels are affected by the **Process maximum white as** pop-up menu in the Video Processing tab of the Sequence Settings. If it is set to White, then the brightest white in the graphic will appear at 100% when viewed on FCP's Waveform Monitor. If the sequence is set to Superwhite, then the brightest white of the graphic will register 109% on FCP's Waveform Monitor.

Use the Superwhite setting to match the brightness of imported graphics to video that was shot and captured with the superwhite luminance levels. This is generally the case with many consumer camcorders. If the video was shot under controlled conditions, a maximum white level of 100 IRE in the recorded video signal, you should have **Process maximum white as** set to White. This will help ensure that the white levels of the graphics match properly.

If an imported graphic triggers Final Cut Pro's **Range Check** feature, you should adjust the graphic's levels or saturation back in Photoshop. While using the **3-way Color Corrector** may seem desirable, you are adding unnecessary render time. The quickest fix is to reopen the graphic in the appropriate external editor.

You can define which applications will open for editing specific kinds of clips. Set the **Still Image** tab to open Adobe Photoshop. To open the clip in Photoshop, do one of the following:

• Control-click on a clip in the Canvas or Browser. Then select Open in Editor from the pop-up menu.
• Select a clip in the Timeline or Browser. Then select Clip in Editor from the View menu.

Make any changes you need to the graphic. Then close and save changes. As long as you do not change the order or number of layers, the changes will automatically update in Final Cut Pro.

Major Photoshop features that import. Final Cut Pro lets you import multilayered Photoshop files. It is possible to import any version of Photoshop files, but only those features that work in Photoshop 3.0 features are supported. Supported features include opacity, composite modes, layer order, and layer name.

The following properties transfer correctly into Photoshop:

Opacity. The imported layer's opacity becomes the Opacity control in the Motion Tab.

Blending Modes. The following blend modes transfer correctly: Add, Subtract, Difference, Multiply, Screen, Overlay, Hard Light, Soft Light, Darken, and Lighten.

Layer Group. Layer grouping is ignored. However, all layers, including grouped layers, are imported as individual layers.

Layer Set. All layers within a layer set are imported to individual layers.

Type Layers. Type is rasterized.

Shape Layers. Shape layers are rasterized.

Solid Color Fill Layers. Solid color fill layers are brought in as a graphic with a full-screen, opaque alpha channel.

Gradient Fill Layers. Gradient fill layers are preserved upon import.

Pattern Fill Layers. Pattern fill layers import.

When importing a multilayered Photoshop document, Final Cut Pro creates a new sequence. All of the layers of the Photoshop file are composited together. The sequence uses a frame size identical to the imported file's frame size.

Photoshop features that do not import

Blending Modes. Merge the blended layers together if an unsupported blend mode is used. The following modes are not supported: Dissolve, Color Burn, Linear Burn, Color Dodge, Linear Dodge, Vivid Light, Linear Light, Pin Light, Exclusion, Hue, Saturation, Color2, and Luminosity.

Layer/Set Mask. Layer and set masks are ignored. To keep the mask's transparency, you must merge the set or layer with an empty layer. Highlight the empty layer as a target.

Layer Effects. Layer effects must also be merged in order to travel.

Adjustment Layers. Merge the adjusted layers together.

How to import graphics. Importing graphics into your system is pretty straightforward. There are a few options, however, that you need to understand. The steps are as follows.

To import a file or folder:

Step 1 At the Finder level, copy or move the files and folders that need to be imported to the project folder and hard disk. It is a good idea to keep all nontimecoded elements—such as graphics, sound files, and imported movies—in one folder. This facilitates the archival and backup procedures needed to preserve a project.

Step 2 In the Browser, select a destination:

- Click on a project's tab in order to import files or folders into the main (root) level of a project or
- To import files directly into a bin within a project, you must first open that bin. Double-click the bin; it will open in a separate window. Import your items directly into this bin.

Step 3 To import, do one of the following:

- Drag the files or folders from the finder to a project tab or bin in the Browser.
- Choose Import from the File menu (Cmd+I). Select File or Folder from the submenu. Select a file or folder in the dialog box, and click Open.
- Control-click in the Browser or a bin's window. Next, choose Import File or Import Folder from the pop-up menu. Select a file or folder; then click Open.

Step 4 Save the project.

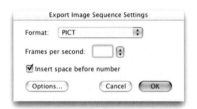

How do you export video frames from your system?

Step 1 In the Canvas or Viewer, place the playhead at the desired frame.

Step 2 From the File menu, choose Export. Then pick QuickTime from the submenu.

Step 3 Select a location and enter a name for the file.

Step 4 Select Still Image from the Format pop-up menu.

Step 5 Pick a setting from the Use pop-up menu. Ignore the frame rate (fps); it doesn't apply to a single frame.

Step 6 You can customize the export setting by clicking on the Options button. Adjust the options and export format; then click OK.

Step 7 When ready to export, click Save.

General tips on usage. It is important to note that:

- An imported Photoshop file becomes a sequence in the project.
- In order to import a layered Photoshop file as a single clip, it must be flattened in Photoshop first.
- A transparent background in the .psd file creates a transparent background in the new sequence.
- Layer opacity settings, some layer modes, fill layers, and visibility are preserved upon import.
- When making modifications to a .psd file that's already used in a Final Cut Pro project, do not add or delete layers.

Glossary

Special thanks to Glen Stephens, from Tools for Television, for help writing the glossary.

16-bit color   65,000 different colors.

24-bit color   16.7 million different colors.

8-bit Color   256 different colors.

action safe area   The action safe area of an image is the outer box of the safe grid. All action taking place on screen should be composed inside this area, or it will not be seen when viewed on a television set.

Actions   Scriptable macros within Photoshop that allow you to record your steps in the design process and easily repeat those steps multiple times. Actions can be assigned to F keys and used to batch process files. Virtually all menu commands and processes are available to be recorded as actions.

additive color model   A color model that creates white when the primary colors of the model are added together. For example, adding red, green, and blue in the RGB model will create white.

adjustment layer   A layer that is placed above an art layer that creates adjustments to the layers below it. Adjustments can be levels, curves, color balance, hue saturation, and many others. Adjustment layers provide a nondestructive way of altering your image.

Adobe Acrobat   Adobe® Acrobat® 5.0 software lets you convert any document to an Adobe Portable Document Format (PDF) file. Anyone can open your document across a broad range of hardware and software, and it will look exactly as you intended—with layout, fonts, links, and images intact.

Adobe After Effects   Adobe® After Effects® 5.5 software delivers a comprehensive set of tools to efficiently produce motion graphics and visual effects for film, video, multimedia, and

the Web. You can explore unlimited creative possibilities with precise control while working in a 2D or 3D compositing environment.

Adobe Illustrator   Adobe® Illustrator® software defines the future of vector graphics with groundbreaking creative options and powerful tools for efficiently publishing artwork on the Web, in print, everywhere.

Adobe ImageReady   Adobe Image Ready is an application by Adobe Systems that prepares Photoshop images and others for web output. Image Ready provides support for GIF animations, rollovers, and a variety of other web-based graphic applications.

Adobe LiveMotion   Adobe LiveMotion is a web animation program for creating animations in the SWF format. It uses a similar interface to Adobe After Effects and allows users to create animations for Internet and multimedia uses.

Adobe Premiere   Delivering unmatched hardware support, Adobe® Premiere® software is the most adaptable DV-editing tool on the market today. Premiere allows you to work more productively with Real-Time Preview. And you can take advantage of the sophisticated new Adobe Title Designer, MPEG-2 export, DVD authoring, powerful audio tools, and more to create extraordinary video productions. Whether you want to edit digital video on your laptop or work with multiple layers of analog footage on a professional, hardware-based, real-time system, Adobe Premiere is the hands-down choice for desktop video editing.

Adobe Type Manager   Adobe Type Manager is an application by Adobe Systems that manages the fonts in your system and allows you to activate fonts and sets of fonts quickly and easily.

aliasing   Aliased images are images that have a rough or jagged edge to them. This is caused by the fact that all raster or bitmapped images are created from tiny square pixels, which inherently cannot create perfectly smooth edges.

Anti-aliased images are images that have a smooth appearance to their edges. Anti-aliasing is achieved by varying the opacity of the pixels on the outer edge of the object, giving the appearance of a smooth edge.

Different tools in the palette window have an anti-aliasing option, such as the **Marquee** tool and the **Text** tool. Your images will look smoother and cleaner if you have this option turned on.

Anti-aliasing introduces the problem of the background color within your image being visible around the edges of your graphic when your graphic is keyed.

Align Linked   Align Linked allows you to link a series of layers and align the contents of each layer to the parent layer. This is the same function as left, right, or center aligning text in a word processor.

alpha channel   An alpha channel is the fourth channel in an RGB image. This channel is used to key out certain portions of your graphic.

The alpha channel acts as a cookie cutter to remove portions of the image and replace them with underlying video.

In most video systems, any area in the alpha channel that is white will show the graphic when keyed, and any area that is black will pass video through. Some systems, however, such as Avid systems, reverse the black and white areas. This is referred to as an inverse alpha channel.

Alpha channels also support varying levels of opacity in an image. Shades of gray in an alpha channel show areas of the graphic as partially transparent. The closer to white the gray area is, the more opaque the graphic is for the corresponding pixels, and the closer to black the gray is, the more transparent the corresponding pixels are.

anamorphic   D1 and DV video signals can be shot for playback in a 16×9 format. Anamorphic 16×9 is video that is squeezed horizontally so that when it is played back in 16×9 mode, it is stretched back to its original size to display a normal-looking image.

Graphics created for an anamorphic output need to be designed at 864×486, and then squeezed down to 720×486 for D1.

Note: For DV, design your files as 864×480 and resize them to 720×480.

For PAL, design your files as 1024×576 and resize them to 720×576.

aspect ratio   An aspect ratio is the general size of a given video format. For example, NTSC has a 4×3 aspect ratio so that all television sets are four units wide for every three units tall.

ATSC   The ATSC (Advanced Television Standards Committee) is the governing body that sets the standards for HDTV.

Bézier curve   A Bézier curve is the curve created in Photoshop using the **Pen** tool that creates vector-based artwork. Bézier curves are the foundation for artwork created in Adobe Illustrator and Macromedia Freehand.

Bitmap   See *Raster Images*.

blending modes   Modes used in Photoshop to mathematically blend a layer with visible layers beneath it.

BMP   BMP is a standard Windows image format on DOS and Windows-compatible computers. BMP format supports RGB, indexed color, grayscale, and bitmap color modes. You can specify either Windows or OS/2® format and a bit depth for the image. For 4-bit and 8-bit images using Windows format, you can also specify RLE compression.

brightness   Brightness is how light or dark a color is. It is independent from saturation.

Button mode   A mode available in the Actions palette that displays all of your actions as buttons. Actions can be executed by clicking these buttons. When in **Button** mode, color labels and keyboard shortcuts are visible on the buttons.

Calculations command   This command lets you blend two individual channels from one or more source images. You can then apply the results to a new image or to a new channel or selection in the active image.

CCIR 601   DV and D1 signals are both NTSC nonsquare pixel video formats. However, CCIR-601 (sometimes called D1) is 720×486 pixels while the DV, or digital video standard, is 720×480 pixels, six fewer than the D1 standard. If this difference is not addressed in your designs, your graphics may not look correct when output to video.

Character palette   The **Character** palette allows you to edit text attributes such as font size, kerning, leading, line spacing, as well as the font name and color.

clipping path   An image clipping path is a path set in Photoshop that lets you isolate certain portions of an image and make everything else transparent when the image is printed or placed in another application.

CMYK   The CMYK color mode is used primarily in the print world. It stands for cyan, magenta, yellow, and black (or key). The images in this color mode are comprised of these four colors. Logos that you receive for your broadcast graphics will most likely be in the CMYK color mode. These need to be converted to RGB before they can be used. Menu: Image>Mode>CMYK Color

Pasting them, or simply moving them to your broadcast graphic will automatically convert it to an RGB color mode.

codec, animation   Codec stands for compressor decompressor. The animation codec is a codec used to encode QuickTime movies in an uncompressed file. This is the highest quality codec you can use that is the most compatible with other systems.

codec, none   When you choose to render a clip without a codec, you are rendering at a quality higher than an animation codec with virtually no compression.

color gamut   Color gamuts are the range of colors that a particular graphics system can display. All hardware differs in ability to reproduce colors.

RGB and CMYK are different color spaces that represent different color gamuts. However, color gamuts go far beyond that. Macintosh and Windows systems have slightly different color gamuts as well. And most importantly, computer and televisions have very different color gamuts. Inevitably, colors may tend to change when viewed on different systems.

Color Picker   The **Color Picker** in Photoshop allows you to select foreground and background colors to be used in your images. Colors can be selected using Lab, HSB, RGB, CMYK, and HEX settings, or simply by clicking on a given color.

color swatches   The Swatches palette is a place to store frequently used colors. You can store any combination of colors in the Swatches palette and save them to swatch files for easy color cataloging.

composition   A composition in After Effects is similar to a canvas in Photoshop in that it is made up of multiple layers. A project can have multiple compositions, and a composition can have multiple layers, which can include other compositions.

conditional mode change   This is a command that allows you to batch convert a series of images to a given color mode, depending on its original color mode. For example, you can tell the dialog to convert all open images with a CMYK or grayscale color mode to an RGB color mode, leaving all other images untouched.

Constrain Proportions Constrain Proportions means to equally scale height and width proportionally to each other. This prevents an image from being stretched when it is resized.

contours You can use contours to shape the appearance of an effect over a given range in the Drop Shadow, Inner Shadow, Inner Glow, Outer Glow, Bevel and Emboss, and Satin effects when creating custom layer styles. For example, a Linear contour on a Drop Shadow causes the opacity to drop off in a linear transition, while a Custom contour can be used to create a unique shadow transition.

contrast See *contrast ratio*.

contrast ratio The contrast of an image is how many steps of gray exist between the white and black areas of the image. This is typically expressed in terms of a ratio. The typical contrast ratio for video is 40:1, meaning that the brightest part of an image can only be 40 times brighter than the darkest area. Some digital cameras with high-quality CCDs can reach a contrast ratio of 100:1.

Copy Merged Copy Merged copies a merged image of the visible layers in your Photoshop document to the clipboard.

crop Cropping an image decreases the canvas size of the image without scaling or resizing pixels.

D1 DV and D1 signals are both NTSC nonsquare pixel video formats. However, D1 (sometimes called CCIR-601) is 720×486 pixels while the DV, or digital video standard, is 720×480 pixels, six fewer than the D1 standard. If this difference is not addressed in your designs, your graphics may not look correct when output to video.

DCS The Desktop Color Separations format is a variation of the standard EPS format. It is for saving color separations of CMYK images. This format has no uses for video applications.

De-interlace filter A filter that removes the interlaced scan lines of an image captured from a video card using either duplication or interpolation.

defringe Defringe replaces the color of any fringe pixels with the colors of nearby pixels containing pure colors (those without background color). For example, if you select a yellow object on a blue background and then move the selection, some of the blue background is selected and moved with the object. Defringe replaces the blue pixels with yellow ones.

Desaturate command The Desaturate command converts a color image to a grayscale image in the same color mode. For example, it assigns equal red, green, and blue values to each pixel in an RGB image to make it appear grayscale. The lightness value of each pixel does not change.

This command has the same effect as setting Saturation to –100 in the Hue/Saturation dialog box.

direct selection Direct selection tools would be the **Marquee** tool, the **Magic Wand**, and the **Lasso** tools. These tools allow you to make a selection directly on the canvas of your image.

dots per inch (dpi) This is considered the resolution of your image, and it is a measurement of the number of dots or pixels displayed per unit. This is referred to as dpi. The screen resolution or dpi of video is often expressed as 72 dpi (although video is really just total pixels used).

duotone This mode creates two-color grayscale images using two inks. Images must first be grayscale before converting to duotone.

DV DV and D1 signals are both NTSC nonsquare pixel video formats. However, D1 (sometimes called CCIR-601) is 720×486 pixels while the DV, or digital video standard, is 720×480 pixels, six fewer than the D1 standard. If this difference is not addressed in your designs, your graphics may not look correct when output to video.

dye-sub printer A printer that uses colored film that is heated and impressed onto the paper as a vapor to achieve color images. Dye-sub printers have better printing quality than ink jet printers because they are continuous tone and undithered.

EPS The Encapsulated PostScript (EPS) language file format can contain both bitmap and vector graphics in RGB, Lab, CMYK, indexed color, duotone, grayscale, and bitmap color modes. It is a widely supported format in the print world. When asking for logo files, an Illustrator file (.ai) or an EPS created in a vector program is desirable. When opening an EPS file containing vector graphics, Photoshop converts the vector graphics to pixels. There are no advantages to the EPS format for video applications.

Equalize command The **Equalize** command redistributes the brightness values of the pixels in an image so that they more evenly represent the entire range of brightness levels. When you apply this command, Photoshop finds the brightest and darkest values in the composite image and remaps them so that the brightest value represents white and the darkest value represents black. Photoshop then attempts to equalize the brightness–that is, to distribute the intermediate pixel values evenly throughout the grayscale.

Export The **Export** function of Photoshop will allow two types of exports: Paths to Illustrator and Zoom View. Paths to Illustrator will create an Illustrator file from any vector-based elements within your file. ZoomView is a format for delivering high-resolution images over the Web. With the Viewpoint Media Player, users can zoom into or out of an image and pan the image to see its various parts.

Eye icon The **Eye** icon turns the visibility on and off for a given layer or channel. Turning the eyeball off will hide the layer or channel, and turning the eyeball on will show it.

Fade Filter command The **Fade Filter** command allows you to fade the effect of a filter that has been applied based on percentages. It also gives you the option to apply a blend mode to the filter that was applied.

Feather The **Feather** function allows you to smooth or soften the edges of a selection.

field All NTSC television signals are made up of 60 fields per second. Television signals are made up of horizontal lines stacked from the top of your television screen to the bottom. NTSC is made up of 525 lines of video. Showing all of the odd lines (1, 3, 5, 7, 9, etc.) at once is one field. Showing all even lines (2, 4, 6, 8, etc.) at once is the other field. It takes two fields of video to make one frame. PAL is made up of 625 lines of video, and interlaces the images the same as NTSC does, only with more lines. This creates an interlaced image, interlacing fields to create frames of video. Fields can create problems when video stills are brought into Photoshop. These lines are visible on your computer monitor and need to be removed by deinterlacing the image.

fill signal The fill signal is the RGB graphic portion of an image. This is the image that you want your viewers to see. The fill signal fills the image where the key signal allows it to pass. This signal is derived from the color information of your graphic.

Filmstrip   The Filmstrip format is used for movie files created by Adobe Premiere. Every frame of video is saved to one file, which you can open in Photoshop for rotoscoping. This generally does not produce smooth results because you lack the ability to keyframe or 'tween items. If you change resolution, delete alpha channels, or alter the color mode, you won't be able to save it back to Filmstrip format. For more information, look in your Premiere owner's manual.

FireWire   FireWire is the brand name for IEEE 1394, a high-performance serial bus for connecting devices such as hard drives and cameras to your computer. Apple computer invented it in 1986.

frame   All NTSC television signals are made up of 30 frames per second. All PAL television signals are made up of 25 frames per second. Frames of video are essentially a series of still images flashed on the screen in rapid succession to create the illusion of movement. Two fields of video make up one frame.

full-screen mode   Full-screen mode in Photoshop allows you to set the entire screen to your canvas, hiding the desktop in the background. You have two full-screen modes available: with and without the menu bar.

GIF   The Graphics Interchange Format (GIF) was originally developed by online service provider CompuServe. (If you remember them, add one point to your Geek IQ.) This format displays 8-bit or indexed-color graphics and images in HTML documents on the Internet. Because of its small color range and compressed images, this format is not very useful for video editing.

Gradient Fill   You fill an area with a gradient by dragging in the image with the gradient tool selected. The starting point (where the mouse is pressed) and ending point (where the mouse is released) affect the gradient appearance, depending on the gradient tool used. Gradients will be applied only to selected areas within your image.

Gradient Map   The **Gradient Map** command maps the equivalent grayscale range of an image to the colors of a specified gradient fill. If you specify a two-color gradient fill, for example, shadows in the image map to one of the endpoint colors of the gradient fill, highlights map to the other endpoint color, and midtones map to the gradations in between.

Group   A layer can be grouped to the layer below it. There are two primary reasons for grouping. The first is to apply an adjustment layer only to the layer directly below it, leaving the other layers down the chain unaffected. The second is to map a texture over text or other object that is in its own layer. Grouping will apply the texture of one image only to the opaque areas of the layer below it.

halftone   Images that are created where detail and tone values are represented by a series of evenly spaced dots in varying size and shape.

hardness   Controls the size of the brush's hard center. Type a number, or use the slider to enter a value that is a percentage of the brush diameter.

HDTV   HDTV stands for High Definition Television and is an emerging video standard. HDTV has a 16×9 aspect ratio. It also has a variety of standards including interlaced signals, progressive signals, and a variety of sizes (either 720 or 1080 horizontal lines.)

The two most common HDTV formats are 720p and 1080i. The *p* refers to a progressive video format and the *i* refers to an interlaced video format.

HDTV formats are set by the ATSC, or Advance Television Standards Committee.

History palette   The History palette is a road map of the work that you do in Photoshop. Each change that you make to your image is stored in the History palette. This is useful for going back to previous states of your image or for creating a new image from a specific history state. You can also paint from one history state to the image using the **History Brush**.

HSB HSB is a color model that generates colors based on the Hue, Saturation, and Brightness of a given color.

hue Hue is the color reflected from or transmitted through an object. It is measured as a location on the standard color wheel, expressed as a degree between 0° and 360°. In common use, hue is identified by the name of the color such as red, orange, or green.

image size Image size is the size of a given image that is determined by the resolution (dpi) and physical dimensions of the canvas.

import Importing allows you to bring a variety of different elements into an open image in Photoshop, or to a new image. You can import anti-aliased PICTs, PDF images, annotations, and PICT resources. TWAIN imports allow you to import images directly from a scanner or digital camera.

indexed color The indexed color mode is limited to 256 colors. This color mode is most commonly used with GIF images and web graphics. Because the number of colors is limited for each image, file sizes remain small. Images that you incorporate into your broadcast designs from the web will most likely be in this format. These images need to be converted to the RGB color mode before they can be used.

Menu: Image>Mode>Indexed Color

intellectual property An intellectual property is any product of the human intellect that is unique, novel, and nonobvious (and has some value in the marketplace). Examples include an idea, an invention, an expression or literary creation, a process, presentation, or a formula.

interlacing Interlacing is combining fields of video to create frames of video.

inverse Inverse is used to convert a selection to its exact opposite. If you have a selection in the shape of a circle and you inverse the selection, you now have a selection of everything but the circle.

Invert command The Invert command inverts the colors in an image. You might use this command to make a positive black-and-white image negative or to make a positive from a scanned black-and-white negative. When you invert an image, the brightness value of each pixel in the channels is converted to the inverse value on the 256-step color values scale. For example, a pixel in a positive image with a value of 255 is changed to 0, and a pixel with a value of 5 is changed to 250.

IRE IRE is the unit of measurement set forth by SMPTE (Society of Motion Picture Television Engineers) that measures the overall brightness of your analog video signal. 100 IRE is pure white, 0 IRE is black.

JPEG The Joint Photographic Experts Group (JPEG) format is used to display continuous-tone images (such as photos) on the Web. Most digital cameras use JPEG because it provides excellent compression; the maximum setting provides comparable quality to much larger files. The JPEG format supports RGB, CMYK, and grayscale color modes, but does not support alpha channels. JPEG is a lossy compression and should not be used as a storage or production file format. If you are using it as a source format, be sure to set the digital camera to maximum quality.

kerning Kerning is the process of adding or subtracting space between specific letter pairs. You can control kerning manually, or you can use automatic kerning to turn on the kerning built into the font by the font designer.

key signal   The key signal is the grayscale image that is sent to a hardware device that tells it what portions of an image to pass video through, and what portions of the fill signal should be visible. This signal is derived from the alpha channel or a matte.

L*a*b color   In Photoshop, Lab mode (the asterisks are dropped from the name) has a lightness component (*L*) that can range from 0 to 100. In the **Color Picker**, the *a* component (green-red axis) and the *b* component (blue-yellow axis) can range from +128 to –128. In the **Color** palette, the *a* component and the *b* component can range from +120 to –120. Lab color is the intermediate color model Photoshop uses when converting from one color mode to another.

layer styles   Previously known as *layer effects,* layer styles allow you to add drop shadows, glows, bevels and a variety of other effects to any layer in Photoshop. Once layer styles have been applied to a layer, they can be removed or edited without permanently altering the contents of the layer.

layers   Layers in Photoshop act like separate images within a given canvas that contain image and opacity information. Layers are visually stacked one on top of another and are used to hold shapes, text, images, and any other element within your designs.

Levels   The Levels dialog box lets you correct the tonal range and color balance of an image by adjusting intensity levels of the image's shadows, midtones, and highlights. The Levels histogram serves as a visual guide for adjusting the image's key tones.

lightness   Lightness is used in the hue saturation and replaces color operations. Lightness moves a given color closer to white as it is increased, and closer to black as it is decreased.

linear key   A linear key is a key that is achieved using an alpha channel or matte. (EX 1)

This type of keying provides the greatest amount of flexibility. Linear keys allow for soft anti-aliased edges, partially transparent portions of your graphic, graphics that fade, drop shadows, and edge glows. Linear keys look to the alpha channel for the opacity level of each corresponding pixel in the image. Most video systems and software packages will support linear keys. If the system you are using does support them, use them. Your keys will be cleaner and more accurate with linear keys than with any other method of keying.

lines per inch   Screen frequency is the number of printer dots or halftone cells per inch used to print grayscale images or color separations. Also known as *screen ruling* or *line screen,* screen frequency is measured in lines per inch (lpi)–or lines of cells per inch in a halftone screen.

link   Layers can be linked in Photoshop by selecting a layer and activating the chain icon on other layers that you wish to link to the parent layer. Layers that are linked can be moved in one operation, moved to layer sets, or deleted as a group.

load selection   You can load the selection of a layer, channel, or layer mask. This operation reads the transparency of a layer or the selection that is represented by a channel or layer mask. You can load the selection of an element under the select menu, or by Cmd+clicking (Ctrl+clicking) on the layer, channel, or mask.

lossless compression   A method of compressing an image where detail is not lost in the compression process.

lossy compression   A method of compressing an image where detail is lost in the compression process. JPEG, TIFF, and PDF are examples of file formats that support lossy compression.

luminance key   A luminance key is a key that is achieved using the black background of an image. Luminance keys are very limiting and do not provide a great deal of creative control over how your graphics are keyed over video. Luminance keys do not allow for anti-aliased edges or partially transparent portions of your image. Luminance keys should only be used if your system does not support linear keys. Graphics that are luminance keyed need to be placed on superblack.

LZW compression   LZW (Lemple-Zif-Welch) lossless compression; supported by TIFF, PDF, GIF, and PostScript language file formats. Most useful for images with large areas of single color.

macro   A small script or routine that automatically repeats a series of operations within an application. Actions are macros that can be recorded and played in Photoshop.

matte   A matte does the same thing as an alpha channel. They both create key signals for a visual element. Mattes are typically not attached to the object that they are creating a key signal for. Mattes are separate files or footage applied to another clip or image. Alpha channels are typically attached to the element they are creating a key signal for.

merge   Combining the elements within multiple layers to a single layer. Merging layers is a destructive function in Photoshop.

moiré   moiré patterns are caused from tight, highly contrasting patterns of objects in your video. The effect is a vibrating rainbow pattern over the top of your video.

multisession CD   A session on a CD includes a lead-in area, a program area (data or audio tracks) and a lead-out area. A multisession disc is one that has multiple sessions on one disc. Each session has its own lead-in, content and lead-out area, and is linked together with other sessions. CD recorders that support multisession recording must also support this feature. In terms of optical storage, this allows the capability of storing more data on a previously recorded recordable media.

Navigator palette   The Navigator palette provides a thumbnail representation of your current canvas and allows you to zoom in and move your visible area around easily.

nonsquare pixels   Pixels that are native to your computer are all square. However, pixels in a few television signals are not, because the image dimensions of the file do not fit in a 4×3 aspect ratio defined by the NTSC. Therefore, they are squeezed taller to fit all the needed pixels into the aspect ratio.

The National Television System Committee, otherwise known as the NTSC, has set the standard that television, as we know it today, has a 4×3 aspect ratio, excluding HDTV, which is 16×9. This means that the size of a television image is three units high for every four units wide.

Video hardware that uses the 640×480 dimension standard is in a 4×3 aspect ratio. 640×480 images have an aspect ratio of 4×3, which means that the square pixels on your computer stay square once converted in your video hardware. This is the easiest system to design for because you don't have to convert your images before going out to video.

However, video hardware that outputs 601 video (sometimes called D1) has a size of 720×486, which does not work out to a 4×3 ratio. This introduces the problem between square and nonsquare pixels. Because the 720×486 image must fit within a 4×3 aspect ratio, the pixels in that image are not square. They are taller than they are wide, roughly 0.9 to 1. Therefore, creating images on your square-pixel computer monitor may look stretched out vertically when they go to NTSC video and stretched out horizontally on PAL video. The same holds true for DV images. They are 720×480, which is not a 4×3 aspect ratio, either.

NTSC NTSC stands for the National Television Standards Committee. This is the governing body that sets the standards for video signals in the United States and North America. It states that video signals in the US must be in a 4×3 aspect ratio and must be 30 frames/60 fields per second, excluding HDTV.

NTSC color filters Restricts the gamut of colors to those acceptable for television reproduction to prevent oversaturated colors from bleeding across television scan lines.

opacity Opacity is a measurement of how opaque or transparent the pixels in your layers are. An opacity setting of 100 will make the elements in your layer completely opaque, and an opacity setting of 0 would be completely transparent.

OpenType font OpenType is a file format for scalable (outline) files that extends the existing font file format used by Microsoft Windows and Apple Macintosh. OpenType was developed jointly by Microsoft and Adobe and allows an Adobe file to be part of a TrueType font file. Prior to OpenType, Adobe did not support TrueType fonts as well it did its own font format, Type 1, for printers that use PostScript. PostScript is an industry standard printer formatting language for higher-quality and more sophisticated printers. OpenType is also known as TrueType Open v. 2.0.

Options palette The Options palette is the palette that sits at the top of your monitor directly under the Application menu. This palette allows you to set the options for all of the tools that are available in the Tool palette.

orphan When laying out text, an orphan is a stranded word on a line by itself. This is something that you want to avoid. Work to balance out word spacing and wrapping so that this doesn't happen.

out of gamut A gamut is the range of colors that a color system can display or print. Different color models include a different set or range of colors. Colors that are represented in one color model may not exist in another. These colors would be considered out of gamut.

overscan Televisions crop the edges of your visuals because of a condition called *overscan*.

The edges of a television set are covered partially by the case of the television, and the ray gun inside the television that generates the image will slightly overshoot the surface of the viewable area of the TV. This keeps unwanted portions of a video signal from being visible to the viewer. However, this will also cut off portions of your signal that you want to be seen. Using safe grids will help you monitor what will be kept and lost during transmission.

Some video monitors have a feature called underscan, which will cause the image on the monitor to be squeezed down so that all of the image can be seen on screen. This is *not* an accurate representation of what the audience will see when they watch your program.

PAL PAL is the most common video format used outside of North America. PAL video signals are a 4×3 aspect ratio and are 25 frames/50 fields per second.

panning A camera movement that adjusts the composition of a shot from right to left. Often photos are taken from Photoshop into After Effects (or another compositing application) so that they can be panned. Be sure you have extra pixel information so you can pan or zoom.

Pantone Used for printing solid-color and CMYK inks. The Pantone Matching System includes 1114 solid colors. To select a color, use a Pantone color guide printed on coated, uncoated, and matte stocks.

Paragraph palette You can use the Paragraph palette to set formatting options such as alignment and line spacing for a single paragraph, multiple paragraphs, or all paragraphs in a type layer.

Paste as Pixels Paste as Pixels will allow you to rasterize a vector object in your clipboard and paste the resulting pixels in your image.

Paste Into Paste Into will paste the contents of the clipboard into the selection of the active layer as opposed to creating a new layer for the pasted object.

PCX The PC Paintbrush format is used by PC-compatible computers. The format is designed to match the standard VGA color palette. PCX supports RGB, indexed color, grayscale, and bitmap color modes, but does not support alpha channels. It is commonly a compressed file and supports bit depths of 1, 4, 8, or 24. Because of its small color range and compressed images, this format is not very useful for video editing.

PDF The Portable Document Format is an amazing, cross-platform, cross-application file format. PDF files accurately display and preserve fonts, page layouts, and both vector and bitmap graphics. You can also transfer Photoshop's annotation notes (both text and audio) into the PDF. The Photoshop PDF format is the only one that Photoshop can save, and it supports layers and other Photoshop features. You do not need to flatten to save a PDF file. This file can then be transferred to others for review and comment using Adobe Acrobat or viewed with the free Acrobat Reader. This is an excellent format for review purposes, but will not be understood by all video-editing applications.

Pen tool Allows you to create Bézier curves for vector objects in Photoshop.

Photoshop Elements Photoshop Elements is the replacement application for Photoshop LE from Adobe Systems. Photoshop Elements provides an excellent platform for editing images. Photoshop Elements is a thinned-out version of Photoshop that provides many of the similar functions as Photoshop, but lacks in the complexity of control that is available in the full version of Photoshop.

PICT file The Macintosh Picture format is widely used by video editors. Its popularity can be traced back to many editing packages, which historically required graphics to be in the PICT format. Its popularity has suffered as other options became available, but the technology behind the format still makes it the best format for video.

The PICT format supports RGB images with a single alpha channel, and is very effective at compressing large areas of solid color. This compression results in huge file savings for alpha channels, which are mostly black or white.

When saving, be sure to pick 32-bit pixel resolution. On the Mac platform, you have choices of additional JPEG compression. Avoid these because they cause import problems on PCs, and the file savings are not worth the quality loss.

PICT resource file The PICT resource is a PICT file which is contained in a Mac OS file's resource fork. This format is often used to create startup screens for software. While similar to a plain PICT file, avoid it. Resource files generally confuse video editing applications. You can edit a PICT resource file by importing it into Photoshop.

Pixar file The Pixar format is designed for high-end 3D applications. It supports RGB and grayscale images with a single alpha channel. If you also create 3D animation, you may use this format.

pixels per inch (ppi) The number of pixels displayed per unit of printed length in an image, usually measured in pixels per inch.

Place You can use the File>Place command to place artwork into a new layer in an image. In Photoshop, you can place PDF, Adobe Illustrator, and EPS files.

PNG   The Portable Network Graphics format provides lossless compression for the Web. The PNG supports 24-bit images and with 8-bit transparency. Because only newer browsers support it (and the file sizes are bigger), you will not find it widely used. If you have to use a web image in your video, look for a PNG.

PostScript font   Each character (or to be more precise, each glyph) in a font has a shape, and there are various ways of describing that shape on a computer. PostScript fonts generally describe the outline of the shape and then color in the interior of that outline; this coloring process is called rasterizing.

PPI   See *pixels per inch.*

premultiplied alpha channel   A premultiplied alpha channel is an alpha channel that follows the edge of your graphic material exactly. This is the type of alpha channel that Photoshop will output from your images. The potential problem from this type of alpha channel is that you run the risk of the background color of your image being present on the edges of your graphic. This is caused by the anti-aliasing that Photoshop does to your images. The edges of your image are partially transparent to give them a smoothing effect. However, this creates partially transparent edges on your alpha channel as well. This will allow part of the background color of your image to be visible when keyed. Some applications, such as After Effects, can address the problem of premultiplied alpha channels. You can tell the software that the image has a premultiplied alpha channel and it will unmultiply the background color from the edge pixels of your image.

primary colors   Primary colors are the colors that all other colors are made up from. Red, green, and blue are the primary colors in the RGB color model; cyan, magenta, yellow, and black are the primary colors of the CMYK color model.

profile mismatch   **Color Settings** lets you specify how Photoshop handles the files it opens and saves. It is especially important when opening files that have no embedded profile or that have a profile that doesn't match the current setup profile. Profile mismatch occurs when Photoshop encounters a file with an embedded profile that doesn't match the current setup profile. How Photoshop handles the mismatch depends on what you've set in the Profile Mismatch Handling section of the Color Settings dialog box.

progressive scan   A progressive video signal is a video signal that does not have interlaced fields. Computer monitors, some HDTV standards, and some mini-DV cameras display progressive images. That means there are 30 full frames per second, not 60 fields, or half frames per second. Images that were shot in a progressive format are much cleaner and easier to work with inside the computer.

PSD   Photoshop format is the default file format. This format is the only format that supports all of Photoshop's features. Always save your design files in this format for maximum editing ability.

Quark Xpress   Quark Xpress is a page layout application that is used for prepress and page layout for anything from simple brochures to entire books or other publications. These files cannot be opened by Photoshop, so be sure to ask the designer for all of the elements and a PDF file of the layout.

raster graphics   Raster graphics, sometimes referred to as bitmapped graphics, use a grid of colors known as pixels to represent images. Each pixel is assigned a specific location and color value. For example, a circle in a raster image is made up of a mosaic of pixels in that location. When working with raster images, you edit pixels rather than objects or shapes.

   Raster or bitmap images are the most common electronic medium for continuous-tone images, such as photographs, because they can represent subtle gradations of shades and color. Raster images are resolution dependent–that is, they contain a fixed number of pixels. As a result, they can lose detail and appear jagged if they are scaled larger.

rasterize   Rasterizing is the process of converting vector images into bitmapped or pixel-based raster images.

Raw   The Raw format is a flexible (and confusing) file format for transferring between applications and computer platforms. Essentially, a text file is written containing a stream of bytes describing the color information for the image. Every pixel is described in binary format. Avoid this format.

resolution dependent   Resolution dependent means that an image has a fixed resolution. Raster or bitmapped images are resolution dependent because they cannot be enlarged without losing resolution or clarity.

resolution independent   Resolution independent images, on the other hand, can be enlarged infinitely without losing any resolution or image quality. Vector-based artwork is considered resolution independent.

Revert command   The **Revert** command will discard any unsaved changes in your current image and return the image to the state it was last saved in.

RGB   The RGB color mode is the one used for television graphics. All graphics that are displayed on video systems need to be created in or converted to the RGB mode first. Menu: Image>Mode>RGB Color

All colors in the RGB color mode are made from a combination of red, green, and blue. These are the primary colors used to create color images on television. Other color modes will not work for video. The **Channels** palette in an RGB image will have a Red channel, a Green channel, and a Blue channel. It is best to design in the RGB color space because all of the filters in Photoshop work in RGB mode.

Rubber Stamp tool   The **Rubber Stamp** tool is now called the **Clone Stamp** tool in Photoshop 7. The **Clone Stamp** tool takes a sample of an image that you can then apply over another image or part of the same image. Each stroke of the tool paints on more of the sample.

Rubylith mask   Traditional color of masks used in printing.

run length encoding   Lossless compression; supported by some common Windows file formats.

safe grid   It is a grid that shows you what areas of your image will be safe and what areas of your image will be lost when transferred to video. Overscan on television sets will cut off approximately 10% of the edges of your image. All of the action within a given shot must be within the action safe area, and all of the titles or graphics of an image must stay inside the title safe area.

saturation   Saturation is the intensity of a color. A saturated blue has a lot of blue in it; an unsaturated blue has very little blue in it.

Save Selection As channel   This command will take the active selection in your image and store the selection as channel in your **Channels** palette. You also have the option of saving the selection as a channel in other open images.

Scitex file   The Scitex Continuous Tone format is used for high-end print work on Scitex computers. This format needs special scanners and rasterizing formats, and is designed for output of high-quality print such as magazines and art prints. While you may receive this format, you will never need to save in it for video output.

scratch disk   This is the physical hard drive that Photoshop uses to write information to when RAM becomes full.

SCSI SCSI stands for small computer serial interface, and it is a serial bus on computers that allows the connection of external hard drives or scanners. SCSI is starting to phase out and be replaced by USB and FireWire.

sepia tone Conversion of a black-and-white image in silver to sepia (a brownish gray to dark olive brown) by metallic compounds. Sepia was the most common tone used, and was used in black-and-white prints of films for special sequences to enhance the dramatic or pictorial effect.

skew Skewing an image is vertically or horizontally distorting an image. This can be accomplished with the Free Transform tool.

slices Slices are dividers in Photoshop that allow you to prepare or cut up an image for Web deployment. Each slice you create in your Photoshop image can be saved as a separate file with an associated HTML file for the Web.

SRL camera An SRL camera (single reflex lens) is a still camera where the viewfinder is actually looking through the lens at the exact same image that will be exposed to the film.

Snap When **Snap** is enabled, your selections and drawing tools will snap to a combination of guides, grids, selections, and document bounds. Under the View>Snap to... command, you can select what Photoshop will snap to.

Snapshot command The Snapshot command lets you make a temporary copy (or snapshot) of any state of the image. The new snapshot is added to the list of snapshots at the top of the History palette. Selecting a snapshot lets you work from that version of the image.

Sponge tool The Sponge tool subtly changes the color saturation of an area. In Grayscale mode, the tool increases or decreases contrast by moving gray levels away from or toward the middle gray.

square pixels Pixels that are native to your computer are all square. However, pixels in a few television signals are not, because the image dimensions of the file do not fit in a 4×3 aspect ratio defined by the NTSC. Therefore, they are squeezed taller to fit all the needed pixels into the aspect ratio.

The National Television System Committee, otherwise known as the NTSC, has set the standard that television, as we know it today, has a 4×3 aspect ratio, excluding HDTV, which is 16×9. This means that the size of a television image is three units high for every four units wide.

Video hardware that uses the 640×480 dimension standard is in a 4×3 aspect ratio. 640×480 images have an aspect ratio of 4×3, which means that the square pixels on your computer stay square once converted in your video hardware. This is the easiest system to design for because you don't have to convert your images before going out to video.

However, video hardware that outputs 601 video (sometimes called D1) has a size of 720×486, which does not work out to a 4×3 ratio. This introduces the problem between square and nonsquare pixels. Because the 720×486 image must fit within a 4×3 aspect ratio, the pixels in that image are not square. They are taller than they are wide, roughly 0.9 to 1. Therefore, creating images on your square pixel computer monitor may look stretched out vertically when they go to NTSC video and stretched out horizontally on PAL video. The same holds true for DV images. They are 720×480, which is not a 4×3 aspect ratio, either.

straight alpha channel A straight alpha channel is an alpha channel that does *not* follow the edge of your graphic material. An example would be an image of a green circle. Instead of the shape of the circle being determined by the color information of the graphic, it is defined by the alpha channel. The graphic would look like a solid green canvas, and the alpha channel would be in the shape of a circle.

This allows the edges of the color to extend outside of the alpha channel, giving you a much cleaner key without the chances of a thin black or white line around the edge of the circle.

This is the preferred type of alpha channel. However, Photoshop cannot calculate this for you. If you want to obtain this type of alpha channel out of Photoshop, you need to plan your design ahead of time to be this way. To achieve this kind of alpha, you must place a solid color layer into your background that matches the color of your glow/drop shadow/soft edge.

After Effects is one application that can take an image file with an alpha channel and turn the image into a new file with a straight alpha channel.

Note: When referring to a straight alpha channel, the alpha channel is actually no different than any other alpha channel; it is the color information in your image that is different.

subtractive color model A color model that creates black when the primary colors of the model are added together. For example, adding Cyan, Magenta, Yellow, and Key (black) in the CMYK model will create black.

superblack Superblack is a level of black below 7.5 IRE, usually at 0 IRE. This is used for luminance keys. The areas of your image that you want to be keyed out should be superblack, and the areas of your image that are black that you want to keep should be at 7.5 IRE.

tablet A tablet is a secondary input device that uses a pen to control the computer as opposed to a mouse. This is extremely useful in Photoshop because it allows for pressure sensitivity and the feel of drawing with a pen instead of a mouse.

TARGA The TARGA format was designed for systems using Truevision video boards. It has become a standard format for PC users because it supports 24-bit RGB images (8 bits × 3 color channels), and 32-bit RGB images (3 color channels plus an alpha channel). Photoshop 7.0 shipped with a bug in its TARGA module that improperly saved the alpha channel. The free update to 7.0.1 or a separate TARGA download fixes this.

TIFF The Tagged-Image File Format is a common cross-platform format that is supported by several applications. Several scanners can create TIFF files as well, and it is a more efficient format for saving nonlayered images. The TIFF format supports RGB, CMYK, Lab, indexed color, and grayscale images with alpha channels. Photoshop can also save layers in a TIFF file; however, other applications only see the flattened version. TIFF is a good format for storing source photos.

title safe area The title safe area of an image is the portion of the image where all of the titles or graphics should be. This is the inner box on a safe grid. Any graphical elements that extend outside of the title safe area run the risk of being cut off by the viewer's television set.

TOYO TOYO Color Finder 1050 consists of more than 1000 colors based on the most common printing inks used in Japan. The TOYO Color Finder 1050 Book contains printed samples of TOYO colors and is available from printers and graphic arts supply stores.

trackball An computer input device similar to a mouse. Instead of moving the mouse, you roll a ball in a cradle to make equivalent mouse movements. Trackballs provide more sensitivity and accuracy than a mouse, and some have four buttons that can be assigned to various functions.

tracking Tracking is the process of creating an equal amount of spacing across a range of letters.

TrueType font   A scalable font technology that renders fonts for both the printer and the screen. Originally developed by Apple, it was enhanced jointly by Apple and Microsoft. TrueType fonts are used in Windows, starting with Windows 3.1, as well as in the Mac System 7 operating system.

Unlike PostScript, in which the algorithms are maintained in the rasterizing engine, each TrueType font contains its own algorithms for converting the outline into bitmaps. The lower-level language embedded within the TrueType font allows unlimited flexibility in the design.

Type Mask tool   The **Type Mask** tool will create a selection of the shape of the text when type is entered as opposed to a color.

underscan   Televisions crop the edges of your visuals because of a condition called overscan.

The edges of a television set are covered partially by the case of the television, and the ray gun inside the television that generates the image will slightly overshoot the surface of the viewable area of the TV. This keeps unwanted portions of a video signal from being visible to the viewer. However, this will also cut off portions of your signal that you want to be seen.

Using safe grids will help you monitor what will be kept and lost during transmission.

Some video monitors have a feature called Underscan, which will cause the image on the monitor to be squeezed down so that all of the image can be seen on screen. This is *not* an accurate representation of what the audience will see when they watch your program.

Ungroup   Once a layer has been grouped to another, it is possible to ungroup the layer and return it to its normal state. *See Group for more information.*

Unsharp Mask filter   Unsharp Mask locates pixels that differ from surrounding pixels by the threshold you specify and increases the pixels' contrast by the amount you specify. In addition, you specify the radius of the region to which each pixel is compared.

USB 1   USB stands for universal serial bus. USB 1 was the original version of USB that had a maximum data transfer rate of 12 mbits/second. USB is used primarily for connecting keyboards and mice to computers. However, there are USB scanners, cameras, and hard drives.

USB 2   USB stands for universal serial bus. USB 2 is a high-speed serial bus that has a maximum data transfer rate of 480 mbits/second. USB is used primarily for connecting keyboards and mice to computers. However, there are USB scanners, cameras, and hard drives.

Variations command   The Variations command lets you adjust the color balance, contrast, and saturation of an image by showing you thumbnails of alternatives. This is a good method for beginners, but does not offer the precise control of the other adjustment methods.

vector graphics   Vector graphics are made up of lines and curves defined by mathematical objects called vectors. Vectors describe an image according to its geometric characteristics. For example, a circle in a vector graphic is made up of a mathematical definition of a circle drawn with a certain radius, set at a specific location, and filled with a specific color. You can move, resize, or change the color of the circle without losing the quality of the graphic.

Vector graphics are resolution independent, i.e., they can be scaled to any size and printed at any resolution without losing detail or clarity. As a result, vector graphics are the best choice for representing bold graphics that must retain crisp lines when scaled to various sizes—for example, logos.

video filters   Filters in Photoshop that are video specific, such as De-interlace and NTSC colors.

Web Photo Gallery Web Photo Gallery can be found under File>Automate. This function will automate Photoshop to generate a web gallery of a folder of images on your machine. It will generate thumbnail, HTML files, and the full-size images. You can control the layout, image sizes, and content within the pages.

white point The white point of an image is a reference for what Photoshop believes to be the brightest portion of your image that is white. From this white point, Photoshop can adjust the color balance of your image. The white point is set in the levels or curves palette.

Wide Gamut RGB Wide Gamut RGB provides a very wide range of colors by using spectrally pure primaries. The downside is that most of the colors in this gamut cannot be displayed on standard computer monitors or printed. When editing a file, colors are often forced into the display space (clipped) and, consequently, your color adjustments may not appear as visible changes on the screen.

WORM disc WORM stands for Write Once Read Many. Any single-session CD-R would be considered to be a WORM disc.

YCC Color space developed by Eastman Kodak that defines colors by luminance (Y) and two levels of chrominance (C and C). This is the color mode that video signals are stored in.

Index

Numerics

The Authority on Digital Video Technology
DV MEDIA GROUP

DV Digital Video

PRINT

DV expo Digital Video

EVENTS

DV .com Digital Video

ONLINE

w w w . **DV** . c o m